# CABINETS IN WE

# Cabinets in Western Europe

Edited by
**Jean Blondel**
*Professor of Political Science*
*European University Institute, Florence*
and
**Ferdinand Müller-Rommel**
*Akademischer Rat of Political Science*
*University of Lüneburg*

**MACMILLAN**

First published 1988 by
THE MACMILLAN PRESS LTD
Houndmills, Basingstoke, Hampshire RG21 2XS
and London
Companies and representatives
throughout the world

ISBN 0–333–46208–4 hardcover
ISBN 0–333–46209–2 paperback

A catalogue record for this book is available
from the British Library.

Printed in China

Reprinted 1993

# Contents

# List of Tables

# List of Figures

# Notes on the Contributors

**Rudy B. Andeweg** is Associate Professor of Political Science at the University of Leyden. His publications include *Kabinetsformatie* (1977).

**Antonio Bar** is Professor of Constitutional Law at the University of Zaragoza. His publications include *El Presidente del Gobierno en España: Encuadre constitucional y práctica política.*

**Jean Blondel** is currently Professor of Political Science at the European University Institute in Florence. Among his recent publications are *Government Ministers in the Contemporary World.* and *Political Leadership.*

**Martin Burch** is Lecturer in Government at the University of Manchester. His publications include *British Cabinet Politics.*

**Maurizio Cotta** is Professor of Political Science at the University of Siena and author of numerous works on Italian politics including *Classe politiche e parlamento in Italia 1946–1976.*

**Svein Eriksen** is Deputy Director General at the Ministry of Consumer Affairs and Government Administration, Oslo. He is author of several reports on decision-making in central government departments.

**Brian Farrell** is Associate Professor of Government and Politics at University College, Dublin. His many publications include *Chairman or Chief? The Role of the Taoiseach in Irish Government.*

**André Paul Frognier** is Head of the Department of Sociology and co-President of the Centre for Political Studies at the Catholic University of Louvain. His recent publications include *Corruption and Reform.*

**Peter Gerlich** is Professor of Political Science at the University of Vienna. His recent publications include *Sozialpartnerschaft in der Krise*, co-edited with E. Grande and W.C. Müller.

**Torbjörn Larsson** is Lecturer in Sociology at the University of Stockholm and author of *The Cabinet and its Ministers.*

**Wolfgang C. Müller** is Lecturer in Political Science at the University of Vienna. His recent publications include *Grundzüge des politischen Systems Österreichs*.

**Ferdinand Müller-Rommel** is Lecturer in Politics at the University of Lüneburg. Among his recent publications is *Vergleichende Politikwissenschaft*, co-authored with D. Berg-Schlosser.

**Jaakko Nousiainen** is Research Professor at the Academy of Finland. His recent publications include *Tasavallan presidentit valtiollisina johtajina* (Presidential Leadership in Finland).

**Tove Lise Schou** is Senior Lecturer in Political Science at the University of Copenhagen and author of *Norway and the EEC*.

**Jean-Louis Thiébault** is Senior Lecturer in Political Science at the University of Lille. His publications include *A l'assaut des beffrois – Atlas des élections municipales de mars 1983 dans le Nord-Pas-de Calais*.

# Preface

The cabinet system of government has been praised for generations, as it has enabled Britain and a number of other countries, principally of the Commonwealth and Scandinavia, to move smoothly through the problems faced by industrial nations in the course of the twentieth century. But the cabinet system of government has also been attacked, as it has often proved unable to solve major societal conflicts, especially on the Continent, both before and after the Second World War. Weimar Germany, Third and Fourth Republic France and Republican Spain are the unfortunate examples of the pathology of cabinet government. In between these extremes, other countries are sometimes regarded as providing examples of relative stability, but also of difficulties and perhaps ineffectiveness.

Such an image is in large part correct; it is also partial. It assumes that there is only one model of 'good' cabinet structure and cabinet decision-making, a model largely based on the Westminster pattern. This view was perhaps valid a century ago, when Britain was indeed one of the few countries to practise cabinet government; but, especially since the end of the Second World War and the gradual establishment of cabinet government throughout Western Europe, the approach has to be broadened. The cabinet system now functions – and functions well – with coalitions as well as single-party governments, with strong Prime Ministers as well as with politicians who are only 'chairmen', with ministers who are basically 'amateurs' as well as with specialists. This diversity has naturally led to very different 'types'; and it is increasingly suggested that there might be alternative ways in which cabinet government can be stable and efficient.

It seemed therefore timely to bring together under one cover a summary of these 'experiences' of cabinet government across contemporary Western Europe. This volume is a survey; it aims at giving a first impression of similarities and dissimilarities by presenting sequentially the structure and modes of operation of thirteen cabinet governments across Western Europe, from Britain to Austria and from Finland to Spain. It hopes to indicate how flexible cabinet government is in the contemporary world, while also to suggest the conditions under which this system appears to work satisfactorily and indeed efficiently.

This volume has been made possible because of the existence of a group of political scientists who, since 1986, have worked together in the context of a project on Structures and Decision-making in Western European Governments; this project aims at analysing systematically the problems posed by cabinet government in various countries and to look at factors accounting for similarities and differences, successes and failures. The group has benefitted from the help of a number of institutions, and in particular of the European University Institute in Florence, which we wish to thank formally for the support which we consistently received. We wish also to thank Ms Clare Gardiner for the care with which she worked on the manuscripts of the essays included in this volume and thus contributed to turn the collection into what is, we hope, a truly homogeneous study.

*Florence and Lüneburg*                                    JEAN BLONDEL
                                            FERDINAND MÜLLER-ROMMEL

# Introduction: Western European Cabinets in Comparative Perspective

Jean Blondel

## CABINET GOVERNMENT AS A COMMON WESTERN EUROPEAN EXPERIENCE

For the first time in their history, Western European countries have been ruled during a substantial period by similar types of government. These governments are not only similar in that they are based on general liberal democratic principles which are broadly accepted by the whole population. They are also similar in that they embody institutional arrangements which give to these liberal democracies the same decision-making framework. Authoritarian regimes have disappeared from Western Europe since the mid-1970s and, for the majority of countries, since the 1940s. Moreover, with the exception of Switzerland, all Western European governments have adopted the formula of parliamentary and cabinet rule. After what might be described as a century of soul-searching often marred by internal turmoil and by external wars, Western European countries have finally followed the lead which Britain (and Sweden) gave in the eighteenth and early nineteenth centuries: they are all led by working cabinet governments.

The formula of parliamentary and cabinet rule is organised, in contrast to the presidential system which prevails in the United States and Latin America, on the idea that the executive is linked to the legislature. The government cannot remain in office if it ceases to have the confidence of Parliament but that it can, in fact, remain in being as long as it enjoys this confidence as there is no fixed term to the life of the government. The arrangement is also based, somewhat more technically but none the less quite importantly, on the notion that the government constitutes a collective body: the ministers form a cabinet which is more than the sum of its members as it is ultimately responsible as a body to Parliament and through Parliament to the nation for the conduct of the affairs of the country.

Parliamentary or cabinet government is thus one of the fundamental

1

characteristics of Western European governments. In fact it could be said, without exaggeration, that it is one of the important ways in which Western Europe has political unity, as it follows from the adoption of this system by all Western European countries, except Switzerland, that a large number of rules and of modes of behaviour – of political understandings – are common to Western European countries while these rules, modes of behaviour and understandings do not apply to most other countries of the world. Thus Western Europe is both internally similar and distinct as a group from the rest of the world where, except for some Commonwealth countries, Israel and Japan, systems of government are based not only on different broad principles but on different specific arrangements.

## SUCCESS AND PROBLEMS IN WESTERN EUROPEAN CABINET GOVERNMENT

Since there is this basic similarity among Western European countries about the nature and general characteristics of the executive, it is only natural that one should wish to examine the extent to which the overall similarity in arrangements conceals a number of important differences in practice. This curiosity, moreover, is not an idle one. For, while it is clear that the parliamentary or cabinet system of government seems to have served and to continue to serve Western Europe well, a number of important questions relating to its functioning have been raised in recent years in most of the countries concerned.

That the parliamentary or cabinet system has served Western Europe well is undeniable: no-one believes any longer that cabinet government produces either inevitably or even frequently weak executives. The time when cabinet government was primarily associated with instability or gross ineffectiveness is over. It has long been pointed out that 'Bonn is not Weimar';[1] the obvious impotence of French governments has ceased with the streamlined system of the Fifth Republic, which has strengthened the executive while preserving the basic principle that the government needs to have the confidence of the Chamber (as has been seen clearly after the general election of 1986). The countries of Southern Europe which, in previous decades, were ruled either by weak or short-lived parliamentary cabinets or by authoritarian leaders now have, on the whole, stable and effective parliamentary executives.

Indeed, it seems apparent that the cabinet system, far from being unable to provide leadership to the nation in an effective manner, seems better adapted to the requirements of modern liberal-democratic government than other systems in that it is more flexible and that it ensures better coordination among the various elements of the political chain. For in order to survive, the government has to accommodate itself to a substantial extent to the desires of the legislature and, through the legislature, of a large number of groups, while the presidential system is more prone to produce conflict and to leave the protagonists in their original positions.

Yet this success of the Western European cabinet system has not wholly eliminated problems and difficulties. If the old questions of instability and overt weakness are indeed truly solved, new matters have emerged in the 1960s and 1970s to which cabinet government has so far not given satisfactory answers. Four of these matters are particularly serious and have been frequently raised. The first problem is that of size, since it is often felt that cabinets of eighteen, twenty or more members cannot be expected to take their decisions in a truly collective manner. A second problem arises from the role of Prime Ministers, whose enhanced status, in many countries at least, has been felt to contribute to a demotion of other cabinet members.

Third, there have been misgivings about the rate at which the turnover of ministers, both in general and in a particular job, has weakened their ability to be effective heads of their departments. Such turnover is often concealed behind an appearance of stability, as Prime Ministers may reshuffle their governments while remaining themselves in office for a substantially longer period than their colleagues.

Finally, questions have been raised about the competence of ministers as managers of very large organisations which often deal with highly technical issues.[2] The extent to which any one of these matters are issues of concern varies between countries, but the effectiveness of cabinet government is often questioned with respect to one, more or all of these aspects.

## THE NEED FOR A DETAILED COMPARATIVE ANALYSIS OF CABINETS

Given the fact that these problems are serious and at any rate are perceived as such in many Western European countries, the least that can be done is to explore the ways in which remedies can be provided which will ensure the overall maintenance of the cabinet system, since this system, as we pointed out earlier, has manifestly been beneficial to the citizens of the countries concerned. Fortunately, nearly all Western European countries are ruled by a cabinet system: we can therefore examine in detail, in parallel and ultimately in a fully comparative manner, the experiences which these Western European parliamentary governments provide.

We have available for analysis a substantial number of countries – eighteen if we include all of them, a dozen if we restrict our analysis to the larger countries which have had several decades of unbroken parliamentary rule. These countries can be studied from the point of view of constitutional and legal arrangements and from the point of view of the practices which have gradually developed and become part of the living system. We know that the traditions and the political culture of these countries are different. We also know that these countries vary in the extent to which they have overcome their political, social and economic problems – problems which also vary in kind as well as in magnitude. There is therefore a wealth of experience to monitor and to analyse and through these analyses it will be easier to perceive the manner in which problems can be better handled and perhaps ultimately solved.

In order to undertake these analyses, we must proceed by stages. For this reason it is prudent to begin by undertaking the study on a parallel basis before proceeding to a full-scale comparative investigation. Although we are now appreciably better informed, across Western Europe, about constitutional arrangements and political practice, we are still some way from being able to grasp in detail the subtle ways in which history and culture have combined to give specific solutions to the many problems posed by the workings of cabinets. If we are to be able to say how cabinet government can meet more successfully the challenges which it faces, what needs to be grasped is not just the bare bones of the structure – the relationship between Government and Parliament, the nature of collective responsibility – but also the delicate manner in which the different elements of the cabinet system combine. We need for instance to appreciate better how cabinets are formed – whether this is a slow or a rapid process and, if it is a slow process, what are the gains as well as the losses of such delays. We need to assess what Prime Ministers can effectively do with respect to their colleagues, what ministers feel is their specific role and what relationships they have with each other and with the Prime Minister. We need·to understand the ways in which the meetings of the cabinet are being used, whether these are occasions for debate or merely for formal ratification, whether they are organs of initiative or merely responsive. We need to see to what extent other bodies develop around the cabinet and prepare the decisions.

These are among the questions which have to be explored in depth if we are to see what differences exist in cabinet government behaviour across Western Europe and thus discover which formula appears more effective in confronting various types of problems. Yet these questions cannot be answered without a close examination of the life and 'style' of cabinets in each country. This is what this volume attempts to do by presenting, according to a common framework, the characteristics of cabinets in thirteen Western European countries. By being deliberately based on a description of modes of behaviour in each country, this book aims at ensuring that we at last have a feel for the way the executive behaves currently in each of these countries. We can thus ensure that we fully understand both what the range of variations is and what is the *raison d'être* – and perhaps the value – of these variations.

The essays which are presented here attempt to do so by describing, however succinctly, the main features of contemporary cabinets in Western Europe, on the basis of a common framework. Cabinets are thus considered successively in the context of the general political setting within which they operate, of their current structure, of the main aspects of their life and of the shape which decision-making takes among their members. The picture which emerges is one of considerable variety: common themes are so to speak diffracted by the profound idiosyncrasies arising from a different cultural heritage or as a result of the existence of different problems.

## THE CABINET SETTING

To begin with, cabinet government, as any form of government, is distinctly shaped by the setting within which it develops. If in Western Europe, as we already suggested, the constitutional setting is broadly similar, the socio-political conditions on which the constitutional rules are applied have been rather diverse. Indeed, one of the reasons why the institutional setting is not very different with respect to the cabinet as such is that, by and large, constitutions (or constitutional conventions as in Britain) are relatively silent about the structure and the operations of the executive. Constitutions which devote some space to cabinet life are primarily concerned with the conditions under which governments may be formed or may fall. Largely because of the instability which characterised a number of parliamentary regimes in the past, some constitutions have thus organised the operation of the question of confidence and of the vote of censure rather restrictively: in Germany,

Fifth Republic France and Spain, the cabinet is thus to an extent protected.

Constitutions are less precise, on the other hand, about the organisation of cabinets – it is said that decisions are expected to be taken collectively while some superior role is sometimes recognised to the Prime Minister with individual ministers sometimes fully responsible with respect to the operation of their departments. What this suggests is that constitutions at best recognise a problem rather than provide a solution – this problem being that there has to be a leader – but also that the cabinet deserve its name only if the major decisions are taken collectively, while a further difficulty arises from the fact that ministers are responsible for particular sectors of the government.

Yet while some constitutions in effect state the problem, others – the older ones – do not even do so. For what they are typically more concerned with is with matters of appointment and dismissal and in particular with the role which the Head of State may play in this respect. Texts normally give to the Head of State the power to participate in cabinet formation, though in Sweden even this power has been taken away from the King in the 1975 Constitution.

In the majority of countries this power is of limited real importance, but some multi-party systems, such as the Netherlands, Belgium, Italy or Finland (in this last country the President, as in France, has considerable influence, especially in foreign affairs), the process of government formation is typically long and difficult. In these cases the Head of State does have, as a result, some significant part to play. The French Fifth Republic Constitution also gives the President the power to select the Prime Minister, but this power was truly effective only as long as the President had a supportive majority in Parliament and could, as a result, choose the government leader. Such an opportunity, which De Gaulle decided to seize and which he bequeathed to his successors, was clearly not provided by the constitutional rule itself. It has been valid only as long as the parliamentary majority remained politically in tune with the President.

We have therefore to turn to the socio-political arrangements if we are to begin to understand the framework within which the cabinet is likely to be organised and take decisions. In this respect, the two most important discriminating factors seem to be 1) the extent to which, alongside the representative element, an 'administrative' or even 'bureaucratic' tradition has prevailed in the country until relatively recently and 2) the extent to which the political system, and the party system in particular, operate in what has come to be called a 'consociational' rather than in a 'majoritarian' manner.

At the root of the contrast is the question of whether the cabinet's role is primarily to lead the political life of the country or whether its role is also (and perhaps even to a major extent) conceived as administrative. While the British cabinet has always been in office to govern rather than to administer, at the other extreme the Austrian or Finnish cabinets have inherited markedly from the 'imperial' tradition. Moreover, as Napoleonic influence extended widely in Western Europe, many other countries, while they were gradually introducing representative principles, adopted aspects of both the representative and the administrative approach to government. From this tradition stems the emphasis on rules and the involvement of the cabinet of many countries in large numbers of small legal decisions.

Yet the difference in the setting of the cabinet scene also comes from the fact that the representative tradition itself has tended to differ sharply between what has come to be called 'consociational' and 'majoritarian' approaches to government. While Britain, Ireland, France and, indeed, Spain are currently part of the majoritarian camp, Austria and The Netherlands are the prime examples (alongside Switzerland, which of course is not ruled by a cabinet system of government) of the consociational type.

Here, too, there are intermediate cases. Both majoritarianism and consociationalism affect, to a greater or lesser extent, Belgium, Finland, Denmark, Germany or Italy. The frontier is so vague that even a country such as Sweden can appear consociational, for under the surface of a marked division between Socialist and 'bourgeois' governments lies a general culture in which the main emphasis is to achieve compromises and not to push things too far in a direction in which the country would not willingly go.

In fact, the division between consociational and majoritarian government is but the top layer of a socio-political system in which party divisions and group representation correspond, to a greater or lesser extent, to deep cleavages around which it is best to tread carefully. Thus, while the consociationalism of The Netherlands tends to represent past differences which gradually healed as time passed by, the efforts of Belgian politicians to maintain consensus sometimes seem to constitute a desperate effort to prevent the break-up of a nation which was stable for over a century but which became shaken, since the 1960s, by the language issue.

It may still be that, by and large, multi-party systems such as that of Finland can only operate if at least a degree of consociationalism prevails. Perhaps also if, as is remarked about that country, the cleavage between right and left has become rather small. But, by and large, consensual politics have come to prevail well beyond the area where the multi-party system is the basis of politics. It can even extend to a country such as Austria, where the electoral strength of the two major parties is at least comparable to what it is (or was) in Britain.

Thus the general setting within which cabinets operate is provided in broad terms by the constitution (or the constitutional conventions). However, the concrete contours depend on the extent to which the representative principle is accompanied and somewhat modified by a bureaucratic tradition. The effect of this representative principle may also be different depending on the extent to which democracy is primarily viewed as operating through a majoritarian cabinet or not. Naturally enough, these variations in setting are likely to affect the characteristics of cabinet structure, cabinet life and the process of cabinet decision-making.

## CABINET STRUCTURE

The structure of Western European cabinets is scarcely defined, as we saw, by constitutional documents. This may be because, originally, this structure was simple. A few ministers came together when necessary to discuss matters concerning the whole executive.

This simplicity is no longer practical. Governments have had to become complex in order to cope with the expansion and the increased technical character of governmental activities. The first consequence has been an increase in the size of the cabinet. But other consequences have had a greater effect on the organisation of the cabinet. The meeting of the Council of Ministers, once the central piece of governmental decision-making, has thus become less important and original ideas of collegiality have had to be replaced by less egalitarian and more hierarchical arrangements.

The increased size of cabinets is perhaps the most obvious development of the last decades, and it has directly contributed to changing the nature of government meetings and to altering the ways in which the cabinet system could be organised. Pre-1914 cabinets were composed of about ten ministers. Although the German and Spanish cabinets, among those of the larger countries, are still appreciably below twenty strong, it is now not unusual to see more than this number around the table of the Council of Ministers. Meetings can therefore no longer be informal. In fact, it is *prima facie* surprising that the increase in size has not been greater. This seems to have been possible only because collegiality has been reduced.

A number of developments have indeed taken place which can be said to have given rise to what we have just referred to as a cabinet *system*. The role of the Prime Minister has increased almost everywhere. 'Second-class' government members have been appointed in many countries. Above all, a variety of 'preparatory' bodies have been set up and ministers have tended to restrict their interventions to those aspects of governmental life which concerned them directly. As a result the determination of the position of a given cabinet on a dimension ranging from single leadership to collective decision-making requires a detailed analysis.

The increased complexity of the government is of course materialised by the more exalted position of the Prime Minister in the cabinet structure. This is not surprising since Prime Ministers did not originally have a recognised position at all. Older constitutions, such as the Belgian text of 1830, did not mention the post of Prime Minister anymore than it was mentioned in earlier British statutes. This situation has changed everywhere, in some cases formally (as in the more recent constitutions of Germany, Italy, France or Spain) and in other cases informally. Prime Ministers have thus become a central element in the cabinet system.

Yet the position of the Prime Minister still varies markedly. Not all Prime Ministers have the right to appoint or dismiss ministers. They do not all have a large staff at their disposal. They do not all have a real control over the agenda. Overall, in The Netherlands, Finland, Belgium or Italy, it is difficult to describe the Prime Minister as being appreciably more than a *primus inter pares*.

At most it can perhaps be tentatively suggested that, in the 1980s, Prime Ministers have been better able to exercise influence over the cabinet, even in those countries where they had traditionally played a rather smaller part. However, cabinet government without strong prime ministerial leadership is not a thing of the past and cultural factors as well as deep cleavages seem able to prevent the ascension of many Prime Ministers towards a 'presidential' or near-presidential stature.

Meanwhile, around the Prime Minister, an oligarchy sometimes emerges at the top (although a formally constituted inner cabinet is relatively rare). Belgium is one of the few examples where the practice regularly occurs. There have been similar attempts in The Netherlands and in Britain, but they have either been temporary or have met with little success. In this respect at least, ministers have been generally able to maintain their status. The only minister to whom a general coordinating role has been conceded is the Minister of Finance.

Formal equality among the ministers no longer means formal equality within the whole government. However, in the majority of countries (not in all, admittedly), there now exists a second tier of ministers usually known as Secretaries of State (although not in Britain, where the Secretaries of State are cabinet ministers and where junior ministers are often named Ministers of State). This is indeed one of the ways in which it has been possible to keep the cabinet to a manageable size. The Scandinavian countries have so far resisted this development. The desire to maintain the principle of collective government has proved sufficiently strong in these countries for the structure to remain egalitarian. Elsewhere, as far as the government as a whole is concerned, it is not.

Yet the emergence of cabinet committees is perhaps the most interesting development, as it has contributed to increasing the complexity of the cabinet and to reducing the role of the cabinet meeting without altogether abolishing (or by undermining only in part) the idea of collegiality. The practice of setting up these committees is a characteristic of many cabinets, although it is not universal (Ireland, for instance, does not have them). These committees vary widely in number and status across countries, but they usually include the relevant ministers – junior ministers – and may or may not include civil servants as well. Their function is to 'prepare' (or in some cases even to 'take') decisions for the cabinet meeting. Often the result is that they tend to take decisions and filter to the cabinet meeting only those matters on which agreement has been achieved. On this, too, there are substantial differences across countries.

The structure of cabinets is thus in a state of flux, state of 'development'. The collegial principle which was embodied in the meeting of the cabinet is eroded, although to a different extent across Western Europe. It is eroded from the top, from the bottom and, so to speak, from inside. Yet there are forces – traditional but also contemporary, juridical as well as political – which ensure that collegiality is not wholly abandoned. This makes for variations across countries, as problems and traditions are different. The structures respond to these situations and provide a framework to the cabinet life.

CABINET LIFE

There is both an external and internal aspect to the life of cabinets. Externally, cabinet life is affected by the way the government relates to the main actors with which it has to deal – Parliament, the parties, the groups and the bureaucracy. The strength of the relationships and the forms which these relationships take are affected by the extent to which an 'administrative' tradition exists and by the configuration of the socio-political forces. As a result, Parliament can play a minimal part in the preoccupations of ministers in Austria, while in Britain and some other countries the House can at least place important hurdles which governments have to overcome (or attempt to by-pass).

It is true that nowhere does Parliament have the strength and autonomy of the US Congress but, as most ministers proceed from Parliament (to a varying extent, admittedly, this being probably one of the reasons why the role of Parliament is somewhat reduced in Austria), governments are physically related to what goes on in the House. The point has often been noted for Britain or Sweden but, in other countries too, Parliaments exercise some pressure which governments cannot ignore.

In fact, the part played by Parliament is closely tied to the role of parties. Parties are the institutions which really count, but Parliament provides the forum where they can fight and ultimately destroy governments. Thus efforts made to court Parliament are part of a general design to prevent party revolts from erupting. But these efforts are no substitutes, especially in coalition governments, for parallel efforts designed to ensure that the leadership of the parties of the majority support the government. This could of course be best achieved, in a coalition in particular, through party leaders joining the government, as has occasionally occurred in Belgium or Italy. But these leaders often do not wish to be closely tied to the cabinet's action.

The battle between cabinet and parties is a battle to occupy the centre of the political terrain. The traditional (British) view suggests that the cabinet is central, yet even in Britain, when Labour is in power, this 'axiom' becomes a mere postulate about which there is some doubt. The validity of the postulate is even more questionable when one considers Belgium, Finland, Italy, Germany, or The Netherlands (although the greater discipline of political actors in these last two countries seems to reduce the magnitude of the problem).

The role of groups in the life of cabinets can perhaps be viewed in the same light as that of parties. For the most important groups are, in many cases, linked to the parties, albeit often in an uneasy manner. The civil service, on the other hand, poses different problems which are perhaps understandably more acute in countries where neither the 'representative' nor the 'administrative' principles are fully adopted, whereas in Belgium (but also in Spain and Italy, albeit in a different manner) a mixture of 'representative' and 'bureaucratic' tradition prevails.

In a 'representative' cabinet (in Britain or in Ireland, for instance) the function of administration is squarely within the civil service, since the government is expected to 'govern'. 'Demarcation disputes' are relatively rare. In an 'administrative' system, such as that which broadly prevails in Austria, ministers and civil servants are close to each other and ministers can be expected to administer. Where the lines are less clearly drawn the relationship may be more difficult. This explains in part the expansion of the personal staffs of ministers in some countries, although these staffs are often unable to bridge the gap fully and problems between cabinet and administration periodically occur.

Thus the external life of modern Western European cabinets creates many tensions. So does the internal life, which appears increasingly dominated, and this time universally, by coordination problems. The acuteness of the difficulties arises from the increased complexity of governmental decisions, but the collegial character of cabinet structures – even if this character is partly undermined – tends to multiply difficulties in decision-making. Bureaucracies everywhere develop empires with closely-guarded borders, to be sure. But the fact that Western European cabinets are ostensibly not, and cannot be, wholly hierarchical tends to reinforce these 'natural' tendencies. This is why the various cabinet committees have been set up. The Council of Ministers could no longer, in the course of two to three-hour weekly meetings, coordinate effectively the activities of departments (especially where, as in many Continental countries, the Council has also to take large numbers of formal decisions).

Coordination takes place mainly through cabinet committees. This is true in most countries, whether the cabinet is 'representative' or 'administrative', 'majoritarian' or 'consociational' (although one of the most 'representative' cabinets, that of Ireland, does not operate through committees). But coordination also takes place by other means. Ministers of Finance are everywhere major agents of coordination. This has the effect of increasing their importance, while the Prime Ministers see their influence expand because they usually chair the most important committees. Yet, in these committees as well as in the cabinet meeting, 'ordinary' ministers can ensure to an extent that the issues for which they care are closely examined and bargains are struck which are acceptable to them. The leadership through and by committees which Prime Ministers exercise is limited by the (vested or other) interests for which ministers (and the civil servants who often accompany ministers) naturally fight.

## CABINET DECISION-MAKING

Decision-making in the cabinet has therefore to be seen as arising from many patterns of relationships. The cabinet system is a network composed of the Prime Minister, the Minister of Finance, the party leadership outside the government, the ministers individually and in groups, as well as some ministerial advisers. The shape of this network varies from country to country, because of the setting and structure of the cabinet. The network also varies over time, partly because the setting changes gradually and because of differences in the personalities involved.

There are thus variations in the extent to which the Council of Ministers is able to be genuinely involved in these decisions and not just to take a large number of formal decisions and to ratify the proposals made by other groups. In some countries the committee system is not highly developed and many coordination problems are discussed and resolved in the Council. In some countries, longer-term policy developments are also occasionally debated in full cabinet meetings. Perhaps most importantly, major conflicts among ministers and among coalition partners will eventually find their way to the cabinet meeting. The result will be either a compromise or the collapse of the government. Conflicts of this magnitude are rare, admittedly. Cabinet members can be expected to agree on many issues in single-party governments while, in a coalition, problems are either ironed out in advance when the cabinet is set up (this being the rationale for the lengthy process of government formation) or settled by party leaders over and above the heads of many cabinet members.

Thus the Council of Ministers is somewhat restricted in its decision-making scope. However, it remains an arena in which final appeals can be and are made, as well as (at least in some countries) a place where ideas are discussed. It is also where, as in Sweden or Finland, occasions such as informal lunches or dinners of ministers tend to foster collegiality.

Yet, for most matters most of the time, the cabinet decision-making process includes a long 'preparation' of solutions, which is often supervised or directed by the Prime Minister or the Minister of Finance. Thus even when the cabinet meeting remains important, a considerable weight is placed on formal and informal mechanisms which involve only part of the cabinet. At the root of the willingness of ministers to agree to what is, in effect, reduced collegiality, is the fact that government members are mainly involved in the work of their department. In countries in which the governmental tradition is more 'administrative' and/or where ministers are more frequently drawn from a variety of technical groups, this tendency towards what might be called 'ministerial sectionalism' is likely to be particularly strong.

Thus the cabinet does not appear to be necessarily, or indeed perhaps even frequently, truly dominated by the Prime Minister. For this to happen, special circumstances must boost his or her leadership, however strong his or her personal prestige may be and even if he or she is helped by a favourable institutional structure. By and large, cabinets where consociationalism prevails are less likely to be moving towards 'prime ministerialism'. 'Majoritarian' cabinets foster prime ministerial leadership, on the other hand, as these have to continuously fight battles against the opposition.

Adversary politics naturally results in the need for a 'chief' rather than for a 'chairman'.[3] This can be seen in the case of the 'pure majoritarian' cabinet, such as that of Britain, as well as in post-1975 Spain or indeed in post-1958 France. In the case of France, however, the President, rather than the Prime Minister, has been the beneficiary. In Germany and Austria, on the other hand, despite the strength of many Chancellors, the situation varies appreciably as a dose of 'consociationalism' prevails alongside the 'majoritarian element'. Indeed, in these two countries, the strength of the Chancellor is also boosted by the tradition of 'administrative hierarchy' which somewhat counter-balances 'consociational' trends.

Cabinet decision-making is not a myth or a pious hope, but it can be wider or narrower in terms of the persons involved and dependent on the shape of the cabinet network at a given time or place. For, to be efficient, cabinet decision-making requires a combination of factors to be simultaneously present. There has to be Prime Ministerial leadership to give some impulse and to prevent conflicts from provoking delays and a loss of morale. The help of a few of the more senior ministers and especially of the Minister of Finance can be of major value.

There has also to be a spirit of compromise and an acceptance of the part to be played by 'partial' cabinets, by informal committees and by negotiations. There has to be a desire on the part of ministers to be involved in the general life of the cabinet, although this must be combined with a policy of relative non-interference in the affairs of colleagues. There has, above all, to be an acceptance of the political role of the cabinet on the part of party leaders outside the government even if, especially in coalition cabinets, these party leaders have to exercise influence at critical moments in the life of these cabinets.

It is not surprising to see these conditions fulfilled only to an extent and in some countries. All the actors concerned must show considerable flexibility – a flexibility which may be difficult to achieve, particularly in times of great stress. Thus there are many cases where individuals, small groups or the Prime Minister have reduced, separately or together, the scope for collective action. Yet cabinet government still displays, in some countries often and in almost all the others occasionally, a substantial degree of collegial decision-making.


CONCLUSION

Cabinet government in Western Europe is complex to analyse. So complex that few efforts have been made to examine carefully the multitude of elements which need to be taken into account if we are to describe adequately, and subsequently attempt to explain, the behaviour of these executives.

What is clear is that this account and this explanation depend on the careful analysis of such elements as the composition and role of the cabinet meeting, the part played by committees, the position of the leader, the relationship between government and parties, the view which ministers have of their functions and the extent to which government members have a managerial or technical background. By attempting to describe these elements in a parallel manner, and by looking in a similar fashion at the questions which cabinets pose, this volume hopes to represent at least a first step towards a general understanding of the way cabinets operate in contemporary Western Europe.

**Notes**

1.  Allemann, F.R. (1956) *Bonn is nicht Weimar* (Cologne and Berlin: Kiepenheuer & Witsch).
2.  See for instance Kellner, P. and Crowther-Hunt, L.D. (1980) *The Civil Servants* (London: Macdonald).
3.  Farrell, B. (1971) *Chairman or Chief, The Role of Taoiseach in Irish Government* (Dublin: Gill & Macmillan).

# 1 The United Kingdom

## Martin Burch

### INTRODUCTION

The cabinet is often characterised as the supreme decision-making body in central government (Haldane, 1918). Some have seen it as the 'major instrument of government', the source of most legislative and administrative decisions, and the body that is most fully involved in the major decisions of government (Hanson and Walles, 1984; Mackintosh, 1977). This conventional view of cabinet emphasises its position 'at the apex of the executive' (Gordon Walker, 1973) and its control over policy-making and the oversight of government business (Bagehot, 1963). In practice the cabinet's position is not always as substantial as the conventional view suggests. There are very clear limits of competence and capacity which constrain the cabinet's decision-making potential. Moreover, the importance of the cabinet varies according to its complexion, the circumstances in which it operates and the style of leadership to which it is subject. It is this inherent variability that is one of the most remarkable features of cabinet government in Britain.

The variable nature of cabinet in part reflects the fact that it, in keeping with most other British political institutions, has no legally defined responsibilities and rules of procedure. In Britain there is no written, codified constitution setting out the structure of government and the powers, rights and obligations of those who work within it. Some aspects of government are covered by laws, but cabinet is only mentioned in passing in three pieces of legislation and was never mentioned at all in the laws of the land until 1937 (de Smith, 1981). Consequently nearly all of what is done is governed by a mixture of convention, past precedent and present practice (Hartley and Griffith, 1981).

There are three particularly important conventions or accepted ways of doing things which affect the operations of the cabinet. First, the convention of collective responsibility implies that decisions once reached should be supported by all members of the government and that dissenting ministers should either concur or resign (Marshall, 1984). Second is the convention that individual ministers are responsible to Parliament, at least in the sense of being answerable, for the work of their departments and may be expected to resign in the case of a major shortcoming (Wright, 1977; Marshall and Moodie, 1971). Hence the usual practice that all members of the government are also members of one of the two Chambers of Parliament. Finally, there is a convention of confidentiality whereby the business, operations and discussions of cabinet are expected to be kept private. These conventions serve to create three central features of cabinet government in Britain: its unity, its accountability and its secrecy. But because they are not legal rules they are often widely interpreted, frequently breached and gradually altered in the course of being applied. Today's convention may be tomorrow's past practice. This lack of clear and binding rules not only allows great variety, but also ensures flexibility and preserves the piecemeal way in which the institution has evolved in response to changing circumstances.

## 1   CABINET STRUCTURE

### Origins and development

The cabinet can be traced back to the councils of advisers that served the King in medieval times. Most historians, however, locate the antecedents of the modern cabinet amongst the group of advisers that were drawn about him by Charles II in the late seventeenth century. It was at this time that the idea of a group of senior ministers meeting together became established, but there was no Prime Minister and little in the way of collective decision-making as the ministers' sole function was to serve and to be answerable to the monarch. Thereafter there were a number of important developments. The decline of monarchical influence was complemented by the rise of the Prime Minister, an office which was fully established by the premiership of William Pitt the Younger from 1804 (Mackintosh, 1977; Rush, 1984).

During the remainder of the nineteenth century two important changes took place. First, rather than being accountable to the monarch, ministers became answerable to Parliament and, increasingly within Parliament, to the House of Commons. This change relfected the growth in popular suffrage through the extension of the franchise, a development which also contributed to the emergence of a mass two-party system with increasingly cohesive voting behaviour along party lines in the House of Commons. The consequences of the growth of party has been that the cabinet's true power base has become the majority party in

Parliament, while control over party voting in Parliament by party leaderships has meant that the cabinet has generally been able to dominate the majority party (Hailsham, 1976).

In the present century another factor, also with nineteenth century origins, has helped to shape the operation of cabinet – namely the growth in the size, complexity and specialised nature of government and the consequent increase in the workload undertaken by ministers. In order to ensure the handling of business two important adjuncts to cabinet have been developed. First, a Secretariat providing secretarial and administrative help. This was initiated in 1916 and today it forms the central part of a much wider Cabinet Office with its staff of around 600 civil servants (Mosley, 1969). Second, the establishment of a system of cabinet committees to decide on or prepare issues for cabinet. The first permanent committee was established in 1906, but apart from a temporary extension in the number of committees during World War One, the major development did not take place until World War Two. And it is this structure, substantially reformed during the Attlee administration (1945–1951), that forms the basis of the present system (Hennessey and Arends, 1983).

So, while the origins of the cabinet can be traced back many centuries, its present structure reflects the demands of changes in Parliament and party and in the scale of government which emerged during the latter part of the nineteenth century. The consequence of these changes has meant that it is necessary to speak, not simply about the cabinet in isolation, but to place it in the context of the wider set of institutions, especially its committees and Secretariat. We can refer to this as the cabinet system, and it is this system and the relationships within it that needs to be considered in any attempt to understand cabinet government in Britain.

## Features and rules of the cabinet

Since 1945 the cabinet has usually had around 20 members. But there have been some variations as the figures in Table 1.1 show. A short period of experimenting with a smaller cabinet of 'overlord' ministers was tried by Churchill, but this was unsuccessful. The numbers involved began to grow slightly in the 1960s and, with the exception of Mr Heath's initial cabinet, membership has remained above 20 until the present day. At the same time the number of ministers in the government has grown from 66 under Attlee to 85 under Thatcher (these figures exclude Whips and Members of Her Majesty's Household, but include Junior Ministers).

Given the growth in the number of ministers the main reason that
cabinets have not grown even larger is that in the late 1960s and
throughout the 1970s a series of amalgamations of ministries took place
(Pollitt, 1984). It is the senior Minister or Secretary of State in each of
these ministries that nowadays has the cabinet post.

TABLE 1.1    Cabinets in Britain: 1945–1987

| PM | PM Party | Date in | Size |
|---|---|---|---|
| Attlee | Labour | 07.45 | 21 |
| Attlee | Labour | 02.50 | 18 |
| Churchill | Conservative | 10.51 | 16 |
| Eden | Conservative | 04.55 | 18 |
| Eden | Conservative | 05.55 | 18 |
| Macmillan | Conservative | 01.57 | 19 |
| Macmillan | Conservative | 10.59 | 20 |
| Douglas-Home | Conservative | 10.63 | 22 |
| Wilson | Labour | 10.64 | 22 |
| Wilson | Labour | 03.66 | 22 |
| Heath | Conservative | 06.70 | 18 |
| Wilson | Labour | 03.74 | 21 |
| Wilson | Labour | 10.74 | 23 |
| Callaghan | Labour | 04.76 | 23 |
| Thatcher | Conservative | 05.79 | 22 |
| Thatcher | Conservative | 06.83 | 21 |
| Thatcher | Conservative | 06.87 | 21 |

The cabinet consists of the senior figures in government, those
heading the major departments as well as some non-departmental
ministers. It always includes the senior Treasury or Finance Minister,
the Chancellor of the Exchequer and, since 1977, another Treasury
minister, the Chief Secretary. Other positions always represented are
those of the Secretaries of State for Foreign and Commonwealth
Affairs, Home Affairs, Scotland, and Defence and, since 1964, the
Secretary of State for Wales, while the Secretary of State for Northern
Ireland has been in the cabinet since 1972. In addition, the Lord
Chancellor, who is the head of the judiciary, is always a member as are
one or two non-departmental ministers such as the Lord President of the
Council and the Lord Privy Seal. These ancient titles involve limited
duties and the ministers are free to take on tasks as they arise or to chair
cabinet committees. Other departmental ministers are appointed to the

cabinet in accordance with the importance of their department. This varies from government to government, but nowadays nearly all departments are included.

Cabinet meetings are held on a weekly basis, on a Thursday morning for one-and-a-half to three hours. Usually no formal cabinet meetings are held for four to six weeks during the parliamentary recess (Wilson, 1976). The number of meetings of cabinet has tended to decline in the post-war period. Under Attlee and Churchill it met regularly twice a week on Tuesdays and Thursdays with an annual total of about 90 formal meetings. Heath seems to have adopted a similar twice weekly schedule (Heath, 1976). Under Wilson, Callaghan and Thatcher the once-weekly regular meeting has been the norm. Both Wilson and Callaghan, however, tended to hold extra meetings on particular issues. Under Thatcher extra meetings are comparatively rare and Hennessey has calculated that she probably holds about 40 to 45 meetings a year which is an all-time low over the post-war period (Hennessey, 1986). Of course as cabinet meets less frequently and for only a short time, its capacity for taking a wide range of decisions is bound to be limited. By necessity much business has to be decided outside the cabinet or at least largely determined by the time it reaches it.

As there are no constitutional precepts or legal statutes governing the operation of the cabinet, rules are partly derived from past practices. These are laid out in a confidential document entitled 'Questions of Procedure for Ministers', which is given to each cabinet member by the Secretariat when he or she joins the cabinet or a new cabinet is formed following a General Election. This document originated in the period immediately after World War One and has been greatly expanded since then to cover more than 130 paragraphs of text. The document states that matters which fall wholly within the departmental responsibility of a single minister and do not engage the collective responsibility of the government should not be brought to cabinet or its committees, though if there is any doubt the minister is advised to bring the matter forward.

All items coming before the cabinet or its committees have to be discussed with the Treasury beforehand if they involve expenditure for extra staffing or affect general financial policy. Also any consequences for Britain's obligations as a member of the EEC must be laid out in any proposal, while the government's Law Officers have to be consulted about any matters involving legal considerations. 'Questions' makes clear that committees have full power to make decisions without reference to cabinet, while appeals to the cabinet by committee members against decisions reached in committee are only allowed by the Prime

Minister after consultation, and sometimes agreement, with the committee chairman. Other parts of the rules deal with the doctrine of collective responsibility, the recording of cabinet proceedings, the manner of presenting documents to cabinet, the confidentiality of cabinet and committee proceedings and papers, the circumstances under which advisers and departmental civil servants are allowed to see cabinet papers and how ministers should handle their private interests while they are members of the government (*New Statesman*, 1986; Gordon Walker, 1973).

The precise status of these informal rules is not clear. Certainly they are used as a basis for cabinet practice, but they are not binding and they are not always applied rigidly. Some argue that the formal rules tend to strengthen the position of the Prime Minister and the Secretariat (Crossman, 1972). For it is the Prime Minister, advised by the Secretary to the Cabinet (the civil servant who heads the Cabinet Office and the Secretariat) and other Cabinet Office officials, who adapts and applies the procedure. And formally speaking it is the Prime Minister who decides which committees are to be established, their terms of reference and their membership. However, the Prime Minister does not have a completely free hand in these matters: certain committees are always established and those ministers with departmental interests in the area covered by the committee are bound to be included (Brown, 1968). The important point is that within the confines of cabinet tradition and subject to the advice of the Secretary to the Cabinet, it is the Prime Minister, and not the other members of the cabinet, who controls the composition, structure and procedures of cabinet.

In order to reach a decision cabinet hardly ever votes, but when it does vote it is usually only on minor procedural matters (Heath, 1976; Wilson, 1976). The usual approach is for the Prime Minister to sum up the sense of the meeting and if this is not challenged it forms the basis for the Secretariat's recording of the decisions reached. The way of weighing up the cabinet's view varies. On many issues only a few ministers make a contribution; in these instances the Prime Minister may attempt to indicate the trend of the views expressed. Where issues involve wider discussion one technique is to 'collect the voices' by going around the table and working out who is for and who is against a proposal (Heath, 1976).

The cabinet agenda is drawn up by the Prime Minister in consultation with the Secretary to the Cabinet. Two items are usually on the agenda of each cabinet – a report on forthcoming parliamentary business and a report on foreign affairs. Matters for inclusion on the agenda can be originated by the Prime Minister or at the request of a minister. Most commonly items arise from cabinet committees or inter-departmental discussions though they may be introduced in response to an immediate and developing series of events and there are some items which are regularly considered such as the annual review of public expenditure. To a large extent many of the items coming to cabinet work their way up the system and this limits the Prime Ministers freedom to keep items off the agenda. Materials are prepared for cabinet and its committees either within the department principally concerned or through inter-departmental groups of officials and ministers. Because of the workload most of the necessary preparatory work is undertaken by civil servants, though the initiative is expected to come from ministers.

All these rules about the conduct of cabinet business remain informal and adaptable. This inherent flexibility partly reflects the necessity of adapting rules to rapidly changing circumstances and requirements. Different Prime Ministers wish to run their cabinets in different ways and the variety of personalities and power relationships in different cabinets require some variation in approach. Moreover the wider political circumstances in which each cabinet operates helps to condition and shape the application of rules.

## 2 CABINET LIFE

### The political context

Since 1945 at the parliamentary level Britain has had a stable two-party system in which governments have been dominated by one or other of the major parties – Conservative or Labour. Since the mid-1960s there has been a growth in electoral support for other parties, but because of the even distribution of this support and the non-proportional nature of the electoral system changes in electoral support have had little consequences for the overall distribution of parliamentary seats. Since 1945 no government has been elected with a majority of the votes cast – the highest percentage achieved by a single party was the 49.7 per cent gained by the Conservative Party in 1955. So, characteristically, Britain has a cabinet system that enjoys majority support in the House of Commons and minority support amongst the electorate. Minority electoral support has neither served to weaken nor limit the operation of cabinet government.

However, there have been two exceptions to this pattern in recent years. From February to October 1974, a Labour government with a minority of seats (three less than all other parties combined) held office. Secondly, the Labour government returned in the October 1974 election had a majority of three which was soon whittled away through losses in by-elections; so in March 1977 the government formed a parliamentary pact with the third largest party, the Liberals, whereby they supported the government in Parliament in return for consultation on policy matters. This was a parliamentary pact and no Liberals entered the government.

The power base of the cabinet is thus not principally the electorate, but the majority party in the House of Commons. The role of party differs according to whether the government is Labour or Conservative. In the case of Labour, the party outside Parliament has a formal role to play in party policy-making both through the Annual Conference and the party's National Executive Committee. In practice the opinions of these bodies is something that Labour cabinets have to be aware of, though they are not obliged to accept them (McKenzie, 1963; Minkin, 1978). Nor do these bodies have any formal_role in determining ministerial appointments in government, though in 1981 the Labour Party adopted a new method of electing its leader whereby instead of leaving the task to the Parliamentary Party the leader is chosen by an electoral college consisting of 40 per cent trade unions, 30 per cent members of the mass party in the country, and 30 per cent MPs. This would obviously have consequences for the operation of cabinet government if a Labour Prime Minister resigned in office and a new Prime Minister had to be chosen. However, as Labour has been out of office since 1979, such a situation has not yet arisen. The Conservative Party outside Parliament has no formal role in the shaping of policy and personnel. Conservative leaders are given a free hand in these matters, though obviously to some extent they are bound to take into account party opinions when considering possible policy options (Norton and Aughey, 1981).

It is the parliamentary parties especially in the House of Commons and on the governing side that are the most significant sources of party influence. Important channels of communication exist between ministers, the party whips (who help organise party support in Parliament) and the other MPs and backbenchers belonging to the governing party. A further link is provided by Parliamentary Private Secretaries (PPSs), who are MPs who serve each minister and help to maintain contact between them and the backbench members of their party. In addition to these contacts, both party leaderships when in government maintain formal connections with various Parliamentary Party committees and their officers such as those from the Parliamentary Committee in the Labour Party, the 1922 Committee and its subject committees in the Conservative Party. The extent of the influence of backbench MPs in the major parties upon their respective cabinets has changed in recent years. The Parliamentary Labour Party has always been influential, while Conservative backbenchers traditionally played a less central role. In the 1970s and 1980s, however, the influence of Conservative backbenchers increased. This change followed the 1965 and 1974 reforms in the Conservative Party's leadership selection process, which for the first time gave Conservative MPs responsibility for the election and dismissal of the party leader. Subsequently Conservative leaders have attempted to develop closer liaison with their MPs (Burch, 1983). This growth in backbench influence has not been unique to the Conservative Party and Norton has documented a general decline in party discipline in the Parliaments since 1970 (Norton, 1980). Yet this decline, though significant, should not be exaggerated. Judged in terms of the extent to which MPs follow the party line in voting, cohesion in both Parliamentary Parties has remained well above 90 per cent (Rose, 1983).

Outside interests also impinge upon the work of the cabinet, but usually in an indirect manner and through the agency of civil servants in the ministries. When it comes to the formation of policy proposals it is they who liaise with the representatives of interest groups, some of whom are involved on a formalised basis as members of advisory bodies attached to the various departments (Marsh, 1983). However, some interest groups may liaise directly with the minister, and this tends to occur when there is a close connection between the minister's party and a particular set of interest groups, as is the case within the Labour Party and some trade unions.

Relations with the media are either handled through public statements usually announced in Parliament or, more commonly, on an unattributable basis through meetings with the Parliamentary Press Corps or 'lobby' (Tunstall, 1970; Seymour-Ure, 1968). This lobby consists of representatives from the major broadcasting companies and newspapers, who are briefed in private by government-appointed information officers and press secretaries. The most important of these briefings, on a twice daily basis, is held by the Prime Minister's Press Secretary (Cockerell, Hennessey and Walker, 1985). The cabinet itself does not have a Press Secretary, though members of the cabinet have press and information officers attached to their departments and they may, unofficially and surreptitiously, 'leak' information to members of the lobby or other journalists.

While relations with outside interests and the media are important conditioning influences, it is really party in the House of Commons that forms the bedrock of cabinet power. It ensures the survival of the Prime Minister and the cabinet and imposes limits on their areas of manoeuvre. This, and the need every four or five years to face the test of electoral opinion, provide the most important elements in the framework of political constraints within which cabinet operates.

## Coordination

Coordination of the work of the cabinet is achieved through a number of formal mechanisms such as committees and the Secretariat. The exact number, terms of references and composition of cabinet committees varies from Prime Minister to Prime Minister. There are two basic types of committee: standing or permanent committees and *ad hoc* or temporary ones. The latter are usually established to handle a specific issue and are given a number rather than a title. Standing committees are designated with initials such as EA for Economic Strategy Committee. Ministers who are not in the cabinet are often members of cabinet committees. Some committees consist solely of ministers, but these are usually backed up by committees of civil servants who feed information through to the ministerial committee. There are also one or two mixed committees of civil servants and ministers dealing with matters to do with national security. Committees vary in terms of their size, some involving three of four persons, others, such as Mrs Thatcher's Economic Strategy Committee, contain more than half the cabinet. Some of the more important committees are chaired by the Prime Minister, others are chaired by non-departmental ministers and, occasionally, departmental ministers (Mackie and Hogwood, 1985).

The number of committees, their composition and terms of reference are closely-guarded secrets. Hennessey calculates that between 1964 and 1969 the Labour government under Wilson established 235 *ad hoc* committees. Between 1974 and 1976 Harold Wilson set up about 120 *ad hoc* groups, while his successor, James Callaghan, established around 160 during his three-year tenure as Prime Minister. After six and a half years in Office, Thatcher had by early 1986 created 43 standing committees and 122 *ad hoc* committees. These calculations can be compared to those officially available for the Attlee (1945–51) and Churchill (1951–55) administrations, which respectively accumulated

148 standing plus 313 *ad hoc* and 137 standing plus 109 *ad hoc* committees (Hennessey, 1985).

The committees as well as the rest of the operation of cabinet is coordinated by members of the Secretariat. The Secretary to the Cabinet works very closely with the Prime Minister both in drawing up the agendas for cabinet and some of its committees, in advising about the establishment and composition of committes, and in helping to monitor the development of business within the cabinet system. Central to this coordinative role are a number of management committees which meet on a weekly basis and involve the Secretary to the Cabinet and officials from the Secretariat and the Prime Minister's Office. The process begins early in the week with the formulation of proposals for the business to be handled by cabinet and its ministerial and official committees over the coming weeks. Periodically this is supplemented by a 'forward look' of up to six months ahead. This provisional programme is then discussed on the Thursday at a meeting of officials from the Secretariat plus officials from the Prime Minister's Office under the chairmanship of the Secretary to the Cabinet. The proposals arising out of this discussion are then placed before the Prime Minister, who usually discusses the proposals with advisers and the Chief Whip on the Friday morning (Donoughue, 1987).

Apart from time-tabling and planning the operation of the cabinet and its committees, the Secretariat circulates information and advise and records and monitors the application of decisions. Its coordinative function needs to be set alongside that of the Prime Minister and his or her staff. The Prime Minister is the only member of the cabinet who is fully informed about what is happening in the cabinet system. Prime Ministers are assisted by members of their Office, especially their five or six Private Secretaries. Most communications to the Prime Minister are directed through these civil servants and they are involved on behalf of the Prime Minister in the Secretariat's planning and coordination functions (Jones, 1985).

Coordination is also achieved through regular meetings of the top civil servants who head each of the ministries. These Permanent Secretaries meet formally once a week to discuss the business that will come before cabinet and how Ministers are to be advised on it (Haines, 1977). Finally, coordination in a formal manner across departments is achieved through meetings between two departments, their ministers and officials.

These formal means of coordination are supplemented by less formal mechanisms. Personal contacts, bargaining and so forth are a central

part of any policy process and no less so than in the highly political
environment that operates within and around cabinet. The most
important of these is what might be termed Prime Ministerial intervention. In theory the Prime Minister can become involved in any area of
policy-making, though in practice most Prime Ministers will avoid
unduly upsetting powerful departmental ministers. A good deal of
business is conducted through discussions between the relevant minister
and the Premier. The extent to which this takes place varies from
administration to administration. When it comes to taking initiatives the
modern Prime Minister is assisted by a small political and personal
advisory staff of about fifteen people including, since 1974, a Policy Unit
of specialist, party appointees.

The exact way in which a particular cabinet works depends very much
upon the style of leadership developed by the Prime Minister. A major
distinction can be drawn between the Chairman and Leader styles of
conducting business. These are perhaps best illustrated in the cases of
Callaghan and Thatcher. Callaghan fitted into the 'chairman' mould
with his desire to achieve agreement and a united cabinet. He tended to
allow relatively lengthy discussions on important issues and to wait to
hear the views of ministers before revealing his own position (Donoughue,
1987). Thatcher has taken more of a leading role in cabinet by pre-
empting the initiative in cabinet discussion and by expressing her views
at the outset. She has tended to restrict the discussion of some important
matters and has shown a preference for settling issues outside cabinet.
She has proved more willing than most previous Prime Ministers to put
at risk the unanimity of cabinet (Burch, 1983; King, 1985). Of course, the
style of a cabinet also depends on the other members of the cabinet, their
approaches to business and what they will allow their colleagues,
including the Prime Minister, to get away with.


3   CABINET DECISION-MAKING

**Techniques and methods of decision-making**

Those items that are brought before cabinet are subject to certain
procedures which help to restrict extraneous business and discussion.
Members of cabinet are expected to stick to the agenda before them and
to the examination of items that have been fully and properly notified. It
is generally the practice that when a minister wishes to raise a matter
orally in cabinet the Prime Minister's consent has to be sought through

the Secretary to the Cabinet. Items brought to the cabinet are usually in the form of 'memoranda'. According to 'Questions', the model memorandum does 'not exceed two pages at maximum', and 'explains at the outset what the problem is, indicates briefly the relevant considerations, and concludes with a precise statement of the decisions sought' (*New Statesman*, 1986). Summaries are expected to be only a few lines in length and covering notes are discouraged. 'Questions' goes on to say that memoranda should be circulated at least a week and never less than 48 hours beforehand. These tight procedures are not, however, always followed. Memoranda are often more than two pages long, often have lengthy appendices attached, and are sometimes circulated just before the meeting. Nevertheless, the aim of limiting the material presented to cabinet members is paramount.

The circulation of cabinet and cabinet committee memoranda is nearly always in the hands of the Secretariat. In the case of cabinet memoranda the Secretariat is normally also responsible for reproducing the memoranda sometimes on the basis of the text sent to it by the originating department. As already noted, the Secretariat will only circulate a memorandum if certain preconditions are met. 'Questions' is very specific on the role that the Secretariat plays in controlling the circulation of cabinet and committee memoranda, stating that if any 'memorandum is reproduced by the originating department, all copies should be sent to the Cabinet Office, and application should be made to the Cabinet Office for any additional copies required by the reproducing Department' (Hennessey, 1986). This control by the Secretariat of the flow of material within the cabinet system helps to coordinate decision-making and to preserve the confidentiality of government business. It can also serve to strengthen the centre against the departments.

Discussions in cabinet take place on the basis of the submitted memorandum. Usually they are opened by the chairman of the cabinet committee from which the item may have emerged, or sometimes the minister from the originating department. Who speaks and when is a matter for the Prime Minister, though obviously those ministers most involved in the item under discussion can expect to be called. All contributions are expected to be to the point (Home, 1985). There is a precedent in cabinet in that more senior ministers can be expected to make a fuller contribution and to be called on first to speak outside their departmental areas (Wilson, 1976; Morrison, 1964). The record of cabinet proceedings is taken by the Secretary to the Cabinet and two officials from the Secretariat. The record is limited to the decisions taken and such summary of the discussion as may be necessary for the guidance of those who have to take action on them. Summaries are given of the item under discussion, the points made by the sponsoring minister, an outline of the points raised in discussion without attribution to individuals and the decision reached. This record is referred to as the Cabinet Conclusions (Wilson, 1976).

Cabinet Conclusions serve as 'instructions for action to departments' (Gordon Walker, 1973). The decisions reached by the cabinet are monitored and followed up by the Secretariat who periodically circulate reports on the implementation of decisions (Morrison, 1964). In order to facilitate this process the Secretary to the Cabinet keeps a full index of Conclusions with a network of cross references (Mackenzie and Grove, 1957). In recent years under Thatcher's premiership, the monitoring of some decisions has also been undertaken by members of her Policy Unit and political office. Otherwise the responsibility for carrying out policy is in the hands of departmental officials.

**What does cabinet decide?**

Clearly, because of limits on time and capacity cabinet is able to handle, only a small amount of the potential decision-taking at the higher levels of government. The bulk of business is handled elsewhere in departments and committees. This much is self-evident. Where the difficulty arises is in assessing whether cabinet effectively oversees and controls decision-taking in the cabinet system as most conventional theories would suggest. There are two criteria by which cabinet's competence in this matter might be judged. First whether it decides nearly all the major and significant issues and, second, whether it subjects to scrutiny nearly all the decisions made elsewhere.

Cabinet's competence in handling both these tasks is open to argument. In the first place it is not always clear as to what are the major and significant issues. Any definition is bound to be subjective and the significance of many issues will be a matter of opinion. Moreover, some matters that later turn out to be of great importance may not have appeared so at the time of decision. For these reasons alone it is certain that some major and significant decisions will not come before cabinet. It is also clear that some obviously major issues never come to cabinet (Burch, 1987). For instance, since at least 1977, major decisions about financial policy have been handled at meetings between Treasury ministers, the Prime Minister, Treasury officials and officials from the Bank of England (Donoughue, 1987). As far as cabinet's facility to scrutinize decisions made elsewhere is concerned, this is limited by the time available and the ability of the non-involved members of cabinet to make useful contributions. The evidence of those who have served in cabinet suggests that such scrutiny when it operates is erratic and of a very general nature – usually amounting to simply being informed about some of the things that have been decided elsewhere.

The limits of time and capacity also apply to the cabinet's ability to handle effectively all those major decisions that do reach it. With a constrained timetable, time taken up deciding one issue means less opportunity to deliberate over another. So, while cabinet may oversee some major decisions, it is not able to do so effectively in every case. Moreover, those matters that do reach cabinet for decision are often largely predetermined by the time they get there. They arrive with a weight of opinion behind them which often precludes wide-ranging discussion and effective decision-making. Detailed policy matters are usually settled in departments or between departments or at cabinet committee level. There are cases of policy issues being considered in detail in cabinet, especially those involving important changes in the framework of government such as the proposal to create elected regional governments in Scotland and Wales in 1978 and 1979. But these are the exception rather than the rule and most policy issues are examined in detail before they reach cabinet.

Cabinet may occasionally get involved in solving conflictual matters regardless of their intrinsic importance – but this is unusual. Business is more likely to be sent back if there is not agreement amongst departments. Indeed it is a function of the Secretariat to ensure that all disputes are settled and or ironed out by the time an issue reaches the cabinet or even one of its committees (Morrison, 1964). So conflictual matters only arrive at cabinet if all other means of resolving them have been exhausted. The main means of solving conflicts tends to be through either discussions between departments or arbitration by the Prime Minister or a committee chairman. Occasionally the cabinet may establish a committee with the function of arbitrating between the demands of competing departments, such as that used by the Thatcher government to iron out disagreements over public expenditure details (Jenkins, 1985).

In essence cabinet tends to resolve those issues that cannot be resolved elsewhere. It may also, depending upon the complexion of the government and the style of leadership, lay out broad strategy and take a very general oversight role in relation to policy-making. It is, however, misleading to suggest that the cabinet collectively and persistently controls policy-making. Because much decision-making on major items is spread outside the cabinet it is essential to place it in the context of the wider cabinet system. It is this system which is the locus of decision-making. The cabinet can be seen as playing an important and central part in this system, but it is not the only arena for decision-making. Many matters are decided amongst only a small group of cabinet members or between ministers and civil servants or between a minister and the Prime Minister.

Once placed within these parameters cabinet begins to make sense as a central part of a wider process of decision-making. The next step is to realize that the precise nature of the cabinet system varies from time to time and from premiership to premiership. Even within a premiership different strategies of managing business may be used depending upon the influence of the various factions within a government. So the range of major decisions into which cabinet is drawn very much depends upon the position and approach of the Prime Minister and the other members of the cabinet.

# 2 Ireland. The Irish Cabinet System: More British than the British Themselves

Brian Farrell

## 1 CABINET SETTING

### The constitutional position

Article 6 of *Bunreacht na hEireann* (the Irish Constitution) declares that:

> all powers of government legislative, executive and judicial, derive, under God, from the people whose right it is to designate the rulers of the State and, in final appeal, to decide all questions of national policy, according to the requirements of the common god.

This robust republicanism is, however, disciplined within the customary institutional restraints of a Westminister-style system of cabinet government. The term 'cabinet' does not occur in the Constitution, which refers to 'the government', and provides a basic but incomplete – and in some ways misleading – description of the role of the executive in the Republic of Ireland (Chubb, 1976; Chubb, 1983).

The principal provisions are in Article 28, headed 'The government'. This specifies that the government shall consist of not less than seven and not more than fifteen members. All are required to be parliamentarians. No more than two may be members of *Seanad Eireann* (the Senate – a relatively powerless, indirectly elected and appointed upper house). The *Taoiseach* (Prime Minister), *Tanaiste* (Deputy PM) and the Minister for Finance must be members of *Dail Eireann* (the popularly elected Chamber of Deputies). All members of the government have the right to attend and be heard in both *Dail* and *Seanad*.

Section 4 of Article 28 makes the government 'responsible to *Dail Eireann*', and requires it to present annual estimates of receipts and expenditure to the *Dail*. It also requires that 'the government shall meet and act as a collective authority, and shall be collectively responsible for the Departments of State administered by the members of the government'.

33

The *Taoiseach*, described as 'the head of government', is nominated by the *Dail* and, in turn, nominates the other members of the government for parliamentary approval. The *Taoiseach* 'may at any time, for reasons which seem to him sufficient' request ministerial resignations; failures to comply may lead to dismissal. The *Taoiseach* also nominates the Attorney-General and eleven of the sixty-member *Seanad*. On the resignation of the *Taoiseach*, 'the other members of the government shall be deemed to have resigned'. The *Taoiseach* presents bills to the President for signature and promulgation and is required to keep the President 'generally informed on matters of domestic and international policy'.

The President is accorded a largely ceremonial role and typically acts on the binding 'advice' of the government or of the *Taoiseach* (for example in summoning and dissolving the *Dail*, or appointing the duly nominated ministers). The President has three discretionary powers. Bills (other than money bills and bills proposing a constitutional referendum) may be referred to the Supreme Court to test their constitutionality. This requires prior consultation with the Council of State (an advisory body of senior politicians, including *Taoiseach, Tanaiste* and Attorney-General) and has been used sparingly. The President may, 'in his absolute discretion', refuse a parliamentary dissolution to a *Taoiseach* 'who has ceased to retain the support of a majority in the *Dail Eireann*'. This right has never been exercised. The President may also resign and thus produce a constitutional and political crisis (Gallagher, 1977).

The last section of Article 28 catalogues a series of matters to be 'regulated in accordance with law', including the organisation, distribution and designation of ministerial responsibilities for the Department of State. These statutory provisions are principally enshrined in the Ministers and Secretaries Act, 1924, and its subsequent amending acts. These provide for specified Departments of State with stated responsibilities in functional areas (for instance, Finance, Agriculture, Foreign Affairs, Education and Justice), each headed by a minister who is described as 'a corporation sole'. That is, all the Department's acts are the acts of its minister . . . he is not empowered by statute to delegate his power to his civil servants . . . the personal and final responsibility of the minister is in every instance stressed' (PSORG, 1969, 61). Typically, each member of the government is responsible for a single department or a small group of cognate departments. In recent years the number, titles and functions of departments have been altered and amalgamated more frequently.

The principal act and its amendments also provide for the appointment of parliamentarians as junior ministers. Initially, the number of these 'Parliamentary Secretaries' was limited to seven; the maximum has now been increased to fifteen and the title changed to 'Minister of State'. Despite efforts to give them greater specific responsibilities, they have remained junior and dependent upon their senior ministerial colleagues for access to, and involvement in, cabinet decision-making. They do not normally attend meetings and cannot have the same depth of understanding of government policy as a minister.

**Duration in office**

In the first 25 years of the state's existence there was little alternation of parties in government and single-party government was the norm (see Table 2.1). Ten years of *Cumann na nGaedheal* in office (1922–1932), were followed by an unbroken period of sixteen-rule by *Fianna Fail*. Since 1948 there has been an irregular transfer of power between single-party *Fianna Fail* cabinets and coalition governments formed by *Fine Gael* and Labour (sometimes involving, or supported by, smaller parties and independent deputies). These changes occurred at three-yearly intervals between 1948 and 1957. *Fianna Fail* then had another uninterrupted sixteen-year period in office. Since 1973 every general election has been followed by a change of government – and noticeably by internal changes of personnel within parties and governments – with a particularly acute volatility leading to three general elections between June 1981 and November 1982. The most recent general election in February 1987, led to the creation of a minority *Fianna Fail* government.

## 2  CABINET STRUCTURE

**Historical origins**

Even prior to the formal establishment of the new Irish state an embryonic cabinet system was established and in place (Farrell, 1969; Farrell, 1971a).

The United Kingdom general election of 1918 was fought on a greatly enlarged franchise which trebled the electoral register. This offered an opportunity to the coalition of political forces merged in the newly created *Sinn Fein* party to implement its policy of immediate separation from Britain. The *Sinn Fein* members refused to take their seats in

TABLE 2.1   Irish Governments: September 1922 to December 1982

| Date in | Government | Government Type in years | Duration |
|---|---|---|---|
| Sept. 1922 | Pro-Treaty (1) | Single Party Majority | 01.0(2) |
| Sept. 1923 | Cumann na nGaedheal (2) | Single Party Majority | 03.7(2) |
| June 1927 | Cumann na nGaedheal (2) | Single Party Majority | 00.3 |
| Oct. 1927 | Cumann na nGaedheal (3) | Single Party Majority | 04.4 |
| March 1932 | Fianna Fail | Single Party Majority | 00.9 |
| Feb. 1933 | Fianna Fail | Single Party Majority | 04.4 |
| July 1937 | Fianna Fail | Single Party Majority | 00.9 |
| June 1938 | Fianna Fail | Single Party Majority | 05.0 |
| July 1943 | Fianna Fail | Single Party Majority | 00.9 |
| June 1944 | Fianna Fail | Single Party Majority | 03.7 |
| Feb. 1948 | Inter-party (4) | Coalition | 03.3 |
| June 1951 | Fianna Fail | Single Party Minority | 03.0 |
| June 1954 | Inter-party (5) | Coalition | 02.8 |
| March 1957 | Fianna Fail | Single Party Majority | 04.6 |
| Oct. 1961 | Fianna Fail | Single Party Majority | 03.5 |
| April 1965 | Fianna Fail (6) | Single Party Majority | 04.2 |
| July 1969 | Fianna Fail | Single Party Majority | 03.7 |
| March 1973 | National Coalition (7) | Coalition | 04.3 |
| July 1977 | Fianna Fail | Single Party Majority | 04.3 |
| June 1981 | Coalition (8) | Coalition | 00.7 |
| March 1982 | Fianna Fail | Single Party Minority | 00.7 |
| Dec. 1982 | Coalition (8) | Coalition | 04.2 |
| March 1987 | Fianna Fail | Single Party Majority | |
| Totals | | Single Party Majority | 34.7 |
| | | Single Party Minority | 14.7 |
| | | Coalition Government | 15.4 |

SOURCES: derived from Chubb, *Cabinet Government in Ireland*, with additional material by author.

NOTES:
(1) From Spring 1923 called Cumann na nGaedhael
(2) Government majority due to fact that Fianna Fail, the biggest opposition party, did not take their seats.
(3) The Government had the support of the Farmers' Party which, however, ceased to operate as a party and its members for all intents and purposes became members of Cumann na nGaedheal. In 1930 the Government resigned after a parliamentary defeat.
(4) A coalition of all parties except Fianna Fail. It also included Independents.
(5) A coalition of Fine Gael, the Labour Party and Clann na Talmham.
(6) Fianna Fail won exactly half the seats.
(7) A coalition of Fine Gael and the Labour Party.
(8) A coalition of Fine Gael and Labour.

Westminister and instead formed *Dail Eireann*, an independent Irish parliament in Dublin. The *Dail* adopted a simple constitution based on the Westminister model, elected a Prime Minister and approved his nomination of four other ministers.

During the troubled years 1919–1922, despite a guerilla-type war of independence, this small cabinet of *Sinn Fein* party leaders, under de Valera, set out to establish the framework of the new Irish state within the shell of the old British regime in Ireland.

The negotiation of a treaty with the British government in 1921 precipitated a cabinet crisis. When the issue was put to the *Dail*, the treaty was carried against de Valera's advice. The split within the cabinet, parliament and party quickly spilled over beyond constitutional limits and led to a short but bitter civil war in which de Valera and the forces of republican *Sinn Fein* were defeated and laid down arms in May 1923.

In the meantime, the other wing of *Sinn Fein* (soon to become *Cumann na nGaedheal*) had formed a new cabinet and framed a Constitution for the Irish Free State (Farrell, 1970–71). This, again, adopted a Westminster-style model of government. Following negotiations with the British government the draft Constitution was amended to bring it into line with Commonwealth dominions, but the incorporation of archaic Crown symbols of allegiance made in unacceptable to republicans. However, it survived, though much amended, until the adoption of a new Constitution in 1937.

The Irish Free State Constitution in theory and in practice incorporated the central features of the British model: a popularly elected chamber chose a Prime Minister who in turn chose party parliamentary colleagues and formed an executive which effectively ruled as long as it retained a parliamentary majority. There were a number of safeguards against undue executive dominance which deviated from the British model: a written Constitution, proportional representation, an elected second chamber, provision for popular referendum and initiative and the introduction of 'extern ministers' (to be chosen by the *Dail* and not bound by the conventions of collective responsibility. In reality, these provisions had little effect. Few 'extern ministers' were appointed, none could be regarded as specialists and all were active members selected by the government party. Taking advantage of the provision for flexible amendment of the Constitution, most of these institutional innovations were gradually abolished.

Despite continuing unrest and challenges to the legitimacy of the state, the system quickly settled down. In 1927 de Valera led his party, now called *Fianna Fail*, into the *Dail* and formed an effective opposition. Five years later his party won the general election and formed a new cabinet. The transfer of power was affected without disruption. The inherited conventions of cabinet government were continued.

*Bunreacht na hEireann*, the new Constitution introduced by de Valera in 1937, did not significantly alter the structure, nor affect the operation of the firmly established cabinet government system. Its main provisions have been sketched out above. Perhaps the most important aspect of the change from the Irish Free State Constitution has arisen from the rigidity of *Bunreacht na hEireann*, the timidity and indifference of legislators on constitutional changes and the increased exercise of judicial review, particularly since the 1960s (Kelly, 1984; Doolan, 1984). It is these constitutional constraints, rather than the theory of parliamentary answerability or practice of opposition politics, which have curtailed any unbridled exercise of executive power

### Size and membership of cabinet

For twenty years after the foundation of the Irish Free State the cabinet was usually limited to ten members. The number gradually expanded after the mid-1940s, but it was not until 1973 that the full cabinet membership of fifteen was achieved. It has been maintained ever since. Typically, all ministers have been *Dail* deputies; only three senators have ever served – all briefly – as ministers. All members of the government have been departmental ministers with the solitary exception of the appointment of a Minister Without Portfolio, designated Minister for the Coordination of Defensive Measures from 1939–1945.

Eleven departments were provided for in the original Ministers and Secretaries Act. These were: Prime Minister/Cabinet Office, Finance, Justice, Local Government and Public Health, Education, Lands and Agriculture, Industry and Commerce, Posts and Telegraphs, Defence, External Affairs and Fisheries. With the exception of Fisheries, each of these departments (sometimes with minor changes of title and function) has been represented in all Irish cabinets. Some have sub-divided to provide major new departments and a number of totally new departments have been added to the cabinet list. Figure 2.1 charts these developments.

Only three non-members attend cabinet regularly. These are: the Attorney-General (sometimes though not usually an elected deputy), who by convention offers legal, and perhaps political, opinions usually

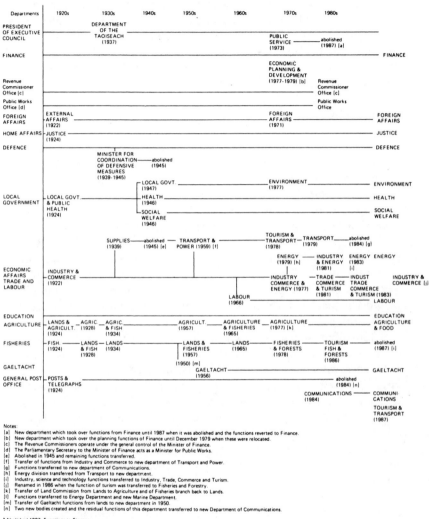

Notes:
[a]  New department which took over functions from Finance until 1987 when it was abolished and the functions reverted to Finance.
[b]  New department which took over the planning functions of Finance until December 1979 when these were relocated.
[c]  The Revenue Commissioners operate under the general control of the Minister of Finance.
[d]  The Parliamentary Secretary to the Minister of Finance acts as a Minister for Public Works.
[e]  Abolished in 1945 and remaining functions transferred.
[f]  Transfer of functions from Industry and Commerce to new department of Transport and Power.
[g]  Functions transferred to new department of Communications.
[h]  Energy division transferred from Transport to new department.
[i]  Industry, science and technology functions transferred to Industry, Trade, Commerce and Turism.
[j]  Renamed in 1986 when the function of turism was transferred to Fisheries and Forestry.
[k]  Transfer of Land Commission from Lands to Agriculture and of Fisheries branch back to Lands.
[l]  Functions transferred to Energy Department and new Marine Department.
[m]  Transfer of Gaeltacht functions from lands to new department in 1950.
[n]  Two new bodies created and the residual functions of this department transferred to new Department of Communications.

[a] Abolished 1987. Functions to Finance.
[b] Abolished 1984. Functions to Communications.
[c] Renamed Trans., Comm. and Tour. 1981; Industry Function to Energy. Renamed Ind., Trade, Comm. and Tour. 1983.
   Renamed Ind. and Comm. 1986. Tourism Function to Fish. and For.
[d] Renamed Industry and Energy 1981; Renamed Energy 1983; Industry, Science and Technology functions to Ind., Trade, Comm. and Tour.
[e] Renamed Agriculture and Food 1987.
[f] Renamed Tourism, Fish. and For. 1986. Abolished 1987; Forestry functions to Energy. Fisheries functions to new Dept of Marine.
[g] Abolished and two new bodies created in 1984, An Post and Bord Telecom. Residual functions to new Department of Communications.
NOTE: New Department of Tourism and Transport 1987.

FIGURE 2.1   Development of the central administration in Ireland: 1922–1987

on request; the government Chief Whip (designated Minister of State at the Department of the *Taoiseach* and at the Department of Defence), who arranges the details of the parliamentary time-table and the Secretary to the Government, who prepares the minutes of cabinet decisions.[1] Occasionally, junior ministers or civil servants are summoned to attend cabinet for a single item.

**Cabinet rules**

The Secretary is also the head of the Cabinet Secretariat and responsible for drawing up the agenda and for maintaining the formal rules of cabinet procedure, which are outlined in Section 4. While these specify how matters should be submitted in an orderly way to government meetings, they do not constitute a set of standing orders. In practice, the *Taoiseach* determines the order of business. Certain matters of a routine nature are, in effect, 'reported' rather than discussed; but, as head of government, the *Taoiseach* chairs meetings, manages the agenda and guides decision-making. He calls on ministers to speak and indicates when it is time to conclude discussion. By convention, votes are not recorded in the minutes of decisions and there is no established provision for recording dissent.[2]

Before submission to government, proposals are prepared by officials of the sponsoring department. They may arise from administrative experience with particular problems, be initiated by special interest groups or even be prompted by expressed media concern. Sometimes, especially in the case of incoming new governments, party manifestos identify policy priorities demanding action. Sometimes proposals have arisen from a consensus generated between government and various 'social partners' which might be seen as approximating some model of a corporate state (Barrington, 1982; Farrell, 1986; Chubb, 1987). Only rarely do government backbenchers through parliamentary party meetings, opposition parties or general interest groups not identified as clients of a particular department succeed in promoting, or even significantly altering the shape of, new policies.[3]

Normally the cabinet meets twice a week and perhaps once a year has an intensive annual two-to-three day session over a weekend. Duration of meetings is much influenced by the personality of the *Taoiseach*; some prefer a brisk, business-like pace, while others favour a more discursive discussion that extends meetings. The number of items on the agenda varies considerably, from 10 to 50.

## 3 CABINET LIFE

### Parties and governments

Although political parties are not even mentioned in the Constitution, they are an integral part of the political system which determines the composition of the cabinet. Despite the adoption of the single-transferable-vote mode of proportional representation, the Irish party system has been remarkably stable (Mair, 1987). In essence, three parties have dominated: *Fianna Fail* (formerly republican *Sinn Fein*) has been the largest party for nearly 60 years, always securing over 40 per cent of the national first-preference vote; *Fine Gael* (formerly *Cumann na nGael*) has been in second place, fluctuating more widely around 30 per cent; Labour typically has secured about 10 per cent. Neither of the two major parties fit comfortably into a neat comparative typology; the description 'politics without social bases' still applies (Whyte, 1974; Laver, 1986; Laver, Mair and Sinnot, 1987).

The basic party cleavage is rooted in historical circumstances. The legacy of bitterness and distrust engendered by the Civil War was translated into adversarial parliamentary politics. The norm of single-party (*Fianna Fail*) government has been often attenuated by the failure to secure an overall majority, as already indicated in Table 2.1. Similarly, *Fine Gael* has had to share governmental power with the Labour Party. The result of these arrangements has been to emphasize compromise and pragmatism rather than ideological programmes in formulating policy. While coalition arrangements have more frequently revealed in a public way internal cabinet disagreements, these have rarely been along simple party lines (Cohan, 1982; Farrell, 1983; Laver and Higgins, 1986). Single-party governments have also experienced such internal disputes, though they have surfaced less often.

Political parties are typically vehicles for securing support. Policy discussions at annual conferences are largely rhetorical exercises. They provide opportunities for politicians to exhibit their capacity and enlarge their personal constituencies. Although outstanding electoral performance may have some influence on ministerial selection, it is not a primary consideration. The party at large has virtually no role in cabinet composition and decision-making.

Similarly, the parliamentary party – like the *Dail* itself – has little more than a ceremonial role. Tight discipline ensures that deputies support their party; governments, once elected, can largely ignore their backbenchers; electoral circumstances reinforce the limited role of the *Dail* deputy (Farrell, 1985). However, ministers and governments that do not devote time, energy and trouble to regular contacts and consultation with backbench party colleagues can run into trouble with their proposals.

Neither parliamentary institutional arrangements nor small party headquarters provide much encouragement for deputies to challenge the cabinet's apparent monopoly of public policy-making.

The cabinet is a closed group of senior party colleagues chosen by the *Taoiseach*, bound together by shared experience and by an often excessive concern for executive secrecy, indisputably in charge of the executive organs of the State and usually able to push through its own legislative programme.[4] The *Taoiseach* is at the apex of this political hierarchy. The centrality and dominance of the *Taoiseach*'s role is enhanced by his responsibility for the coordination of the cabinet's work.

## Coordination of cabinet work

Dr Maurice Moynihan, who served as Secretary to the Government for nearly a quarter-century from 1937–1961, has given a classic description of 'the special position of the *Taoiseach* as head of the government – the captain of the team':

> he is the central co-ordinating figure, who takes an interest in the work of all departments, the figure to whom ministers naturally turn for advice and guidance when faced with problems involving large questions of policy or otherwise of special difficulty and whose leadership is essential to the successful working of the government as a collective authority, collectively responsible to *Dail Eireann*, but acting through members each of whom is charged with specific departmental tasks (Moynihan, 1960).

This delineation, based on personal experience of working with three Prime Ministers, remains valid. There has been no institutional development to match the growth in the size and scale of government functions. All ministers sit at the cabinet table. There are no 'overlords' to coordinate a range of departments. Given the relatively small scale of Irish government, it has not seemed necessary to develop any formal cabinet committee system.

Ad hoc committees (sometimes mixed committees of ministers and civil servants) are sometimes established to carry out specific tasks, usually to coordinate or finalise the bringing forward, within a given time limit, of government policies on complex issues involving a range of departments. Some of these may continue in existence over the greater part of the life of a cabinet or even through several successive cabinets; an example is the long-standing Security Committee, suspected by some non-members of being an inner cabinet. Effectively, it is left to the *Taoiseach* in cabinet, or in informal meetings with individual ministers, to coordinate both the day-to-day work and long-term policies of government. Decentralisation of decision-making is further discouraged by the doctrine of collective responsibility, defined in the cabinet rules as requiring that:

> each minister should inform his colleagues in government of proposals he or a Minister of State at his Department intends to announce and, if necessary, seek their agreement. This applies, in particular, to proposals for legislation which can be initiated only after formal approval by government.

This narrows the scope for individual kite-flying, let alone decision-making, by ministers.

There are other rules – relating to absence from cabinet meetings, conflicts of interest, and gifts – which reinforce the particular importance of cabinet membership and ministers' responsibilities to the *Taoiseach*. Above all else, perhaps, the emphasis on confidentiality differentiates membership of 'the cabinet club' from all other relationships. Even the close relationship of minister and senior departmental civil servants is reduced by their absence from, and lack of information about, this exclusive political circle. Parliamentary colleagues, interest groups and favoured journalists are all alike covered by the rubric that ministers should not divulge any information about cabinet discussions without specific authority. Cabinet rules provide for one minister (sometimes the *Taoiseach*) to be charged with responsibility for briefing the Government Press Secretary on cabinet affairs. There are, of course, 'leaks' – deliberate or inadvertent – but only those participating can have a full and informed appreciation of the realities of cabinet life.

**Leadership styles**

Political skills, personality and luck are defining characteristics of the Irish governmental élite. There is little emphasis on technical capacity or professional qualification in either selection or deployment of ministers (Farrell, 1987a; Farrell, 1987b; Coakley and Farrell, forthcoming). As a general rule, a minister will be a relatively senior party member, bringing political experience and maturity to office. Specialisation is scarcely regarded as a significant criterion. Although a certain amount of change is customary following a general election, there is little of the mid-term shuffling of portfolios that occur in other systems and ministerial resignations and dismissals are sufficiently unusual to be considered political crises. As a result it is not easy to codify the ministerial hierarchy, although certain posts (noticeably Finance but also Foreign Affairs, Agriculture and Industry-Commerce) are recognised as senior. Appointments to, or removal from, such portfolios is seen in terms of promotion and demotion, though never officially acknowledged as such.

At cabinet, the seating arrangements favour such senior office-holders and they will normally make more frequent and authoritative interventions in discussion. Specifically, the Minister for Finance, who sits facing the *Taoiseach*, is likely to participate on most topics. Ministers who have a long record of service, have experience in a number of departments, or have been in charge of a matter currently being considered, will also tend to have their views sought and listened to. Above all else, personality comes into play. Naturally intelligent, energetic ministers are prone to cover a wider range of issues, well outside their own particular brief. Ministers who have, or can establish, a particular bond with the *Taoiseach* of the day acquire additional influence.

It is the *Taoiseach* who exercises ultimate authority. It is a function not merely of the office but of the multiplicity of roles thrust upon him – simultaneously chief executive, government chairman, party leader, national spokesman, principal legislator, electoral champion and media focus. The precise mode of cabinet management and government direction varies. Some leaders are more active and interventionist, others more cautious. Some press for decisions, others are ready to defer or postpone if disagreements arise. Some 'take soundings' (although the order in which cabinet opinions are solicited varies), others are quicker to put matters to the vote or even assert, after an issue had been introduced, that everyone agrees (meaning that the *Taoiseach* agrees with the minister's proposal) and assume consent (Farrell, 1971b; Farrell, 1983a; Farrell, 1985b; Farrell, 1987b).

While it is possible to distinguish 'chairman' and 'chief' models, in the real world of politics leaders switch roles according to circumstance. In the past, a combination of factors tended to limit the exercise of executive leadership and suggest the utility of the chairman style. Newer circumstances (including more competitive elections and sophisticated campaigns, government overload and the demands of retrenchment, and the emphasis on summitry in EC and Anglo-Irish negotiations) have nudged incumbents in the other direction. There is constant pressure to play the role of chief.

## 4 CABINET DECISION-MAKING

Instructions on cabinet procedure, originally developed in the early 1920s, have evolved over the years. There are detailed rules for the submission of memoranda, proposed legislation and ministerial orders which provide for processes of consultation with, and circulation of observations by, other departments. They are designed to give ministers sufficient time to consider suitably brief, comprehensive and accurate proposals from colleagues in advance of government meetings. They are also intended to check the tendency to raise matters without due notice; documents may not be circulated in the course of cabinet meetings without specific direction of the chairman. There is a mechanism for ministers to use a Certificate of Urgency to have late memoranda circulated in advance, at the direction of the *Taoiseach*. It is also recognised that, for reasons of urgency or confidentiality, certain matters may have to be raised orally but, again, prior notice should be given to the *Taoiseach*. For convenience, an informal '12 o'clock rule' is operated to permit brief mentions of matters not on the formal agenda that may be dispensed with quickly.

Since there is no system of standing committees, a very wide variety of items have to be raised at cabinet. These include matters as trivial as the dismissal of even minor civil servants, appointments ranging from the most senior members of the judiciary to the least important state-sponsored boards, the formation and deliberations of inter-departmental committees and proposals for ministerial visits. Government decisions are notified formally to the minister and department concerned. It is then the responsibility of the minister to ensure that decisions are implemented at the earliest practicable date. Computerisation has facilitated the mechanism for follow-up by the Cabinet Secretariat which prepares a regular schedule of outstanding decisions, indicating the current position in each case. At an informal level a *Taoiseach* who takes a particular interest in a specific policy or functional area may press the minister concerned.

The available evidence (and it remains scanty) suggests a considerable degree of overload in the Irish cabinet system. The complex, the controversial and the insoluble compete with the current, the commonplace and the critical for scarce time and attention on the government agenda. The intractable problem of Northern Ireland, the latest transport strike, the painful disciplines of controlling public expenditure, the dismissal of a postman, the effects of technical developments in EC policies, the appointment of a Supreme Court judge, the timing of a bye-election, the detailed discussion of major legislation and a myriad other items crowd out consideration of longer-term strategic planning. Without much more extensive research it is impossible to judge how thoroughly the cabinet is able to consider the matters on which it must decide, as it is impossible to determine the extent to which departmental officials rather than their political masters shape and direct public policy. The Irish cabinet, even more than the British model from which it derives, has managed to preserve the secret garden of government decision-making from prying eyes.

## Notes

1. The practice of circulating a copy of the cabinet minutes to each minister was discontinued in 1922. The minutes are checked with the *Taoiseach* and ministers are supplied only with extracts particularly affecting them. The full minutes are read out at the subsequent meeting.
2. Although isolated examples did occur in the 1920s, it is assumed that ministers who cannot accept policy should resign.
3. On a more direct involvement by interest groups in recent referenda see Girvin (1986) and Girvin (1987).
4. It is also accepted that ministers should not express disagreement with government policy in public.

# 3 The Netherlands: Coalition Cabinets in Changing Circumstances

Rudy B. Andeweg[1]

## 1 CABINET SETTING

'The Government shall comprise the King and the Ministers. The Ministers, and not the King, shall be responsible for acts of government.' – (Article 42 of the Dutch Constitution)

This article of the Dutch Constitution determines both the legal and political setting of the cabinet. The King or Queen may still formally appoint the Ministers, sign the bills and give the annual address to Parliament outlining the government's plans, but the Ministers are answerable to Parliament, and in practice only Parliament can dismiss them.

In the Netherlands there is no separation of powers as in the United States, but neither are the powers fused as in the United Kingdom. Ministers cannot be Members of Parliament, except for the duration of an *interregnum* between successive governments. They can and do, however, participate in parliamentary debates, seated behind a separate table facing the Speaker. Both Ministers and Members of Parliament can introduce legislation, but parliamentary initiatives are rare and it is exceptional if they succeed. Most legislation originates from within the government. The courts offer little in terms of checks and balances, as laws are not subject to judicial review.

Today the cabinet is without doubt the most powerful political institution: it has replaced the King as the effective, if not as the dignified part of the state, and it has replaced Parliament as the supreme policy-making body. No wonder that one constitutional scholar spoke of the 'Sovereignty of the Council of Ministers' as the most important characteristic of the Dutch political system (Van Maarseveen, 1969).

However, the cabinet remains dependent on the continued support of Parliament. To ensure its survival, it will try to anticipate the reactions of

TABLE 3.1 Dutch cabinets: 1945–1986

| Date in | PM | PM Party | Govt. Composition | Duration in days |
|---|---|---|---|---|
| 24-06-45 | Schermerhorn | PvdA | PvdA/KVP/ARP/non-partisan | 374a |
| 03-07-46 | Beel I | KVP | PvdA/KVP/non-partisan | 766 |
| 07-08-48 | Drees I | PvdA | PvdA/KVP/CHU/VVD/non-partisan | 950b |
| 15-03-51 | Drees II | PvdA | PvdA/KVP/CHU/VVD/non-partisan | 537 |
| 02-09-52 | Drees III | PvdA | PvdA/KVP/ARP/CHU/non-partisan | 1502 |
| 13-10-56 | Drees IV | PvdA | PvdA/KVP/ARP/CHU | 800b |
| 22-12-58 | Beel II | KVP | KVP/ARP/CHU | 148a |
| 19-05-59 | De Quay | KVP | KVP/ARP/CHU/VVD | 1527 |
| 24-07-63 | Marijnen | KVP | KVP/ARP/CHU/VVD | 630b |
| 14-04-65 | Cals | KVP | PvdA/KVP/ARP | 587b |
| 22-11-66 | Zijlstra | ARP | KVP/ARP | 134a |
| 05.04.67 | De Jong | KVP | KVP/ARP/CHU/VVD | 1553 |
| 06-07-71 | Biesheuvel I | ARP | KVP/ARP/CHU/VVD/DS70 | 380b |
| 20-07-72 | Biesheuvel II | ARP | KVP/ARP/CHU/VVD | 295a |
| 11-05-73 | Den Uyl | PvdA | PPR/PvdA/D66/KVP/ARP | 1683 |
| 19-12-77 | Van Agt I | CDA | CDA/VVD | 1362 |
| 11-09-81 | Van Agt II | CDA | PvdA/D66/CDA | 260b |
| 29-05-82 | Van Agt III | CDA | D66/CDA | 159a |
| 04-11-82 | Lubbers I | CDA | CDA/VVD | 1348 |
| 14-07-86 | Lubbers II | CDA | CDA/VVD | |

PPR = Radicals
PvdA = Social Democrats
D66 = Progressive Liberals

KVP = Catholics
ARP = Protestants } CDA = Christian Democrats
CHU = Protestants

VVD = Conservative Liberals
DS70 = right-wing split-off from Social Democrats
a = interim cabinet, intended for short duration
b = life of cabinet, shortened by a political crisis

Parliament to its proposals. More importantly, the political composition of the cabinet is dictated by the political situation in Parliament. Since the introduction of universal suffrage and proportional representation, no single party has ever enjoyed a majority in Parliament. To muster the support of a parliamentary majority, all governments have to be coalition cabinets. In the comparative literature there is often a fear that proportional representation and a multi-party system lead to unstable government.[2]

There is no objective definition of political stability, and the duration of a cabinet in itself is an imperfect indicator. Nevertheless, Table 3.1 gives no cause for great concern in the Dutch case. The maximum duration of a cabinet is roughly speaking four years. From 1945 to 1986 there have been nineteen cabinets, lasting an average of 789 days (or two years and two months). However, five of these cabinets were caretaker administrations holding office prior to new general elections. If we exclude these cabinets, the average Dutch cabinet survived for more than two years and eight months. Even then, the life-span of a cabinet may be cut short for reasons other than political conflict: only six cabinets perished prematurely for political reasons.[3] The duration of cabinets is not much influenced by the composition of the coalitic n. Contrary to popular belief, cabinets including the Social Democrats do not have a shorter average life span (829 days) than cabinets without them (753 days).

The most prominent explanation for this relative governmental stability is given by the theory of consociational democracy. Until the 1960s Dutch society was characterised by a strong segmentation or pillarisation (*verzuiling*). Catholics, Protestants, Social Democrats and, to a lesser extent, Liberals formed clearly identifiable subcultures, each with its own infrastructure of social organisations (schools, parties, health organisations, mass media, and so on), isolated from and relatively hostile towards each other. According to Lijphart (1975e), the Dutch elites realised the dangers inherent in the deep religious and socio-economic cleavages, and acted to compensate the centrifugal forces at the mass level by a 'politics of accommodation' at the elite level. Cooperation in the cabinet was one of the ways in which the leaders of the various social groups tried to stabilise an inherently unstable political situation.[4] According to others, elite concurrence and political stability were not so much the result of a self-denying prophecy as of the old Dutch tradition of bargaining and compromise, which had developed in the days of the confederal Dutch Republic and which now applied to a new political situation.[5] Whatever the correct explanation may be, until recently the result was 'government above politics' – a cabinet removed from the heat of party conflict. After all, Ministers represent the King in Parliament, and there is an old adage that 'the closer to the throne, the less partisan'.

## 2 FORMAL STRUCTURE

### History

The Dutch cabinet started as a loose combination of individual advisers to the King, each heading one of his departments.[6] Only since 1983 has the Constitution recognised that 'The Ministers shall together constitute the Council of Ministers . . . The Council of Ministers shall consider and decide upon overall government policy and shall promote the coherence thereof' (Article 45). Before that time the Constitution mentioned only individual Ministers. In 1901 the Prime Minister even refused to discuss cabinet procedures in Parliament because, constitutionally, the cabinet did not exist.

Although the legacy of strong ministerial autonomy and weak collective decision-making still haunts the Dutch government, there have been important changes since the introduction of ministerial responsibility in 1848. In 1848 only about 11 per cent of the adult male population was enfranchised and therefore mass political parties had yet to develop. Without parties the ties between cabinet and Parliament were weak. Ministers were often individually recruited by the King, and when Parliament passed a motion of no-confidence it was usually directed against an individual Minister, who was then replaced without consequences for the cabinet as a whole. Within the cabinet, Ministers fiercely protected their autonomy, even after 1850, when cabinets were allowed to take decisions by majority vote and dissenting Ministers had to resign or publicly support the decision.

A Prime Minister existed in name only, and sometimes not even that. Until World War Two the Council of Ministers only had a temporary chairman for a period of three months for a year. Sometimes this temporary chairman was elected by all cabinet Ministers; at other times the chair rotated in order of seniority. Any attempt to introduce a Prime Minister worthy of that title met with strong opposition. Ministers saw it as a violation of the principle of ministerial equality. Members of Parliament feared it would destroy the individual responsibility of Ministers, and would thereby weaken Parliament's influence.

Moreover, there was some anxiety that it would restore influence to the King, as he would appoint the Prime Minister.

However, two attempts have been made. In 1860 the King appointed the Baron Van Hall as chairman of the Council of Ministers for a period of one year. When Van Hall insisted on prolongation, the rest of the cabinet rebelled and he was forced to resign. In 1901 the Standing Orders of the Council of Ministers were changed to establish a chairman for the duration of the cabinet. The first chairman was Abraham Kuyper, one of the most formidable political figures of that time. As soon as he left office the temporary chairman was restored, although in practice there was little turnover.

With the gradual extension of the suffrage in the late nineteenth and early twentieth century, well organised political parties developed. This altered the relationship between King, cabinet and Parliament. In the first place, the parliamentary parties took over from the King as the selector of cabinet personnel. The last time the Queen tried to impose her own choice on Parliament, in 1939, a vote of 'no confidence' forced that cabinet to resign upon its first appearance in the Second Chamber. Secondly, the cabinet became a coalition of parties instead of a collection of individual Ministers. Hence collective responsibility took precedence over individual ministerial responsibility.

Since World War Two there have been only isolated instances where an individual Minister was forced to resign without an ensuing cabinet crisis. During the 1973–1977 government the Christian Democratic Minister of Justice was held accountable for the escape of a war criminal. During the parliamentary debate, the spokesman for the Social Democratic coalition partner openly admitted that his party only abstained from a vote of censure against the Minister because that would bring down the entire cabinet. During the 1982–1986 cabinet, a parliamentary inquiry found the Conservative-Liberal Minister of Economic Affairs guilty of having lied to Parliament, but he was allowed to continue in office to protect the Cabinet.

Today, Parliament can no longer censure an individual Minister without risking the downfall of the entire cabinet. Likewise, an individual Minister can no longer use the threat of resignation as a weapon in Parliament without the prior approval of the cabinet.

A third result of the changing political circumstances for the cabinet was that the temporary chairman slowly evolved into a Prime Minister (Van Raalte, 1954). When a strong party leader entered a cabinet, he automatically assumed a position of leadership in that cabinet. An increasing number of cabinets routinely re-elected their chairman or, under the system of rotation, the other Ministers simply forfeited their turn.[7] During World War Two the Dutch government was exiled to London and imitated many aspects of English cabinet government, including a more prominent position of the chairman. After the war, the Queen appointed the Prime Minister and later changed the Standing Orders to legitimise the new practice. Even before the war, in 1937, a small Department of General Affairs had been set up to act as an office for the 'temporary chairman'. Before that time the Prime Minister had the responsibility for one of the departments. This severely restricted his role, not only because he had to devote a considerable amount of time to the management of his department, but also because he had departmental interests to defend and was not seen by his colleagues as an objective arbitrator. The combination of Prime Minister and Minister of Finance was viewed with particular suspicion. In 1946 the Prime Minister briefly attempted to combine the chair with the position of Minister of Internal Affairs, but this restoration lasted for little more than a year.

In summary, as a result of political developments the King and the individual Ministers lost ground. Meanwhile the parliamentary parties, the cabinet as a whole and the Prime Minister became more important. Yet as we shall see in the remainder of this chapter, the King still exercises some discretionary power, and individual Ministers still jealously guard their departmental turf.

**Formal composition**

Dutch cabinets have always been comparatively small. Until World War One the size of the cabinet oscillated between seven and nine Ministers, with so-called confessional cabinets sometimes adding separate Ministers for the Dutch Reformed and Catholic churches and secular cabinets discontinuing these departments. During the *interbellum* the number of cabinet members gradually increased to twelve. That figure rose sharply to eighteen under the government in exile during World War Two. In the postwar period the average cabinet has consisted of fifteen members, occasionally less when one Minister simultaneously holds more than one position. As a rule, only the heads of all the departments are members of the cabinet. The growth of the cabinet therefore reflects the increasing number of departments as the role of government in society expanded. At present there are thirteen departments, and an illustration of the composition of the Dutch government can be seen in Table 3.2.

In 1938 the Constitution was altered to make room for Ministers

Without Portfolio in the cabinet. This change was intended to free the Prime Minister from departmental management, but that problem had already been taken care of. The term 'Minister Without Portfolio' is something of a misnomer: these Ministers do have a portfolio, but one for which the creation of a separate department is not deemed necessary. Since 1965, for example, all cabinets have included a Minister Without Portfolio for Development Aid, assisted by civil servants in the Foreign Office and a huge budget (as one former such Minister quipped: 'I may have been without a portfolio, but I certainly was not without a purse').

Sometimes Ministers Without Portfolio are added for reasons of political balance. In 1952 the Catholic Party claimed Foreign Affairs, but the Social Democrats feared a papist Europe as all the Foreign Secretaries in the budding European Community were Catholics. As a compromise a non-partisan Minister of Foreign Affairs was appointed, in addition to whom the Catholic Joseph Luns became Minister Without Portfolio with the right to call himself Minister of Foreign Affairs when abroad. When asked why the Netherlands had two Ministers of Foreign Affairs, his stock reply was that, Holland being such a small country, the rest of the world was too large an area to be covered by only one Minister. No cabinet has included more than two Ministers Without Portfolio.

TABLE 3.2    Composition of the Dutch government in 1987

| Department | Minister with Portfolio | Minister without Portfolio | Secretary of State |
|---|---|---|---|
| General Affairs | 1 | | |
| Foreign Affairs | 1 | 1 | 1 |
| Justice | 1 | | 1 |
| Internal Affairs | 1 | | 1 |
| Education | 1 | | 1 |
| Finance | 1 | | 1 |
| Defence | 1 | | 1 |
| Housing, Physical Planning and Environmental Environmental Protection | 1 | | 1 |
| Transport and Waterworks | 1 | | |
| Economic Affairs | 1 | | 2 |
| Agricultural and Fisheries | 1 | | |
| Social Affairs and Employment | 1 | | 1 |
| Welfare, Health and Culture | 1 | | 1 |

Numerically more important has been the introduction of Secretaries of State (*staatssecretarissen*) in 1948. Their number has rapidly risen to equal or even surpass the number of Ministers. Secretaries of State are junior ministers: they are assigned part of a Minister's portfolio without in any way diminishing the Minister's own responsibility for the entire portfolio.[8] They are not members of the cabinet, although a Secretary of State is usually invited to attend whenever the cabinet discusses matters pertinent to his portfolio. Only the Secretary of State for Foreign Affairs, who is responsible for European Affairs, customarily attends every cabinet meeting.

When ill, Ministers are not substituted by their Secretary of State but by a colleague. Sometimes Secretaries of State are appointed to relieve Ministers with an extensive portfolio (the Minister of Finance generally delegates taxation to a Secretary of State); or they may represent specific interests within the department (in the past there were Secretaries of State for each of the three services in the Department of Defence); occasionally they provide expertise where a Minister feels he needs it (one Prime Minister had a Secretary of State to assist him with economic problems). Often Secretaries of State are appointed for reasons of overall political balance, or even as one party's watchdog over another party's Minister. As Secretaries of State share the cabinet's collective responsibility, but do not take part in its collective decision making, their role is an ambivalent one. Their position is sometimes critised for seeming to be underdeveloped and undervalued, and sometimes it is even seen as redundant. In the 1986 cabinet formation the latter view prevailed and the number of Secretaries of State was reduced from sixteen to eleven.

Presiding over Ministers, with or without portfolio, and over Secretaries of State is the Prime Minister. He still has few formal powers. He draws up the agenda and chairs all meetings of the cabinet and its committees. He casts the deciding vote when there is a tie. The Prime Minister does not, however, appoint the Ministers: appointments are formally made by the Queen after negotiations between the parties forming the government. The Prime Minister cannot remove a Minister or 'reshuffle' the cabinet by assigning Ministers to other portfolios. The Prime Minister of the wartime government in exile twice dismissed a Minister without even consulting the cabinet. He was immediately criticised for such 'Persian constitutional morals', and after the war a parliamentary inquiry repudiated the claim that the Prime Minister should have the power of dismissal. The Prime Minister can ask the Queen to dissolve Parliament when there is a political crisis or at the end of a regular parliamentary term. It is dubious, however, whether the Queen would honour such a request simply because the electoral prospects of the governing parties look favourable.

Although the Prime Minister is entrusted the task of coordinating cabinet policy, he has no authority to settle conflicts between Ministers unless they agree to his arbitration.[9] He cannot give any directives to Ministers. The Prime Minister's staff is relatively small. Today about 350 civil servants are employed by the Department of General Affairs, but most work in the Government Press Office, on the staff of the Scientific Council for Government Policy, or for one of the intelligence services. Only ten to twelve are acting as advisers to the Prime Minister. All are career civil servants, and only occasionally does a Prime Minister bring in some political appointees. The Cabinet Secretariat is part of the Department of General Affairs, but has a semi-independent position. Except for the Cabinet Secretary, the Secretariat is formed by a handful of young civil servants seconded from other departments for no more than a few years (Van der Voet, 1974).

Despite the paucity of staff and formal powers there is a feeling among many Dutch commentators that the position of the Prime Minister has been strengthened over time, even though the use which is made of this position varies considerably with the personality of the Prime Minister and the political situation of the moment. The impression of a stronger Prime Minister is largely fed by his increasing external role. Since the 1967–1971 cabinet the Prime Minister has given a weekly press conference and television interview, in which he explains and defends the cabinet's decisions. Increasingly the Prime Minister represents the country at EEC and other summit meetings. Even then, however, the collegiate nature of Dutch cabinets is noted: in 1983 the European Summit in Stuttgart issued a declaration: 'The European Council brings together the Heads of State or Government and the President of the Commission *assisted by* the Foreign Ministers of the member states and a member of the Commission.' At the insistence of the Dutch delegation it was added that this statement '*ne saura porter atteinte aux competences du ministre des Affaires Etrangères dans l'exercise de ses competences nationales*' (will in no way restrict the powers of the minister of foreign affairs with respect to his national attributions) (Hoekstra, 1983).

To complete our description of the formal composition of the cabinet, we should mention the Deputy Prime Minister(s). This office grew out of rather informal arrangements for substituting the Prime Minister during illness or absence. In 1948 a status-conscious substitute chairman had stationery printed calling himself 'Vice Minister President' (Van Raalte,

1954). The title stuck and eventually found its way into the Standing Orders. Generally, a Deputy Prime Minister is the leading Minister of a major coalition partner of the Prime Minister's party. They are in charge of one of the regular departments, but also act as their party's chief spokesman in the cabinet. Occasionally Prime Ministers have formed a *presidium* with the Deputy Prime Minister(s) to prepare cabinet meetings and to anticipate or avert conflicts.

**Formal procedure**

The Dutch cabinet meets at least once a week, normally on a Friday. The average meeting starts at 10 am and is closed by late afternoon. In the 1970s it was not uncommon for cabinet meetings to continue into the early hours of the next day, but nowadays the meeting may be concluded by teatime. Extraordinary sessions of the cabinet occur quite often, in fact whenever the Prime Minister or any two Ministers seek a meeting. On average, a Dutch Minister may spend some 30 hours a month in meetings of the full cabinet, which is considerably more than his colleagues in most other countries.

The amount of time spent in cabinet is at least partially explained by the fact that the agenda is relatively long. The Prime Minister draws up the agenda, although most items are put on the agenda automatically. Article 4 of the Standing Orders lists the kind of items that need the approval of the full cabinet: all legislative proposals, all proposed Orders in Council, all treaties and international agreements, instructions for delegations to international organisations, all white papers, the publication of any policy plan that has financial repercussions or may otherwise affect the position of the cabinet, all policy plans on which the Ministers involved have failed to reach agreement bilaterally, all conclusions reached by cabinet committees, the establishment of advisory councils, important requests for advise and the publication of such advise, important appointments (senior civil servants and judges, mayors of large municipalities, and so on) and all other matters affecting 'overall government policy'. A Minister who is in doubt about whether something belongs in this broad but vague latter category is obliged to inform the Prime Minister, who then decides whether or not to put the matter on the agenda. The scope for cabinet decision-making is therefore quite wide.

Officially, papers relating to any given cabinet meeting have to be circulated at least ten days in advance, but in practice this rule is not always adhered to. Attached to each paper is a standard form summarising the proposal contained in the paper, reviewing its procedural status (for example, whether inter-departmental consultation has led to an agreement) and listing the consequences of the proposal in terms of finance, the labour market and government personnel. Each department has its own way of briefing its Minister on papers submitted by other departments, but generally these briefs look at the cabinet agenda only from a rather narrow departmental point of view. The Minister of Defence, for instance, would not expect a substantial briefing from his department on a proposal concerning euthanasia. Ministers are allowed to appoint a political adviser but few do so, and political advisers àre employed more as liaison to the party and to Parliament than as counsellor on cabinet matters.

If at least half of its members are present the cabinet can take decisions by majority vote. In cases where the vote is a tie, and only if the matter is urgent and all Ministers are attending, the Prime Minister casts the deciding vote. However, formal voting is relatively rare. Votes are taken to shorten long debates on minor issues, but on major issues a vote signals the start of divorce proceedings between the coalition partners. Normally, the Prime Minister sums up after two or three rounds of discussion, and if no one challenges his conclusion it is recorded as the decision of the cabinet. In the case of strong opposition to a proposal the Prime Minister will defer a decision and form a small *ad hoc* committee of the Ministers most concerned (often including himself) to work out a compromise.

Throughout the meeting the Cabinet Secretary and one of his assistants are present to take rather elaborate minutes. The cabinet minutes remain an official secret for 50 years. After 20 years one can apply for limited access for research purposes, but anything written on that basis is subject to censorship. Ministers themselves have become more open about discussions and conflicts in the cabinet, but information of this kind is often leaked to influence a decision that has yet to be taken. Once agreement has been reached, the doctrine of collective responsibility is generally adhered to.

## 3 CABINET LIFE

### Cabinet formation

At least as important as the historical legacy and the formal structure is the fact that Dutch cabinets are invariably coalition governments.

Although the political parties increasingly express their coalition preferences during the campaign, the election outcome usually leaves many options open. As a result of the party and electoral system, the Dutch voters do not decide who will govern and which election manifesto will become the government programme. These decisions are taken by politicians *after* the elections (Andeweg *et al*, 1980).

The *interregnum* between two cabinets is therefore of crucial import -ance. It is also a time when the Queen becomes more than a constitutional ornament. She is no longer in a position to form the cabinet herself but, after consultations with all party leaders and some other advisers, she will appoint someone to preside over the negotiations – a *formateur*. Due to the often complicated political situation it is uncommon that a cabinet is formed at the first attempt. To reduce the ignominy of failure, the Queen in most cases appoints an *informateur* rather than a *formateur*: information can always be obtained, whereas a cabinet cannot always be formed. In practice there is very little difference between the two offices.

The choise of *(in)formateur* is entirely dependent on the Queen. The outcome of the formation process will normally be a coalition of Christian Democrats and Social Democrats, or a coalition of Christian Democrats and Conservative Liberals (both combinations may also include smaller parties). The Christian Democrats have been part of all Dutch governments since 1918, and their pivotal role has been strengthened by the fact that Social Democrats and Conservative Liberals *de facto* exclude each other from participation in a cabinet. In recognition of this situation, the Queen will often appoint a Christian Democrat as *(in)formateur*. However, as a centre party the CDA is ambivalent about its coalition preferences and the Queen's choice is sometimes interpreted as a royal preference for one of the two most likely combinations.[10]

In negotiations with the parliamentary leaders of the *Koalitionsfähige* parties, the *(in)formateur* (or *(in)formateurs*: sometimes two or even three are appointed when no single person is acceptable to the antagonistic parties) narrows down the range of possible coalitions to the most feasible. Once that is settled, the negotiations focus on the formulation of a government programme and on the distribution of ministerial and secretary of state posts among the coalition partners. The programme is usually first on the agenda and it has evolved from a broad outline of the principles of the new government's policy to an elaborate enumeration of detailed plans and drafts for new laws in the most recent cabinets.

The distribution of ministerial portfolios over the parties is roughly proportional to their strength in Parliament, with the Prime Minister usually, but not necessarily, coming from the largest party. Care is taken that all parties are represented in all major policy areas, so that no one party has all the key socio-economic positions or another all those in international affairs. Parties also have traditional preferences: the Christian Democrats are always keen on Education (to protect the parochial schools) and Agriculture (because farmers form one of their most loyal constituencies. The Social Democrats have a traditional claim on Social Affairs and the Conservative Liberals on Economic Affairs.

When the programme and the apportionment of the seats are agreed upon by the parliamentary parties concerned, an *informateur* will usually make way for a *formateur* if he has not already done so. The final task for the *formateur*, usually the Prime Minister designate, is to staff his government with Ministers and Secretaries of State. They are nominated by their party leader, but must be acceptable to the coalition partner(s). After that the new cabinet can be sworn in at the Royal Palace.

At any of the stages just described the parties may be unable to reach a compromise. Usually a 'fresh' *informateur* is then called upon to 'glue the rift' or 'put the train back on track' as the jargon has it. In 1977 this proved to be necessary several times when negotiations between the Social Democrats and the Christian Democrats broke down over plans for an 'excess profit-sharing' law, on abortion legislation and on the distribution of ministerial posts. Each time a compromise was eventually hammered out, but after 163 days of negotiations the parties failed to reach agreement on the appointment of one Christian Democrat as Minister of Economic Affairs. Ultimately, negotiations between the parties collapsed and were begun anew between the Christian Democrats and the Conservative Liberals. The total *interregnum* lasted 208 days, and witnessed nine attempts by *(in)formateurs* to form a government.

This record is still unbroken, but there is no doubt that the formation of Dutch cabinets is time-consuming – the average postwar cabinet formation took 67 days and on average a month per year is spent on forming a government. Although the duration of the cabinet formation is cause for some concern, it should be clear that the process leads to relatively stable governments. Many conflicts that may arise during a cabinet's reign are anticipated and dealt with during the painstaking and time-consuming negotiations over the government programme.

Moreover, the sitting government stays on as a caretaker government during the *interregnum*. As a rule such a *demissionaire* government does not introduce important new legislation or take controversial action, but it is far from being a lame duck. During its time pending legislation is routinely brought to an end, budgets are introduced, subsidies are handed out and appointments are made. If the process is criticised it is more for its rather undemocratic nature than because of its duration.[11]

The cabinets formed by this process are interesting in at least two respects. In the first place, many coalitions were larger than would be strictly necessary in order to secure a parliamentary majority. The classical game-theoretical model predicts that coalitions should be 'minimal winning' because it would not be rational to add 'extra' parties. That would mean sharing power among more parties, thus reducing each party's share. Having confronted rational coalition theory with actual cabinet formations, De Swaan noted the deviation of the Dutch case and gave it a game-theoretical explanation. He pointed to the fulcrum position of the Catholic Party (now part of the Christian Democratic Party): 'The most effective way to exploit this position was for it . . . to carry the advantages of a pivotal position into the government coalition itself. By including both Social Democrats and centre-right parties, the Catholics could play both sides against the middle at every cabinet meeting' (De Swaan, 1982).

Another explanation for the large size of many Dutch coalitions is that coalition parties not only share power, but also share responsibility – a feature commonly overlooked in game-theoretical models. Political parties may be less anxious about letting extra parties share in their responsibility, especially at times when difficult and unpopular decisions have to be taken. This was certainly the case during the first postwar years when decolonisation and economic hardship were the central problems and coalitions were particularly large.

A third explanation for the wide-spanning coalitions refers to the theory of consociational democracy mentioned at the beginning of this chapter. To counteract social and political instability the leaders of the social groups cooperated rather than competed with each other. The cabinet formation epitomised the politics of accommodation, and elite cooperation is greatly facilitated when most of the social groups are represented in the cabinet.

Next to the larger-than-necessary size of the coalitions, the result of the cabinet formations is non-obvious in another sense. As we have seen, a cabinet formation is an intensely political process. Yet, paradoxically, it results in relatively technocratic appointments. Even before the Constitution prevented Ministers from simultaneously holding a seat in

Parliament it was customary for a member of Parliament to resign his seat upon being raised to government rank. Of all Ministers appointed between 1848 and 1983 only 42 per cent had prior parliamentary experience. At each cabinet formation there are rumours that some newly-nominated Ministers had hastily to become party members before taking the oath of office. Many commentators have pointed to the high number of outside specialists being appointed Minister in the Netherlands: a lawyer at Justice, a banker or economist at Finance, someone with trade union credentials at Social Affairs, and so on (Dogan and Scheffer-Van der Veen, 1957–58).

The ratio of technical expertise to political experience in ministerial appointments varies considerably across policy areas. A study of all ministerial appointments since 1848 shows that specialist appointments are particularly common at the departments of Justice, Agriculture and Economic Affairs, whereas appointees of political pedigree can most often be found in younger departments such as Social Affairs and Welfare, Health and Culture. The Department of Internal Affairs also has a high intake of politicians, largely because this was a natural department for the Prime Minister until the establishment of the Department of General Affairs. Surprisingly, two departments that are often mentioned as strongholds of non-political specialists, Foreign Affairs and especially Transport and Waterworks, do not live up to their reputation. At the latter department barely half of all Ministers brought any technical skills to the job (Bakema and Secker, 1988).

Over the years political experience has gained in importance as a criterion for recruitment to ministerial office. But it has not replaced the requirement of technical expertise, as can be seen from Table 3.3.

TABLE 3.3    Technical expertise and political experience in ministerial (first) appointments in The Netherlands: 1848–1986

| Period | Technical Expertise % | Political Experience % | *n.* |
|--------|-----------------------|------------------------|------|
| 1848–1888 | 71 | 36 | 118 |
| 1888–1918 | 79 | 50 | 72 |
| 1918–1940 | 72 | 41 | 61 |
| 1940–1946 | 59 | 14 | 29 |
| 1946–1967 | 72 | 57 | 68 |
| 1967–1986 | 65 | 73 | 75 |

SOURCE:    Bakema, W.E. and Secker, I.P. (1988).

The figures for any given period add up to more than 100 per cent because Ministers may have both specialist qualifications and political credentials. It is interesting to see that only since 1967 have political appointments overtaken technical appointments. The year 1967 is usually associated with the beginning of the end of consociational democracy in the Netherlands. It may be that with the demise of the politics of accommodation the rule of 'government above politics' also disappeared, making the cabinet a much more political arena.

**Parties in cabinet**

That impression is certainly reinforced by the fact that more and more the parties continue to play a role in the cabinet after it has been sworn in. Not only has the government programme become more extensive and detailed, it is also adhered to more strictly than was the case in the past. Interestingly, although the programme undoubtedly serves to bind the Ministers to the policies agreed upon by the parties, it also functions to limit the parties' freedom of movement in Parliament and to increase party discipline.

In the same way, Ministers are not only more often recruited from the political class, but are also expected to act as their party's bridgehead in government. This has had a profound impact on decision-making in cabinet. In the 1950s and 1960s, for example, the whole cabinet met once a week for an informal dinner. Only on the day of the cabinet meeting itself did Ministers from each governing party lunch separately. As a first sign of the 'politicisation' of the cabinet, it became customary for the parliamentary leader of a governing party to attend his party's Ministers' lunch. This lunch became so important that hardly any decisions were taken by the cabinet *before* lunch. In 1973 the lunch was replaced by a dinner on the eve of the cabinet meeting, during which a party's Ministers, Secretaries of State, the Party Leader in the Second Chamber of Parliament and sometimes also the Party Leader in the First Chamber, as well as the Party Chairman, discuss the next day's cabinet agenda. Occasionally party discipline is enforced and the decision taken by cabinet differs from the one that would have emerged had all Ministers followed their individual judgement.

As with the programme, the increasingly political nature of ministerial office bound both the Ministers to the parties and the parties to their Ministers. The change can perhaps be illustrated by looking at cabinet crises. Before 1965, cabinet crises did not arise from disagreements among Ministers but rather from conflicts between Ministers and their own party! In 1951, for example, a motion of censure against the government fell short of a majority in Parliament, but the motion was supported by the Conservative Liberals. The only Minister from that party then resigned, and a cabinet crisis ensued. In 1960 the Protestant Anti-Revolutionary Party collided with its own Minister of Housing over the number of subsidised houses to be built, causing a temporary cabinet crisis. Other crises resulted from the withdrawal of support for the cabinet by one or more of the governing parties in Parliament.

Between 1945 and 1965 no cabinet fell because of internal disagreement. Since 1965 all cabinet crises but one have been caused by disagreement along party lines within the cabinet. In 1965 a Christian-Democratic/Conservative-Liberal coalition split along party lines over media policy. In 1972 a five party centre-right cabinet collapsed when the Ministers from the smallest coalition partner did not agree with the proposed budget. In 1977 a five party centre-left coalition broke up after an internal disagreement over an expropriations bill. In 1982 a cabinet made up of Christian Democrats, Social Democrats and Progressive Liberals failed to reach agreement on socio-economic policy after having overcome an earlier internal crisis. In the meantime there have been no further cabinet crises resulting from a rift between a Minister and his own party, such as the ones mentioned for the pre-1965 period.

In summary, it could be argued that the history of the Dutch cabinet is best interpreted as the gradual, but irreversible, colonisation of the government by the political parties.

## 4   CABINET DECISION-MAKING

Yet, despite the growing influence of the parties on the cabinet, the cabinet remains to a surprising degree a meeting of heads of departments. In the cabinet, as former Prime Minister Drees (1965) put it, 'functional conflicts tend to be more important than political conflicts'. He stepped down in 1958, but even today most Ministers agree that departmental interests guided their behaviour and structured conflicts in cabinet for most of the time. This phenomenon can be traced back to the origins of the cabinet as a collection of individual advisers to the King, but the fact that 'departmentalism' in the cabinet has largely withstood the rising tide of politicisation means that it is reinforced by current circumstances. The relationship of Ministers with civil servants, and of Ministers with interest groups are of particular relevance in this respect.

Let us first look at the civil service, or rather the lack of it. Each department has its own personnel policy and criteria for recruitment. Civil servants are formally employed by a department and do not join a civil service encompassing the whole of central government. Most Dutch civil servants spend their entire career within the walls of a single department. Experienced observers have noticed signs of distinct departmental cultures in jargon and even in dress, ranging from corduroy at Welfare, Health and Culture, blue blazers at Internal Affairs or pin-striped suits in the Foreign Office. Lawyers sometimes refer to thirteen 'legal families' because departments have different legislative traditions. One prominent politician concluded that the Netherlands are no longer the 'Republic of the Seven United Provinces' but are now the 'Republic of the Thirteen Disunited Departments'.[12] As a result, the Minister is advised and briefed by civil servants whose knowledge, loyalty and identity is confined to their department, and does not extend to the government as a whole. Moreover, the distinction between politics and administration is not very sharp in the Netherlands, and occasionally Ministers and Secretaries of State are recruited from the ranks of civil servants. Then, of course, the danger of a Minister 'going native' in his own department is most acute.

Another reinforcement of ministerial departmentalism is the important role interest groups play in policy-making. Corporatism has strong roots in the Netherlands, and after World War Two an attempt was made to reorganise economic life along corporatist lines. In 1948 a Secretary of State for Corporatist Reform was appointed, followed by a Minister Without Portfolio from 1952 to 1956. Although this attempted reform was not very successful, there has been a proliferation of advisory councils, bipartite and tripartite commissions, and many more informal venues for consultations and negotiations between government and interest groups. Ministers of Justice or Foreign Affairs may have fewer contacts with such organisations, but for Ministers of Social Affairs, Education, Welfare, Health and Culture and Agriculture, such contacts may be more intensive and time-consuming than those with Parliament. These Ministers and their civil servants will rarely use the word 'pressure groups', preferring instead to speak of 'our clients'. Most interest groups and advisory councils concentrate their efforts on one department and one Minister (the employers on Economic Affairs, the trade unions on Social Affairs, and so on). When Ministers are recruited from these organisations, the 'departmentalising' effect is strongest.

In structural-functionalist terms, the function of interest articulation is well cared for in Dutch government, but at the expense of interest aggregation. Most policy coordination takes place at the level of civil servants, but when they reach a deadlock the issue is referred to the Ministers who try to resolve the problem in an informal bilateral meeting. In addition, all cabinets have a system of cabinet committees to promote coordination (Andeweg, 1985). There are now fourteen permanent cabinet committees for policy areas such as European Affairs, the Civil Service, Regional Policy, Physical Planning and Environmental Protection. With one exception, they are all presided over by the Prime Minister. The Ministers and Secretaries of State of all the departments with a stake in the policy area concerned are members.

Sometimes the net is cast rather wide to ensure political balance in the committee. In addition, civil servants can be members. However, membership is not very important as all Ministers can participate in any meeting of each and every cabinet committee. If one Minister so requests, an issue is referred to the full cabinet. All conclusions reached by cabinet committees need confirmation by the full cabinet. The importance of cabinet committees varies considerably from one committee to the next, and from one cabinet to the next. On the whole, however, their role is a limited one and the frequency of their meetings is considerably lower than that of the full cabinet.

More important than these official permanent committees are informal arrangements for coordination – some *ad hoc*, some more permanent. Since the early 1970s a small unofficial committee has formed in the cabinet to discuss socio-economic policy. It started as a 'triangle', comprising the Ministers of Finance, Economic Affairs and Social Affairs, but they have since been joined by the Prime Minister and the Minister for Internal Affairs, forming the 'pentagon'. This pentagon has come to dominate socio-economic policy-making, and as socio-economic problems constitute the bulk of the cabinet's agenda it is sometimes depicted as an 'inner cabinet' and resented as such by other Ministers. Similar, but less prominent and less permanent committees can sometimes be found in other policy areas.

By far the most important coordinating mechanism is still the budgetary process. In the Netherlands the budget is the result of a series of negotiations between each spending department and the Department of Finance (Koopmans, 1969). As a first step in this annual ritual, the Department of Finance issues guidelines to limit the financial demands of the departments. Following these guidelines the departments then draw up their budget proposals, and the negotiations start between civil servants from each department and from the Department of Finance. If the civil servants cannot reach agreement on an item, it is referred to a bilateral meeting between the spending Minister and the Minister of Finance, both accompanied by civil servants.

Many Ministers regard this annual bilateral meeting as more important than any other meeting of the cabinet. There have been legendary Ministers of Finance with whom such a meeting lasted at least a whole day. Sometimes agreement is only reached after the civil servants have been sent out of the room. In practice the full cabinet only decides on the remaining differences between the Minister of Finance and his colleagues. It should be emphasised that, important though the budgetary process is, its coordinating role is still restricted to the financial aspect of government policy.

CONCLUSION

What, then, is the role of the cabinet in decision-making? Ministers may be obliged to seek cabinet confirmation for most of their plans and the cabinet may be collectively responsible for almost any action by an individual Minister, but the Dutch cabinet is still far removed from the ideal of collective and collegiate government. From time to time a politically charged and controversial issue may involve all or most Ministers. Setting aside those cases, it is usually frowned upon for a Minister to join a debate in which his department has no stake. As a consequence, cabinet meetings resemble joint sessions of cabinet committees: a different sub-group of Ministers participates in the discussions on each item, their colleagues leaning back or spending the time in the cabinet room usefully by taking care of departmental business until it is their turn. Only the Prime Minister and the Minister of Finance are *ex officio* members of all these partial cabinets. Cabinet government is sometimes depicted as the 'Government against Sub-Governments', lamentably lacking in presidential systems (Rose, 1980). On the basis of the Dutch experience one might wonder whether that is true in more than just a formal sense.

## Notes

1. The author wishes to thank the Dutch Organisation for the Advancement of Pure Research (ZWO) for its financial support through a Huygens Fellowship, and the Warden and Fellows of Nuffield College, Oxford, for their hospitality when he was an Academic Visitor there during 1987. This chapter builds upon earlier publications by the author especially on Andeweg (1988).
2. See Geismann (1964) with regard to the Dutch case.
3. Non-political causes include urgent changes in the Constitution. Any change in the Constitution requires a dissolution of Parliament and new elections.
4. Paradoxically, however, cabinets lasted longer after 1967, when pillarisation started to wane. See Van den Berg and Visscher (1984).
5. This hypothesis has been put forward by H. Daalder in several publications. See, for example, Daalder (1966).
6. For developments until World War One, see Dooyeweerd (1917). For an English language account of developments before World War Two, see Vandenbosch and Eldersveld (1947). For the situation immediately after the war, see Barents (1952).
7. It is generally assumed that after 1874 cabinets had a permanent chairman.
8. For a discussion of the present position of Secretaries of State, see De Graaf and Versteeg (1985), and W.A. Van den Berg (1985).
9. With one exception: since 1979 the Prime Minister has the power to adjudicate conflicts about the boundaries of portfolios.
10. In recent years H. Daudt has created a controversy among Dutch political scientists and historians, by arguing that the Christian Democrats have always had a natural preference for a coalition with the Right and only governed with the Left in case of 'dire necessity'. See H. Daudt (1982). Even if Daudt's thesis is contested, there can be no doubt that the coalition predilections of the Christian Democrats have shifted to the Right in the 1980s. For an overview of Christian Democratic coalition behaviour, see De Jong and Pijnenburg (1986).
11. These criticisms have led to various unsuccessful attempts at reform. See, for example, Daalder (1986, pp. 512–17).
12. E. van Thijn, as cited in Van den Berg (1985e, pp. 247).

# 4 Belgium: A Complex Cabinet in a Fragmented Polity

André-Paul Frognier

## 1 CABINET SETTING

Belgium is a constitutional monarchy associated with a parliamentary regime where the cabinet is responsible to Parliament. The powers of the King are listed in the Constitution, but he does not have personal responsibility as his decisions must be counter-signed by a Minister in order to be valid. On the other hand, his person is inviolable in both the public and private (civil and penal) fields. The King and the Ministers belong both to the executive and the legislature simultaneously.

The constitution gives the King the power to nominate and dismiss Ministers (Article 65). The cabinet can only remain in office if it has the confidence of the two houses – the Chamber of Representatives and the Senate – which have the same legislative powers. The maximum duration of a cabinet is four years: that is, the constitutional period between two legislative elections.

The Belgian Constitution of 1830, written in the year when Belgium gained her independence, did not acknowledge the existence of a cabinet which would collectively take decisions, except in the case of an *interregnum* or in the case of the Monarch being unable to do so. In practice, however, and as early as 1831, Ministers met together regularly, and it rapidly became the practice that they should meet quite often. Only at the time of the constitutional revision of 1970 was the cabinet officially recognised, although some laws or Royal Decrees (*Arrêté Royaux*), had long since referred to it.

The main reforms introduced in 1970 which related to the cabinet stated that 'apart from the Prime Minister, there must be as many French-speaking Ministers as Flemish-speaking ones' (Article 36 bis). The text recognises the existence of a ˚Prime Minister, although the expression has been in existence since 1890 and was used officially for the first time in 1918. Since 1970, the Constitution has made a distinction between Ministers and Secretaries of State (*Secrétaires d'Etat*) who are

68

assistants to a Minister and are part of the 'government' but not of the Council of Ministers (Article 61 bis). This had in fact been the practice since 1961.

The political system has three main cleavages: religious (Catholic–Free-thinker); socio-economic (Left-Right); and linguistic (Flemish–French-speaking). These cleavages are partially institutionalised in that free 'segments' or, as the Belgians say, 'political families' or 'sociological worlds', have long been recognised. These are the Catholic, Socialist and Liberal segments. The institutionalisation of cleavages, however, is not complete. First, the socio-economic cleavage cuts across the Catholic segment: for instance, there are Catholic trade unionists as well as Socialist trade unionists. Second, the linguistic cleavage took a long time to be recognised. It has in part been institutionalised since the 1960s through the division of the main parties into Flemish and French-speaking wings, but the interest groups are not divided in the same way. The parties kept their names but are wholly independent of each other: the linguistic division of the parties have corresponded to sharp differences with respect to the structure of the state, but less so in other fields.

Three parties (or six since the linguistic division) dominate: they are the so-called 'traditional' parties, the Christian Party (today Social Christian Party), the Socialist Party, and the Liberal Party (today Party for Freedom and Progress). Other parties have fluctuated in strength and do not have a clearly defined social base: they include mainly the 'linguistic' parties which are specifically oriented towards one region and which were established to defend the interests of the French-speaking inhabitants of Brussels (Democratic Front of French-speaking, FDF), the Flemish population (People's Union, VU) or the Walloons (Walloon Rally, RW). There is also a small Communist Party and an Ecologist Party (which is a recent creation). Table 4.1 gives the list of the parties which have taken part in cabinets since 1961.

Belgian political structures bear some resemblance to Dutch-type consociational arrangements. There are indeed many cases of joint decision-making processes in which all three traditional parties take part. Public resources also tend to be allocated according to principles based on proportionality among the segments of the population. In difficult circumstances, parties have come together to take and implement major decisions. This was the case with the Education Agreement (*Pacte Scolaire*) which ended sharp conflicts between Catholics and Free-thinkers. Moreover, alongside each ministry, there is

TABLE 4.1  Electoral scores of governmental parties in Belgium: 1961–1985

| Parties | 1961 | 1965 | 1968 | 1971 | 1974 | 1977 | 1978 | 1981 | 1985 |
|---|---|---|---|---|---|---|---|---|---|
| *Christian* | 41 | 34 | — | — | — | — | — | — | — |
| French | — | — | 12 | 10 | 9 | 10 | 10 | 7 | 8 |
| Flemish | — | — | 20 | 20 | 23 | 26 | 26 | 19 | 21 |
| *Socialist* | 37 | 28 | 28 | 27 | — | — | — | — | — |
| French | — | — | — | — | 14 | 13 | 13 | 13 | 14 |
| Flemish | — | — | — | 16 | 13 | 13 | 12 | 13 | 15 |
| *Liberal* | 12 | 22 | 21 | — | — | — | — | — | — |
| French | — | — | — | — | 5 | 7 | 6 | 9 | 10 |
| Flemish | — | — | — | — | 10 | 9 | 11 | 13 | 11 |
| FDF | — | 1 | 3 | 9 | 5 | 4 | 4 | 2 | 1 |
| VU | 3 | 7 | 10 | 11 | 10 | 10 | 7 | 10 | 8 |
| RW | — | — | 3 | 2 | 6 | 3 | 3 | 2 | — |

NOTES:
(1) The percentages are computed on the Belgian electorate taken as a whole. Before the splitting of the parties, the results are given *in toto* for each political family. After 'French' means the French-speaking party of this family (for Wallonia and for the French-speakers of Brussels) and 'Flemish' the Flemish party (for Flanders and the Flemish-speakers of Brussels.)
(2) The percentages have to be read in column. They do not reach 100 per cent because we should add the results of the other parties as well as the void and nil votes. In 1968 and 1971 the lists 'Christians: French' included Flemish votes in Brussels (a minority), where these lists remained unitarian. We must point out that the results of the FDF in 1977 are mainly due to a cartellisation with a liberal tendency. Moreover, in 1977 and 1978, the French liberal family was divided between a walloon and a Brussels party.

a 'Consultative Committee' which includes the most representative interest groups concerned. These committees thus associate the segments to the decision taken.[1]

However, some aspects of Belgian politics are not consociational. Coalitions are unstable (but this may also sometimes restore in the long term the consociational balance). Social cleavages led to numerous conflicts which ended up in violence and death (the 'Royal Question', the 'Great Strike', the 'Education War'). It is as if the governments which perceived themselves as 'strong' tried to gain decisive advantages without much concern for consociationalism. Consociationalism reappears, however, when conflicts become so deep that they might destroy the political system and none of the conflicting actors is able to overcome his adversaries. Thus agreements are more the result of a stalemate than of a permanent spirit of compromise.

Since the 1960s Belgium has followed a difficult path in the direction of federalism and the balance of power has changed. With the Catholics in the majority in Flanders and in the minority in Wallonia, and the Socialists in the reverse position, the quasi-federalist arrangements have led to the emergence of new political units which are dominated by one party. As a result, opposition has increased and the political style has tended to be less consensual.[2]

Moreover, one of the characteristics of Belgian politics is the relative instability of its cabinets.[3] The level of instability was high immediately after World War Two and during the 1970s. This last period of instability resulted primarily from the impact on cabinets of opposition between the Flemish and French-speaking parts of the country with respect to the move towards federalism. In these circumstances it is only natural that governmental instability should have been high. Yet the phenomenon is not new. In his work on the interwar period, C.K. Höjer (1969) noted that governmental instability was high at that time, although, according to him, this was compensated by the stability of the individual Ministers who remained at the head of a particular department for long periods.[4] There is indeed some evidence that this is still the case:[5] while the average duration of cabinets is 1.4 years (see Table 4.2), the average duration of Ministers in office is 3.8 years.[6] Overall, during the postwar period and up to 1984, 15.5 per cent of the Ministers[7] remained in office less than a year, 21.6 per cent between one and two years, 37 per cent between two and five years, 18.8 per cent between five and ten years and 7 per cent ten years or more.[8] This last group is composed of fifteen Ministers of whom ten belonged to the Christian Party, around which almost all the coalitions have revolved since the war.[9] Yet, although the duration of Belgian Ministers in office is appreciably longer than the duration of cabinets, it is nevertheless less than that of Ministers in most other Atlantic countries. Blondel (1987) estimates the average duration of these Ministers to be four years for the period 1945–1981. Belgian is at about the same relatively low level as France and ranks just above the US, Finland, Portugal and Greece. The duration of Belgian Ministers in office is thus comparatively short.[10]

TABLE 4.2   Average duration of cabinets in Belgium: 1945–1985

| Period | % years |
|--------|---------|
| 1945–1950 | .77 |
| 1951–1960 | 2.32 |
| 1961–1970 | 2.94 |
| 1971–1980 | .82 |
| 1981–1985 | 2.32 |

Moreover, ministerial posts often change hands in Belgium. The effect on duration can be calculated in two ways. On the one hand, one can assess the average number of months during which a post is held by the same person in a continuous or interrupted manner. On this basis, the same post is held in Belgium by the same person, Minister or Secretary of State, for on average 2.1 years. For Ministers alone the average is 2.2 years.[11] Departmental stability is therefore only 1.5 times higher than governmental stability (2.2 years versus 1.4 years) and it is lower than ministerial stability (2.2 years versus 3.8 years). In this respect, too, Belgium is appreciably below the average for Atlantic countries of 3.1 years. Belgium ranks below Canada, Fifth Republic France, Britain, Portugal and Denmark (between two and three years), and is only above Italy, Finland and Greece (less than two years).[12]

We can also measure ministerial stability in terms of the number of portfolios which a member of the government has held while in office. On the basis of an assessment made for Ministers only, Belgian Ministers appeared evenly divided between those who held only one post (50.2 per cent) and those who held two or more posts (49.8 per cent).[13] There is therefore a substantial amount of rotation in Belgian cabinets and we can thus conclude that instability and rotation are two features of the Belgian system.

Belgium has a governmental elite in which only a minority is relatively stable (25.8 per cent of the Ministers remained five years or more in office) and where many move from post to post. Around these is a substantial group who have only a short experience of government.

TABLE 4.3   Cabinets in Belgium: 1945–1985

| Prime Minister | Date in | Party Composition |
| --- | --- | --- |
| Spaak I | 03.46 | Socialist |
| Van Acker I | 04.46 | Soc Lib Communist |
| Van Acker II | 08.45 | Soc Lib Communist UDB |
| Huysmans | 08.46 | Soc Lib Communist |
| Spaak II | 03.47 | Chr Soc |
| Eyskens G I | 07.49 | Chr Lib |
| Duvieusart | 06.50 | Chr |
| Pholien | 08.50 | Chr |
| Van Houtte | 01.52 | Chr |
| Van Acker III | 04.54 | Soc Lib |
| Eyskens G II | 06.58 | Chr |
| Eyskens G III | 11.58 | Chr Lib |
| Lefevre | 04.61 | Chr Soc |
| Harmel | 07.65 | Chr Soc |
| Vanden Boeynants I | 03.66 | Chr Lib |
| Eyskens G IV | 06.68 | Chr Soc |
| Leburton | 01.73 | Chr Soc Lib |
| Tindemans I | 04.74 | Chr Lib |
| Tindemans II | 06.74 | Chr Lib RW |
| Tindemans III | 03.77 | Chr Soc |
| Tindemans IV | 06.77 | Chr Soc FDF VU |
| Vanden Boeynants II | 10.78 | Chr Soc FDF VU |
| Martens I | 04.79 | Chr Soc FDF |
| Martens II | 01.80 | Chr Soc |
| Martens III | 04.80 | Chr Soc Lib |
| Martens IV | 10.80 | Chr Soc |
| Eyskens M | 04.81 | Chr Soc |
| Martens V | 12.81 | Chr Lib |

NOTE: The cabinets are defined by the double criterion of different PMs and/or different coalitions. We did not take into account the linguistic split of traditional parties, since they have never been divided in majority and opposition. The year indicated is this of the official nomination, the first one in the case of successive identical cabinets following our criterion.

The fact that there is considerable rotation at the top has already been pointed out for Belgian elites as a whole,[14] and for Ministers in particular.[15] It is presented as an exception to the theory of the circulation of elites.[16] Our study shows that, for high-ranking Ministers, there is indeed more rotation than circulation of elites. Among the lower ranks there is more circulation than rotation, with rapid returns to the government.


## 2  CABINET STRUCTURE

Just after independence the structure of the cabinet was simple: the King chaired the Council of Ministers, all of whom were equal or near-equal. The Council was led by its 'Chairman' (*President du Conseil*) who was subordinate to the King, particularly at the beginning. Gradually, the King ceased to chair the council. The present King, Baudouin I, has never done so and his father, King Leopold III, did so only twice, in order to issue Royal Declarations, but not to preside over deliberations.[17] At the same time, the Chairman and then the PM became predominant.

Between 1831 and 1847 there was no organised political parties in the strict sense of the word and there were only broad political leanings – Catholic and Liberal – both of which were represented in the government. This period has been known as the 'unionist' period, during which the King dominated the cabinet.

The growing importance of parties and their impact on public life were probably the main factors accounting for the decrease of the part played by the King in leading the Ministers, and for the corresponding surge in the role of the Prime Minister. Meanwhile, the tendency for governments to be coalitions made the presence of a coordinator increasingly necessary. Between the wars, the importance of the Prime Minister grew: he was given responsibility for economic and financial matters as well as for the overall supervision of the administration. In particular he became responsible for the overseeing of the recruitment and management of civil servants. Finally, his powers were further enhanced in the post-1945 period, as a result of the fact that cabinet committees were set up and that he chaired these committees.

The Prime Minister does not lead a group of quasi equals, as did the King in the early post-independence period. Cabinets have become larger and more hierarchical. Whereas Belgium had 6 Ministers in 1831 and 12 in 1900, there were 28 members of the government in 1985, of whom 13 were Secretaries of State. This increase led to the development of cabinet committees whose task is to prepare the decisions of the government.

Some Ministers gained more influence than others: the Deputy Prime Ministers (*Vice Premier-Ministres*); Moreover, a group of second-level Ministers was set up under the title of Secretaries of State.

Overall, the number of Ministers and Secretaries of State has tended to be high (see Table 4.4). Given the high turnover described earlier, it is not surprising that there should have been as many as 210 Ministers and 71 Secretaries of State between 1945 and 1985.[18] This puts Belgium in sixth position among the Atlantic countries in the number of its government members, ranking after Greece, France, Britain, Italy and Portugal.[19] The peak of the 1970s corresponds to large coalitions as well as to the presence of Ministers with sub-national responsibilities within the cabinet. These posts were abolished later as new autonomous political units were set up as a result of the gradual move towards 'federalization' of the country. These units are known as 'regions' for socio-economic matters and 'communities' for cultural matters.

TABLE 4.4    Size of cabinets in Belgium: 1945–1985

| *Period* | *No. Cabinets* | *No. Ministers Secretaries of State* | *No. Ministerial Posts* | *No. Secretary of State Posts* |
|---|---|---|---|---|
| 1945–1950 | 9 | 70 | 35 | — |
| 1950–1960 | 4 | 62 | 31 | — |
| 1961–1970 | 4 | 81 | 45 | 15 |
| 1971–1980 | 10 | 102 | 60 | 39 |
| 1981–1985 | 2 | 53 | 36 | 11 |

NOTE:    We must not confuse these numbers with the total number of different ministers and secretaries of state during the period because in this table the computing is made by decade, which results in the same names being repeated and increases the total.

The cabinet is thus hierarchical, with a Prime Minister, Deputy Prime Ministers, Ministers and Secretaries of State. By and large, the Deputy Prime Ministers owe their influence to the fact that they are the presidents or among the main leaders of the several parties which form the coalition. They will also run one of the more important departments. As the top elite of the parties which belong to the government, they tend to meet as a group in order to discuss the main problems facing cabinet.

Once they have come to an agreement among themselves and with the Prime Minister, this agreement is then proposed to (and occasionally forced on) the rest of the ministers and the Secretaries of State. Sometimes some of the more important Ministers join in the negotiations with the Prime Minister and the Deputy Prime Ministers. There is therefore a real sense in which there is an 'inner cabinet' in Belgium even if it was not always formalised as such.

Meanwhile, the role of 'ordinary' Ministers is to be responsible for a sector of government, though they of course attend cabinet meetings. There are now no 'Ministers without Portfolio', although some did exist before 1968. Finally, the role of Secretaries of State is to assist the Ministers. Secretaries of State do not attend the Council of Ministers, but they have in other respects the same status as the Ministers. They are usually appointed to more technical posts. A position of Secretary of State is viewed as a stepping-stone towards a ministerial career. towards a ministerial career.

There are no texts concerning the formal cabinet rules, except for the articles of the Constitution mentioned in the first section. Linguistic parity in the Belgian cabinet is now a formal rule and is regarded as a symbol of 'consociationalism'. The rule does not apply to the position of Prime Minister, who has usually been drawn from among Flemish politicians since 1970. Nor does it apply to Secretaries of State, among whom there is a Flemish-speaking majority.

Finally, since Secretaries of State do not belong to the Council of Ministers, a 'council of Government' has been set up which includes both Ministers and Secretaries of State. This body meets a few times a year at the most important moments in the cycle of a government – especially at the beginning and at the end, but also when major questions arise. Occasionally Secretaries of State are also asked to attend cabinet meetings.


## 3   CABINET LIFE

### The cabinet and its environment

According to the Belgian Constitution, the cabinet is largely independent of the King. After a governmental crisis or an election, the role of the King is limited to the appointment of a government *formateur* (often preceded by an *informateur* in order to clarify the political situation if necessary). When a governmental crisis is imminent, the King can take time to decide before accepting or refusing the resignation of the cabinet, although he is not entirely free in all circumstances. It would seem that the greater the crisis, the greater the King's freedom of manoeuvre. Cabinets are increasingly autonomous *vis-à-vis* the legislative body considered as an institution. This corresponds to a general trend towards the strengthening of the executive over the legislature. Two specific points need to be stressed. First, the collapse of governments very rarely occurs as a result of an action of the House of Representatives. Since 1945 only once did a government fall after a vote of confidence in the Chamber. The collapse of governments is typically the consequence of internal conflicts between the dominant parties and this illustrates *a contrario* the limited role of Parliament. Second, in recent years, the government has often requested and obtained 'special powers' (*pouvoirs spéciaux*) to enable it to decide on a range of issues (essentially economic and social). These powers are granted under certain conditions and for limited periods only. Nonetheless, the result is that Parliament is to an extent by-passed with respect to the legislative process.

The situation in relation to political parties is different, although here too there has been an evolution in the past few years. It is commonly said in Belgium that the country is governed by a 'partitocracy' – the suggestion being that the traditional parties dominate politics in general and cabinets in particular. Indeed, this was a correct assessment for some time. Parties were the key elements in the decision-making process, often individually, but sometimes collectively through 'party summits' or other forms of 'joint decision-making' such as the *Pacte Scolaire* referred to above. The power of the parties lies in the fact that each of these organisations represents a 'segment' of the population.

In recent years, Prime Ministers have tried to link parties and cabinet by appointing the Presidents of these parties as Deputy Prime Ministers. This was designed to help the cabinet to be the arena in which compromises took place and thus to ensure greater autonomy as well as greater stability to the cabinet. Since the custom does not allow anyone to hold the offices of party president and Deputy Prime Minister simultaneously, party presidents have had to formally resign these positions on becoming Deputy Prime Ministers. Those who replaced them tended to focus their attention on public opinion, while Deputy Prime Ministers have focussed theirs on cabinet matters. The development also had some apparent effect on governmental stability: the 1981 government has been able to reach the end of its four-year term, a development which had occurred only once before since World War Two. However, this type of experience has been too short-lived to justify the conclusion that a lasting reform of political processes has taken place.

Interest groups are very influential in Belgium, as the existence of a number of clearly defined social segments gives them considerable leverage. They often have a very large following: the trade unions, for example, have almost the same percentage of affiliated members as in Sweden – 70 per cent. The Consultative Committees in the ministries have further increased the power of the trade unions. For a long time agreements among the main socio-economic pressure groups were regarded as being as binding as laws. However, this situation has changed somewhat since the mid-1970s as a result of the world economic recession. Agreements became more difficult to come by and the level of *concertation* has decreased. The result was a greater governmental freedom of action with respect to social expenditure. In a number of cases, the government decided to reduce the role of trade unions in negotiations by launching new policies without prior discussion and then confronting the unions with a *fait accompli*. Reactions have been mixed and opposition has not had any significant impact. This has strengthened the government's hand. Here, too, it would be premature to claim that the power of the executive has more than temporarily increased.

The political affiliation of civil servants above a given rank is well-known in Belgium. This means that the relationship is smooth when the head of an agency is of the same political 'colour' as his Minister. On the other hand, the relationship may be more tense and conflicts may arise when political affiliation differs, especially if the civil servant belongs to a party which is in opposition at the time. Often Ministers appoint civil servants who are known to belong to their party as members of their personal staff.

There is no Information Minister and no Information Secretary for the government. Each Minister or Secretary of State has his own press attaché who is mostly concerned with boosting the public image of his Minister and who therefore distributes information on all his or her activities. Leaks from the meetings of the Council of Ministers are said to be frequent. As a result the press rapidly obtains insights in the discussions which have taken place and on the character of the decisions.

**Internal coordination**

The Prime Minister chairs the Council of Ministers and heads its secretariat. His main task is one of coordination. He also has exclusive responsibility for a number of administrative agencies such as the Chancellery and the Centre for Studies on Economic Coordination (*Service d'Études de Coordination Economique*). He shares responsibility with other Ministers with respect to the Office of Planning (*Bureau du Plan*) and the Department of Scientific Research. Politically, he coordinates mainly by means of chairing almost all the standing cabinet committees, although coordination also takes place through the meetings of the personal staffs of the Ministers who prepare the standing committee meetings.

Cabinet committees are composed of the Ministers holding the relevant posts and prepare the decisions of the Council of Ministers. They may be set up by Royal Decree or by an informal cabinet decision. The committees formally in existence in 1987 and set up by Royal Decree are as follows:

Special Committee for Global Policy
Cabinet Committee for Economic and Social Coordination
Cabinet Committee for Institutional Reforms
Cabinet Committee for the Environment
Cabinet Committee for Scientific Policy
Cabinet Committee for Computer Science
Cabinet Committee for External Policy
Cabinet Committee for Women's Status

The first two have a special status and a wider brief and they often include the most important Ministers. All, except the Cabinet Committee for the Environment, are chaired by the Prime Minister and the secretariat of these committees is responsible to the Prime Minister.

The importance of the Special Cabinet Committee for Global Policy has varied. It was established in 1961 as an inner cabinet to substitute the Council of Ministers on the 'hottest' matters coming to cabinet, but it never really replaced the Council of Ministers even though it sometimes played a major part in preparing decisions. It included the Ministers who were also the leaders of the coalition parties. Since 1981 it has not been convened, and was replaced by meetings of the Prime Minister and the Deputy Prime Ministers (sometimes together with other Ministers).

The Cabinet committee for Economic and Social Coordination has considerable prestige as it takes many decisions in social and economic matters. Except when the law formally requires the Council of Ministers to decide, this committee substitutes for the cabinet on the matters which are within its competence. It has a complex structure, being divided into a number of sub-committees. Since the mid-1970s it has been composed of twenty members on the basis of competence. As a result it is more technical than the Special Cabinet Committee for Global Policy.

All Ministers and Secretaries of State have personal staffs (*cabinets*) at their disposal. These *cabinets* have greatly expanded in recent years. A small *cabinet* should include 30 to 40 persons, while a large staff might be composed of over one hundred people. These *cabinets* comprise civil servants who are 'detached' from their original department as well as other members who come from different professional backgrounds. A proportion of this cabinet is employed with a view to cover subjects within the administrative responsibility of the Ministers. Other members of the *cabinet*, often the maj)rity, work for the party and have the task to ensure that relations between the Minister, his constituency and public opinion run smoothly.

From an administrative point of view the *cabinet* has a double role. It acts as a link between the Minister and his civil servants, on the one hand, and between the Minister and the personal staff of other Ministers on the other. The personal staffs of each Minister meet frequently to prepare cabinet committees and to formulate potential compromises. The *cabinet* is led by a *Chef de Cabinet* who is the right-hand-man of the Minister. Sometimes these *chefs de cabinet* participate in the most technical cabinet committees together with, or as deputies to, their Minister.

## Ministerial careers and ministerial background

Belgian cabinets are primarily composed of parliamentarians. Eighty-two per cent of Ministers have been Members of Parliament. In this respect, Belgium is half-way between wholly parliamentary systems such as those of Britain or Italy and systems where there are substantial numbers of non-parliamentary Ministers (such as those of Austria, France and the Netherlands).[20] It is interesting to note that this heavy presence of parliamentarians in Belgian cabinets does not seem to have markedly increased Parliament's role in the decision-making process. Yet there is a symbiosis between the ministerial and parliamentary life of a Minister. Ministers return to Parliament after leaving the government while they wait to be called again to office. The 'rotation' which was mentioned earlier results in intermittent spells on the backbenches between ministerial assignments.[21] Even when Ministers retire from government the majority (two-thirds) continue to sit in Parliament.[22]

There is a substantial proportion of 'managers' in Belgian cabinets. If we define in this way Ministers who have a background in the civil service, in the middle and upper levels of the private sector (*cadres*), in business or in associations or trade unions, about a third (36 per cent) of Belgian Ministers belong to this category. Those coming from the public sector are a small minority (under 10 per cent). But the majority of Belgian Ministers are still 'amateurs' or 'generalists': lawyers are relatively numerous (17 per cent) and university professors are an even larger group.[23] Only one-fifth can be defined as specialists in the strictest sense – that is to say, Ministers whose training corresponds to the department of which they are the heads.[24] Naturally enough, the rotation from one ministerial post to another does not lead to specialisation. In a sense the system *is* coherent: if there is to be substantial rotation 'amateurs' and 'generalists' are better suited than specialists. Overall, Belgium is in this respect close to the average for Atlantic countries, for there are fewer specialists there than in Austria or the Netherlands (but more than in Switzerland).[25]

## 4  CABINET DECISION-MAKING

### The 'consensus rule' and the role of the Prime Minister

The informal decision-making rule in Belgian cabinets is explicitly called the 'rule of consensus'. The Prime Minister is the agent of this consensus. The arrangement has been described in the following way by Wilfrid Martens, who was Prime Minister throughout most of the 1980s:

> First of all he [the Prime Minister] must listen a lot, and when deep disagreements occur, he must suggest a solution to the matter. This can be done in different ways. Sometimes, during the discussion, I note the elements of the problem and think of a proposal which I formulate to the Council, the Secretary taking notes. The Ministers can then insist on changing commas and full stops. The Prime Minister can also make a proposal which leaves enough room for amendments in order to keep the current discussion on the right tracks. When a solution must be found in order to reach a consensus, he can force one or two Ministers to join or resign'.[26]

In the case of the Netherlands, A. Lijphart (1968) describes the role of the Prime Minister as that of '*primus inter pares* without due emphasis on *primus*'[27] *Primus inter pares* is also valid in the Belgian case, but the emphasis has tended to be put more and more on the *primus* since the mid-1970s as the Prime Minister appears to play an increasingly important part. This development has taken place in parallel with the growing personalisation of the power of the Prime Minister. Two recent Prime Ministers, Leo Tindemans and Wilfrid Martens, have benefitted from this increased stability: the former led several cabinets and the latter had led six by the end of 1987.

Yet the Prime Minister is not alone in reaching decisions. As we saw, Belgian cabinets are hierarchical. In the most important fields what counts is the negotiation between the Prime Minister and the Deputy Prime Ministers, who can be regarded as mini-Prime Ministers with respect to their own parties. A strong disagreement from one of the Deputy Prime Ministers means almost automatically the collapse of the government, at least if the Deputy Prime Minister belongs to one of the traditional parties (Christian, Socialist or Liberal). The situation is less clear-cut with respect to the others (that is to say the linguistic parties). Disagreements with the representatives of these parties have been settled by the forced withdrawal of the representatives of that party from the cabinet without being followed by the collapse of the government. Consensus building is thus essentially confined to the representatives of the traditional parties.

### Decision practices

The Prime Minister decides on the points to be debated at the Council of Ministers. The agenda is sent to the Ministers often a few days (but sometimes only hours) before the meeting which takes place usually once a week on Friday mornings. When a Minister wishes to see a point discussed at the next meeting of the Council, although the matter has not been previously decided in one of the cabinet committees, he has to inform the Prime Minister and submit a memorandum. If the question concerns several Ministers, personal contacts will usually have been established between the respective personal staffs of these Ministers.

The 'agenda' covers a large variety of matters from the 'hottest' to the more routine matters (decorations, inaugurations, for instance). The personal staff of a Minister is informed of the agenda of the Council of Ministers and prepares the Minister's brief under the supervision of the *chef de cabinet*. As we saw, some matters are prepared by the coordinating bodies (cabinet committees and inter-staff meetings) and the decision can therefore be reached rapidly. However, the cabinet often discusses delicate problems which divide the majority and the cabinet meeting becomes a forum for debate and negotiation. But it is difficult to keep the discussion under control as the political parties exercise strong supervision and leaks to the media are numerous. Debates are particularly awkward when the Prime Minister and the Deputy Prime Ministers have not been able to reach agreement beforehand, especially if one of the Deputy Prime Ministers feels deeply about the matter. The large size of the cabinet is also an obstacle to effective debate and rapid decision-making. Thus the Belgian cabinet is not only a place where matters which have already been prepared elsewhere are being formally approved. It is also an element in the bargaining process and even displays the characteristics of a small Parliament.

There are no fixed rules specifying the types of decisions which the cabinet can take, except if a law or a Royal Decree states that the Council of Ministers has formally to approve a measure. By an large, however, the Prime Minister is the master of the game. He chooses what he wants to be placed on the agenda and decides when and how he will raise questions. There are, nevertheless, some customary modes of behaviour. For instance, decisions which are politically important, such as those with linguistic implications and which affect relations between the Flemish and French-speaking population, have to be discussed in cabinet as do matters which have an important budgetary impact.

The Council of Ministers has a Secretary who often remains in the post for many years. This parallels the fact that Prime Ministers have for a long period of time been drawn from the Flemish Christian Party. The Secretary is neither a Minister nor a civil servant. He is one of the prime ministerial *chefs de cabinet*. He exercises considerable influence as a result of the fact that he has a long experience in writing the minutes of the meetings (which are not open for consultation by the public) and in summarising the decisions in a short public document which is sent to the Ministers. The agenda and the decisions of the Council of Ministers are – in theory at least – confidential. Once a decision has been reached by the Council of Ministers it is customary for all Ministers to defend it publically – even if they did not originally agree with it.

Party decision-making regularly encroaches on the processes of governmental decision-making in at least two ways. First, party leaders usually have a weekly meeting with their Ministers and with the leaders of their parliamentary party to discuss urgent matters. Second, Ministers also attend the weekly meetings of the 'party bureau' (the committees composed of party leaders and of representatives of the rank-and-file). At these meetings general lines of party policy are debated and decided. Often information on the decisions taken by the government is distributed there and these decisions are presumably discussed. Ministers often include among their staff men and women who are more or less openly representatives of interest organisations. This, too, makes it easier for party and groups to affect governmental life.

The Belgian cabinet is thus striving for consensus in a context in which divisions are strong and indeed touch at the very roots of the existence of the country. As the system is parliamentary and indeed as Parliament plays a substantial part at least in the recruitment and the careers of Ministers and in providing the framework within which parties have a major role, the cabinet can only maintain itself if it displays at least some characteristics of leadership. But the reality of political life is one of divisions which require periodic adjustments and a constant striving for compromise, however, leadership has to be toned down within the cabinet and give way to a broader form of rule based on ministerial oligarchies which are repeatedly engaged in consensus building. This double function – of leadership and of consensus – building – shows how much the cabinet system of government has to be flexible in a country like Belgium in order to survive. However, the problem is to know what the limits of this flexibility are, and when real instability and crisis can undermine it in such a fragmented polity.

## Notes

1. On the consociationalist aspect of the Belgian political system see mainly Lijphart (1981).
2. On the critics of the consensualist aspect of the Belgian political system see, among others, Covell (1982), Huyse (1981), De Ridder, Peterson and Wirth (1978) and Obler, Steiner and Dirickx (1977).
3. When defining a cabinet the legal criterion is the taking of oath.
4. See Hojer (1969) p. 315.
5. For the period 1946–1971 see *Centres de Recherches et d'Information Socio-Politiques* (1972) pp. 18–19.
6. The duration is therefore much shorter for Secretaries of State: 1.9 years. The creation of these posts is more recent and corresponds to periods of low cabinet stability. On the other hand, these data do not consider the fact that Secretaries of State can become Ministers, nor the time spent by Ministers before and after the period in consideration.
7 Exclusively, without taking into account the Secretaries of State.
8. Blondel (1988), Table 1, p. 54.

9. Before and after the split over linguistic problems.
10. Blondel (1985) p. 88.
11. For Secretaries of State the average is 1.59 years. We have considered only the posts which have been cited in the Royal Decree of nomination. In this case, changes of names or regroupings are considered as new ministerial posts.
12. Blondel (1985) pp. 226–227.
13. Blondel (1988), Table 4, p. 57.
14. Blondel (1988), pp. 59–60.
15. Das (1987) p. 218.
16. De Wachter (1982) p. 324.
17. De Lichtervelde (1947) p. 33.
18. Ministers and Secretaries of State taken into account are those whose names had been published in the *Moniteur Belge* when the Royal Decree of nomination was published. If a new person was appointed during the term, we have added the name.
19. Blondel (1985) p. 277.
20. Blondel (1985) p. 277.
21. Blondel (1988) pp. 62–3.
22. Blondel (1988) p. 62.
23. Blondel (1988) p. 65.
24. Blondel (1988) pp. 64–6.
25. Blondel (1987) p. 277.
26. Martens (1985) p. 45.
27. Lijphart (1968) p. 136.

# 5 France: Cabinet Decision-Making under the Fifth Republic

## Jean-Louis Thiébault

When two ministers expressed opposite viewpoints in a conflict over security issues the Prime Minister of the time, Pierre Mauroy, justified the existence of a public debate between the members of the government in an article entitled 'Governing differently' (*Le Monde*, 20th April 1982). This point of view divided the members of the government as well as the majority because it acted counter to the traditional conception of governmental decision-making which dates back to the beginning of the Fifth Republic.

This traditional conception is based on the notion that the debate between the members of the government should not take place in public but should remain inside the government, that the government is not a collegial body, that the Prime Minister has an authority over the other members of government and is the person who resolves conflicts between them. Under the Fifth Republic these principles have accounted for the organisation of the government, the mechanics of the decision-making process and for the relationship between government and administration. Before examing them, however, we should first take a look at the constitutional and political framework within which the system operates.

## 1 CABINET SETTING

A number of provisions of the French Constitution have a direct impact on the structure and processes of government. These relate to the dualism of executive power, to prime ministerial supremacy and to the subordination of ministers to the prime ministerial or presidential will.

### Executive dualism

France has a dual executive based on the President of the Republic on the one hand, and the Prime Minister and his government on the other.

From 1958 France has had four presidents, nine prime ministers and nineteen governments (see Table 5.1).

TABLE 5.1    Presidents and governments in Fifth Republic France

| President | Prime Minister | Date in | Date out |
|-----------|----------------|---------|----------|
| DE GAULLE | Debre | 08.01.59 | 14.04.62 |
| (out 27.04.69) | Pompidou I | 04.04.62 | 10.10.62 |
| | Pompidou II | 28.11.62 | 08.01.66 |
| | Pompidou III | 08.01.66 | 06.04.67 |
| | Pompidou IV | 06.04.67 | 11.07.68 |
| | Couve de Murville | 11.07.68 | 22.06.69 |
| POMPIDOU | Chaban-Delmas | 22.06.69 | 05.07.72 |
| (out 02.04.74) | Messmer I | 07.07.72 | 28.03.73 |
| | Messmer II | 05.04.73 | 27.02.74 |
| | Messmer III | 01.03.74 | 27.05.74 |
| GISCARD | Chirac | 28.05.74 | 25.08.76 |
| D'ESTAING | | | |
| (out 21.05.81) | Barre I | 27.08.76 | 29.03.77 |
| | Barre II | 29.03.77 | 31.03.78 |
| | Barre III | 03.04.78 | 13.05.81 |
| MITTERRAND | Mauroy I | 21.05.81 | 22.06.81 |
| | Mauroy II | 22.06.81 | 22.03.83 |
| | Mauroy III | 22.03.83 | 17.07.84 |
| | Fabius | 17.07.84 | 20.03.86 |
| | Chirac | 20.03.86 | 10.05.88 |
| | Rocard | 10.05.88 | |

The President of the Republic has extensive powers. Moreover, the institution of the presidency was shaped by General de Gaulle's strong personality and was subsequently strengthened by the election of the President by direct universal suffrage as of 1965. We need not deal here with all aspects of presidential power, but only with those which relate to governmental power-sharing. In such matters as the meetings of the Council of Ministers, the preparation of laws and decrees, the appointment of senior civil servants, the defence and foreign policy the President of the Republic, on the one hand, and the government and the Prime Minister on the other, need to intervene simultaneously and therefore cooperate.

Prior to March 1986 the formula which prevailed was power-sharing between the President of the Republic and the Prime Minister, although the President was pre-eminent. This pre-eminence was based on three elements: the institutional powers of the President, his electoral and popular legitimacy and his position as the real leader of the parliamentary majority (Duverger, 1985 and 1986; Quermonne, 1987).

The Prime Minister acted under the umbrella of the leadership of the President. Consequently, the relationship was a hierarchical one and there was an unequal dualism. But this dualism was also ill-defined (Gicquel, 1980). In general, two-level leadership became the practice. The Prime Minister's task was primarily to deal with Parliament, the administration, the political parties, the trade unions and (to an extent) public opinion.

The President of the Republic operated at a more exalted level, avoiding unnecessary political risks. In this type of arrangement the Prime Minister was compared to a shield, a lightning-rod or a fuse. The President of the Republic could, however, always decide to 'descend' to the 'lower' level for, in addition to his constitutional powers, the Head of State assumed a general power of control which enabled him to deal with any issue at any time. This ill-defined power-sharing had many drawbacks, particularly as conflicts easily emerged. The removal of prime minister Chaban-Delmas in 1972 and the dismissal of Chirac in 1976 are examples of such conflicts.

Presidential pre-eminence has given way to a new arrangement as a result of the general election of 1986 when, for the first time under the Fifth Republic, the President ceased to have a supporting majority in Parliament. President and government now proceed from opposite political camps. This led to the so-called *cohabitation*, on the basis of which President and Prime Minister seek to establish their autonomy and rely on the powers which they respectively hold. The Prime Minister has become the real head of the government because of the parliamentary majority which supports him (Duhamel, 1986).

The *cohabitation* system which has prevailed since 1986 has led to a situation whereby the Prime Minister has governmental power and the President has become an arbiter. This is an entirely new formula whereby the Prime Minister has become the centre of the activity of the government. The President of the Republic has accepted the change: internal policy no longer depends on him and he no longer has the power to initiate. He has, however, retained the power to stop proposals or at any rate to delay them. He intervenes by means of comments and criticisms on issues concerned with the allocation of powers beween the executive, the legislature and the judiciary on matters relating to individual liberties, law and order and social welfare (Hadas-Lebel, 1986).

The President of the Republic likewise continues to exercise a power of supervision over the appointments of about twenty senior civil servants in three important areas – internal security, external security and the 'vital' interests of the nation. Meanwhile he accepts that the appointment of other senior civil servants should be the sole competence of the government alone (Coignard and Makarian, 1987).

Finally, the President sees himself as being in charge of foreign affairs and defence, although he has agreed that the Prime Minister should participate with him in the formulation of foreign policy (Fournier, 1987a).

## Prime ministerial authority on the members of the government

Besides dualism, prime ministerial authority on the other members of the government is a feature of the French cabinet. This authority has been established gradually.

At the beginning of the Third Republic, in 1870, the President of the Council, as the Prime Minister was then known, as an ordinary minister without special powers and was more of a peace-maker than a leader. Indeed, the functions of head of government and of leader of the parliamentary majority were then distinct. With the advent of the Fourth Republic, in 1946, the President of the Council became the real head of government and was given constitutional pre-eminence over the other ministers, even though the political practice did not follow suit. Under the Fifth Republic, however, since 1958, the head of the government (now referred to as Prime Minister for the first time) has found a means of asserting his authority which is strengthened both in law and in fact and he is now more powerful than other ministers. The conception of a horizontal or egalitarian government has been replaced by a vertical or hierarchical conception (Gicquel, 1980).

Prime ministerial pre-eminence derives primarily from the important role played by the head of the government in cabinet formation. By being able to propose the names of the ministers to the President, the Prime Minister has acquired a superior position. He also leads governmental action by determining the rules of conduct ministers must follow, and he is the one who resolves conflicts between individual cabinet ministers. Ministers may initiate policies, but their role becomes rather limited afterwards as it is always the Prime Minister (or the President) who has the final say if problems arise. The power of the French Prime Minister over the other members of the cabinet is thus greater than that of many foreign heads of government (Fournier, 1987b), and that power was not diminished as a result of the emergence of a dual executive.

## Ministerial subordination

A final characteristic of the French model is that ministers are wholly dependent on the Prime Minister and the President. As a matter of fact, the French Constitution scarcely discusses the role of ministers. The powers of ministers are two-fold: they jointly participate in the determination and the management of governmental policy and they are heads of departments. But, since the beginning of the Fifth Republic, more importance has been attached to the management of ministerial departments than to political and governmental functions. This is because ministers are no longer allowed to retain their parliamentary seats when they come to office and because a large proportion of members of the government come from the higher civil service.

The autonomy and, therefore, the authority of ministers has diminished as a result. Ministers tend to relate to the President and the Prime Minister in a manner akin to that of civil servants. Although political considerations must still be taken into account in the selection of cabinet ministers, the government is no longer truly a centre of genuine political power and is primarily an administrative body. Governments are no longer threatened by votes of censure on the part of Parliament as the majority has become cohesive and disciplined, and thus their duration has tended to coincide more with phases of presidential action. However, it is interesting to note that although governments are now appreciably more stable than before 1958, the turnover of individual ministers has continued to be high – cabinet reshuffles, individual promotions and other changes of positions occur frequently.

## 2   CABINET STRUCTURE

The French government includes the Prime Minister, the Ministers and a number of junior ministers known as Secretaries of State. There is a tendency towards hierarchy in the positions within the cabinet and there has also been a slow increase in the size of the government – from about 30 under De Gaulle to about 40 afterwards. The first two Mauroy governments were the largest with 43 and 45 members. The Chirac government of March 1986 also had 43 members. In both absolute and relative terms, the bulk of the increase has been due to the Secretaries of State – a trend which continued throughout the period, except between 1981 and 1983. The increase in the number of Secretaries of State is primarily the result of the desire to achieve a balance among the coalition partners. Occasionally it has also been due to the need to give some prominence to a problem which had hitherto been neglected (Tricot and Hadas-Lebel, 1985).

The Council of Ministers is the only collective body of the government which brings together the Prime Minister, the Ministers and a few Secretaries of State under the chairmanship of the President of the Republic. It is important to note that the President has always chaired the Council of Ministers, from 1875 when the Third Republic was born to the present day. In this respect France does vary – and always has varied – from many parliamentary systems where the Head of State has long ceased to chair cabinet meetings (Gicquel, 1980).

The Council of Ministers meets every Wednesday at the Elysée Palace, the official residence of the Presidency of the Republic. The composition of the Council has varied somewhat. At the beginning of the Fifth Republic, during De Gaulle's presidency, all the members of the government attended all the meetings of the Council. Between 1969 and 1972 and from February 1974, Secretaries of State did not attend, except with respect to matters concerning their department. In 1983 the number of ordinary ministers was reduced and that of 'delegate ministers' increased. The latter did not attend the meetings of the Council in order to 'increase efficiency' (Tricot and Hadas-Lebel, 1985), but started to attend meetings again in 1986.

From the beginning of the Fifth Republic meetings of the Council of Ministers have been dominated by the President of the Republic. It is he who determines the agenda. The General Secretary of the Government prepares a draft every week which he submits on Friday morning to the President, the Prime Minister and other Ministers. The agenda is then discussed on Monday evening at the Elysée Palace by the General Secretary of the Government and by the General Secretary of the Presidency of the Republic. Both officials are then received by the President who hears their proposals, makes appropriate changes and finalises the agenda, which is then sent to the Ministers on Tuesday (Py, 1985).

Discussion in the Council of Ministers is led by the President of the Republic with the Prime Minister playing a secondary role, although he is able to intervene when he thinks necessary. General de Gaulle strove, before concluding the deliberations, to give the Prime Minister the last word and this practice seems to have been discontinued after 1969.

The deliberations of the Council of Ministers are an important stage, often the last, of the process of governmental decision-making. The meeting is typically divided into three parts, according to guidelines adopted in 1947, and amended several times under the Fifth Republic (Py, 1985).

1   Draft bills, ordinances and decrees are discussed in part A. Agreement has usually been achieved beforehand and there is no discussion. When the bill is exceptionally important and has political implications for all the members of the government, however, a debate may take place. The President may decide to let ministers express their opinions in a *tour de table* (that is to say, an opportunity for each and everyone to make a short statement). Very occasionally, if criticisms are voiced by some ministers, a draft may be sent back for further discussion with a view to be presented at a later date to the Council.

2   Appointments of a wide range of senior members of the judiciary, the civil service and the military are presented under part B. Questions are rarely raised as potential problems will have been dealt with beforehand.

3   Part C, which is often the most time-consuming part of the Council, is devoted to ministerial statements. Some of these are made on a regular basis. For instance, every week, the Minister of Foreign Affairs makes a statement on the international situation and the President, the Prime Minister or individual ministers may have to report on their visits abroad. The Foreign Minister's statement provides the President with an opportunity to make clear to the Council what his own intentions are in foreign policy matters. The Council of Ministers thus ensures that foreign policy activity is coordinated. There are also other regular ministerial statements on aspects of domestic policy and on parliamentary work. Statements are also made by ministers concerning their departments (for instance to present policy initiatives or to press the case for a particular line of activity). The President normally makes his views known at the end of the discussion which follows these statements (Fournier, 1987b).

The Council of Ministers thus tends to take formal note of decisions which have already been taken elsewhere (Plouvin, 1980). Moreover, traditionally, the Council of Ministers does not decide on a majority basis. The deliberations are said to be collegial and to involve all members of the government on the basis of the principle of collective ministerial responsibility. There are no votes in the Council of Ministers and debates are secret.

Yet there is another, and more political, aspect to these matters. When the presidential majority and the parliamentary majority coincided – that is to say, up to 1986 – the Council of Ministers was a place where consensus prevailed (at any rate between the President and the government). Conflicts were rare. Since 1986, on the other hand, the Council has ceased to be the arena for the formulation of government policy (Fournier, 1987a). The Council of Ministers became less important as a result, and difficult issues are now discussed in cabinet meetings chaired by the Prime Minister. Such meetings had fallen into disuse since 1958, but have become relatively numerous since 1986 (eight in the first eight months of 1987).

Meanwhile, meetings of the Council of Ministers have become shorter since 1986, but they continue to take place frequently as they are constitutionally and legally required to approve legal documents. The President continues to hold two essential powers: those of finalising the agenda and of directing the debate. He could indeed refuse to place some governmental proposals on the agenda, but he has never used this power since March 1986. The power to direct the debate gives the President an opportunity to express his opinion on the issues which are raised. He has indeed done so on a number of matters which were particularly controversial, such as the events in New Caledonia, the bill on the privatisation of firms which had previously been nationalised, and the proposal to privatise prisons (Fournier, 1987a). Ultimately, however, the President has one vote only and the Prime Minister and the ministers could force the issue if they wished. The President has no power of veto – and he has not tried to exercise any such power since 1986.

## 3 CABINET LIFE

Three aspects of French political life have direct consequences on the organisation and the functioning of the cabinet: the fact that governments are coalitions; that the parliamentary majority is disciplined; and that political leadership is exercised by the Prime Minister and the President of the Republic.

### The nature of coalitions in Fifth Republic France

With the exception of the early period (1958–1962), the governments of the Fifth Republic have been able to count on a majority in the National

Assembly although these majorities and these governments have typically been coalitions. Single-party governments might have been theoretically possible at two different periods – during the fourth legislature (1968–1973) when the Gaullist party had an absolute majority (293 seats out of 487), and during the seventh legislature (1981–1986) when the Socialist Party had an absolute majority (285 seats out of 491). Yet, even in these two cases, the majority party did not wish to govern alone. In the first case, the Gaullist party maintained its alliance with the moderate conservatives. From 1981 to 1984 communist ministers were included in the government and only when these resigned in July 1984 did the French government become a single-party government for a substantial period (almost two years).

Although all governments between 1958 and 1984 were coalitions, the nature of these coalitions differed (Duverger, 1985). Some can be said to have been 'unequal' (as from 1962 to 1968 or from 1973 to 1978 when the right governed on the basis of an alliance between Gaullists and moderate conservatives). During the second legislature (between 1962 and 1967) the Gaullist party had an almost absolute majority (233 seats out of 482) and it governed with the support of a small number of conservatives (35 seats). The situation changed during the third legislature (1967–1968) when the Gaullist party only had 200 seats and needed the support of an expanded, though still small, group of conservatives (42 seats) in order to govern. During the fifth legislature (1973–1978) the parliamentary strength of the Gaullist party was further reduced to 183 seats.

Throughout these periods there was a considerable difference in the relative parliamentary strength of the coalition partners. One can thus speak of the 'majority of the majority' (usually the 'party of the President'), and the 'minority of the majority' (constituted by a number of small groupings needed to ensure a sufficient level of parliamentary support). The 'party of the President' was typically characterised by its predominant role in supporting the institutions and by the cohesion and discipline of its parliamentarians (Quermonne, 1987). The 'minority of the majority', on the other hand, sometimes displayed opposition tendencies towards the party of the President, but its criticisms always stopped short of provoking a break-up of the coalition of majority parties.

More balanced coalitions appeared during the sixth legislature (1978–1981) and the eighth legislature which started in March 1986. The parliamentary strength of the Gaullist party has only been slightly stronger than that of the conservative UDF (154 deputies against 123 in

1978, and 155 against 131 in 1986). From 1978 to 1981, however, the weakness of the conservative UDF is compensated by the influence of the President and by the internal divisions of the Gaullist RPR. In return, the position of the Gaullist RPR is stronger since March 1986 because of the part played by the Gaullist leader and Prime Minister, Jacques Chirac, and by the internal divisions of the UDF.

## Discipline and cohesion of the parliamentary majority

General de Gaulle played a considerable part in increasing parliamentary discipline, particularly on the right. He checked the behaviour of Gaullist deputies, who feared the risk of indiscipline. There are now few cases of indiscipline, and they do not affect the outcome (Duverger, 1985). This results in strong majorities and stable governments. The principle of unconditional support to the government is reinforced by the fact that, were difficulties with the parliamentary majority to occur, constitutional means of pressure, such as the procedure of Article 49 paragraph 3, can be and have been used. This was particularly so when parliamentary coalitions were weak or divided, as from 1967 to 1968 and from 1976 to 1981. Under the first part of the presidency of François Mitterrand (1981–1986), the same procedure has been used to hide differences between socialists and communists. It has been also used to force the socialist parliamentarians to toe the President's line.

Parties outside Parliament are equally docile. The most important French political parties (Gaullist RPR, conservative UDF, and the Socialist Party) have been built or rebuilt as a result of and around the direct election of the President by universal suffrage (Portelli, 1980). Each party has to nominate a presidential candidate and this results in what might be called the 'presidentialisation' of each party even before the leader of that party becomes President. The Gaullist party was founded solely to support the political action of General de Gaulle and had no policy other than loyalty to a person. It was in no position to refuse to obey his orders. The conservative UDF was in the same situation *vis-à-vis* Valery Giscard d'Estaing. There was more of a problem with respect to the Socialist Party because of the traditions of that organisation. As Mitterrand had restructured the party in 1971 and then led it in opposition until 1981, however, even the socialists came to accept the logic of 'presidentialism'. The allegiance to Mitterrand, first secretary of the Socialist Party, facilitated the allegiance to Mitterrand, President of the Republic. This was not always sufficient to ensure agreement: the socialists were never quite as docile as the Gaullists. As a matter of fact, during the first years of his presidency, Mitterrand had to convince rather than coerce the members of the Socialist Party.

## Prime ministerial and presidential leadership

The political leadership of the Prime Minister also has a considerable influence on the organisation and the functioning of the cabinet. In general the Prime Minister was not the leader of the major party of the coalition (Quermonne, 1987). Indeed, from 1958 to 1974 the Gaullist party (UNR then UDR) did not even have a leader as such. The first occasion when the Prime Minister combined the functions of govern-mental head with that of party leader was when Jacques Chirac became General Secretary of the Gaullist party, from December 1974 to June 1975. The second occasion was after the 1986 election, when the Prime Minister, Jacques Chirac again, remained president of the Gaullist RPR. Very occasionally, however, the Prime Minister has been the leader of the majority. In one case, under De Gaulle, Prime Minister Pompidou was clearly this leader but, at other times, under the presidencies of Pompidou, Giscard d'Estaing and Mitterrand (until 1986 at least) the real leader of the majority was the President (Quermonne, 1987).

The political leadership which the Prime Minister can exercise has typically depended on the amount of autonomy which the President has given him. This amount of prime ministerial autonomy and initiative is customarily related to the conception which the President has of the government. Until March 1986 there have thus been 'political govern-ments' (Debré, Chaban-Delmas, Chirac and Mauroy), and 'managerial governments' (Pompidou, except his fourth government, Couve de Murville, Messmer, Barre and Fabius) (Quermonne, 1987).

Until March 1986, however, political leadership in the Fifth Republic was primarily exercised by the President. De Gaulle's personal prestige and support were the bases for his strong authority, while he also relied on the loyalty of the Gaullist party. Yet, at the beginning of his presidency, De Gaulle concerned himself primarily with Algeria, defence and foreign policy and left most other issues to the Prime Minister, Michel Debré, in a parliamentary context in which there was no real majority (1959–1962). From 1962, on the other hand, De Gaulle became more generally involved in determining governmental policy: he can be said to have 'presidentialised' the political system.

In 1969 Georges Pompidou appeared as De Gaulle's heir. But, in spite of being able to rely on an absolute Gaullist majority when he came to office in 1969, his position was somewhat difficult and he therefore left considerable autonomy to his first Prime Minister, Jacques Chaban-Delmas, and to the government. His political leadership increased gradually and he was therefore able to reduce the role of the Prime Minister in 1972 when he dismissed Chaban-Delmas and appointed Pierre Messmer.

Giscard d'Estaing won the presidency in 1974 because of his personal skills and in particular because of his remarkable use of television. He never succeeded, however, in forming a large political party to support him and his only firm support came from a small parliamentary group. Yet, during the first two years of his presidency, he exercised strong political leadership despite the difficulty resulting from the strength of the Gaullist party in the coalition. After 1976, when he dismissed Jacques Chirac, his leadership decreased. Raymond Barre, who was overtly a Giscard supporter, nonetheless built up a government which was more independent of presidential control. Although the conservative UDF, nominally composed of supporters of the President, increased its share of the seats at the 1978 general election, Giscard d'Estaing was still not the firm leader that Pompidou had been.

Up to 1986 Mitterrand's political leadership rested on the fact that he relied on a Socialist Party which was very loyal to him and it was strong from the start as a result. But Mitterrand's leadership increased with the Laurent Fabius government (1984–1986) when the Head of State came to have complete control of his party and factionalism (which had been substantial in the early 1980s) was markedly reduced (Duverger, 1985).

## 4 CABINET DECISION-MAKING

When a member of government wishes to initiate a bill or a regulation (*decree*) he has to draft a proposal. Traditionally, the heads of the divisions of the ministries were responsible for the preparation of the draft. The process involved inquiries with those concerned and especially with pressure groups. In recent years these heads of divisions have been increasingly by-passed, unless they have been appointed personally by the minister concerned. Drafts are increasingly prepared by the personal staff attached to each minister, known collectively as the ministerial *cabinet*. On the most important issues, in particular, divisions of ministries are rarely concerned at the initial stage.

Ministerial *cabinets* blend these new policy-making functions with their more traditional political role: thus ministerial *cabinets* are no longer easily distinguishable from the divisions of ministries. This development has led to the presence of a large administrative apparatus at the top of the state machinery. This can be seen as one of the most important changes to have taken place in governmental practice since the beginning of the Fifth Republic (Quermonne, 1987).

Once drafted, proposals are submitted to other ministers. This often leads to the setting up of inter-departmental committees which have become numerous and are one of the key elements of the governmental decision-making process. These committees are chaired by a member of the Prime Minister's personal staff and include higher civil servants and the members of ministerial *cabinets* who are responsible for the proposal.

Inter-departmental committees are concerned with the study of the political, economic or social events. They also discuss the detailed provisions of draft bills or decrees and ensure that the agreement of every minister concerned is sought and obtained, with the advisers stating the position of their minister in the course of the meeting. If the points of view differ, further meetings are scheduled in order to achieve consensus. If disagreement persists between the ministers the matter is referred to the Prime Minister, who takes a decision. As a matter of fact, that decision is usually taken in the name of the Prime Minister by the director of his *cabinet* or by another of his chief advisers. Such decisions, which are called *arbitrages* of the Prime Minister, are a daily feature of the governmental process. The document which states the Prime Ministerial decision is called a 'blue' and is an essential part of French administrative life (Fournier, 1987b).

Inter-departmental committees are increasingly numerous. They multiplied during the socialist governments (141 in 1961, 589 in 1971, 1070 in 1980, but 1855 in 1982, 1500 in 1983, and 1356 in 1984) (Fournier, 1987b). The frequency of these meetings is a result of the involvement of the Prime Minister in issues which were dealt with formerly by a minister or even by the head of a division of a ministry. Such a development suggests that there are transfers of whole areas of ministerial power to the Prime Minister and, in effect, to the advisers of the Prime Minister.

These transfers have given rise to three important characteristics of Fifth Republic governments: the divisions of the ministries have lost their traditional powers; prime ministerial control has extended to all the ministerial departments; and an administrative staff composed of senior civil servants who discuss matters together at the Prime Minister's official residence at Matignon has become a crucial element in decision-making (Quermonne, 1987).

Some important issues, such as the preparation of draft bills or decrees or the determination of broad policy developments, are examined at the inter-departmental committee level. Sometimes senior civil servants have already studied all the possible options, but, if an agreement cannot be reached, the proposals are sent to the ministers who have taken the decisions. In such cases, inter-departmental committees are usually chaired by the Prime Minister and are composed of the Ministers and the Secretaries of State concerned. Some senior civil servants may also attend, but only intervene when invited to do so by a minister. Until March 1986 a member of the President of the Republic's staff was present both to report to the President and to ensure presidential control of governmental policy. Since March 1986, in order to avoid any Presidential involvement in the management of the policies of the Chirac government, Mitterrand's advisers no longer attend these meetings.

There are two types of inter-departmental committees. Some are permanent, have a well-defined membership and often a permanent secretariat. There are about fifteen of these in such fields as regional planning or European integration. Most committees are less formal and are set up *ad hoc* according to the political, economic or social circumstances or the importance of the issue. This type of inter-departmental committee is often called a 'limited committee': their number varies according to the prime ministerial style of leadership. As can be seen, inter-departmental committees are very powerful instruments in the hands of the Prime Minister, who can control ministers better in this way.

Inter-departmental committees and the prime ministerial *arbitrages* are thus the main instruments by which the head of the government can ensure his predominance (Tricot and Habas-Lebel, 1985; Quermonne, 1987). These *arbitrages* occur in all fields. They are, of course, frequent in the budgetary process, but they also occur with respect to appointments of senior civil servants as well as to draft bills and draft regulations.

Nonetheless, Prime ministerial authority does vary. Despite the fact that some Prime Ministers have had many means to establish their influence, there have been marked differences among them in the extent to which they have been able to exercise this influence. The Prime Ministers who had most authority were Michel Debré, Georges Pompidou and Raymond Barre; Maurice Couve de Murville and Pierre Mauroy, on the other hand, were those who had least influence over their colleagues.

Finally, there is one last form of inter-departmental meeting which is 'below' the Council of Ministers but above the inter-departmental committee. These are the inter-departmental councils which meet at the Elysée Palace if and when the President so decides. Before 1986 they could also meet because the President was asked by dissatisfied ministers to 'arbitrate' on prime ministerial *arbitrages* or the decisions of inter-departmental committees. These councils, which are a Fifth Republic innovation, meet under the chairmanship of the President of the Republic and include the Prime Minister and a few senior ministers, sometimes with a few senior civil servants in attendance.

Some of these inter-departmental councils are permanent, such as the Defence Council which is expressly mentioned in Article 15 of the Constitution. Others are called 'limited councils'. Some of them were set up by De Gaulle, as was the Council on Algerian Affairs which was created in February 1960. De Gaulle and Pompidou convened few meetings of these councils. The meetings multiplied under Giscard d'Estaing, when they were convened almost as frequently as the Council of Ministers (between 30 and 50 a year between 1974 and 1981). Mitterrand has made little use of inter-departmental councils since 1982.

Most draft proposals are therefore discussed at length in inter-departmental committees, yet they must also be submitted to the Council of State which gives an opinion. This opinion is sent to the General Secretary of the Government, who thus plays an essential role at the end of the procedure. It is he who sends the text to the sponsoring department, discusses possible amendments and suggests to the President a date at which the proposal can be placed on the agenda of the Council of Ministers (Py, 1985; Institut Français des Sciences Administratives, 1986). Only then does the final deliberation take place in the Council of Ministers.

The work of the Council of Ministers tends to be concentrated on immediate questions. Admittedly, in 1974, Giscard d'Estaing introduced suggestions for programmatic debates. The preparation of these programmes, which settled governmental management for six months, was jointly undertaken by the General Secretary of the Government, the General Secretary of the Presidency of the Republic and the director of the prime ministerial *cabinet*. The final list of drafts to be adopted was decided by the President of the Republic in agreement with the Prime Minister and other ministers were not involved in the process. His successor, Mitterrand, wanted the government to operate on the basis of programmatic actions, but he did markedly alter the procedure by requesting the Prime Minister to ask the opinion of every minister.

Such programmes enable a government to define its activities in the medium-term, although daily questions on foreign or domestic policy tend to wreak havoc to these plans. Indeed, programmes have been constantly modified during the period of their implementation, either because electoral reasons led to the postponement of proposals or, on the contrary, because sudden demands brought hitherto ignored issues to the fore (Py, 1985).

The main difficulties faced by the French model of cabinet decision-making arise, above all, from constitutional constraints and in particular from the dualism of executive power (the so-called *cohabitation*). The risk of strong political differences at the apex of the state apparatus is considerable. Since March 1986 the constitutional constraint has become very important. It seems to dwarf the two other problems of current French cabinets, though these do remain. On the one hand, ministerial staffs (the *cabinets* of the ministers) have become very large and somewhat unwieldy. On the other hand, inter-departmental committees have become so numerous and strong that they have effectively undermined the role of the Council of Ministers as well as the collegial influence of members of the cabinet. It is too early to say whether the new *cohabitation* formula will at least make it more difficult to by-pass the Council of Ministers or whether behind-the-scenes compromises will become, as in some other countries, an established practice for dealing with difficult problems.

# 6 Spain

Antonio Bar

## 1 CABINET SETTING

The distant origins of the Spanish cabinet are to be found in the administrative reforms introduced under Felipe V in 1714. However, it was not until 1834, after several significant changes in its history, that the parliamentary system began to emerge and that the first steps were taken in the direction of a cabinet independent of the monarch. Since then, the Spanish parliamentary system has been interrupted several times and has also appreciably altered. Its working is currently governed by the Constitution of 1978.

The Spanish government is composed of a number of layers which are hierarchically dependent on each other. These layers can be grouped into two main categories. The top group is truly political and includes the Council of Ministers or cabinet proper – the expression cabinet is now rarely used although it was the term originally adopted. The second group of layers is primarily administrative in terms of the functions which its members fulfil, but it is part of the government in that those holding the relevant posts are appointed and dismissed by the government.

The first group is composed of the Prime Minister (*Presidente del Gobierno*), the Deputy Prime Minister (*Vicepresidente del Gobierno*) – there can be more than one – the Ministers (with or without portfolio), the Secretaries of State (*Secretarios de Estado*), the Under-secretaries (*Subsecretarios*) and the General Secretaries with under-secretarial rank (*Secretarios Generales*). The Prime Minister, the Deputy Prime Minister and the Ministers form the cabinet as such and are clearly above those who hold one of the other three types of post. The second group is comprised of the *Directores Generales* and of the *Secretarios Generales Técnicos* (see Figure 6.1).

The cabinet which is discussed here is the cabinet which has emerged after the end of the Franco regime. However, not surprisingly, a number of administrative features of the current government have been inherited from structures which predate the democratic monarchy, especially since the transition was smooth and orderly.

One of the main reasons for such a peaceful change was the presence

102

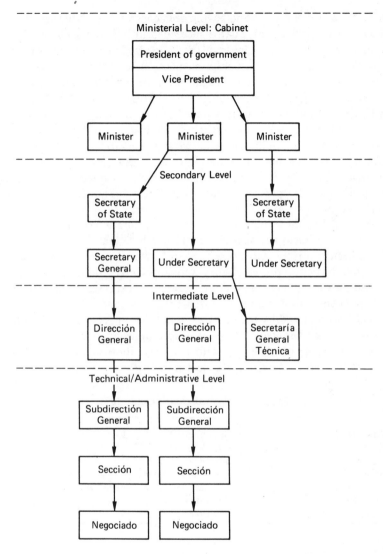

FIGURE 6.1   The Spanish government

of the King, who ensured by his skill and vigilance that the transition to democracy was rapid. This development was also associated by the efforts made by the second Prime Minister of the new regime, Adolfo Suarez (the first Prime Minister having been appointed immediately after the death of Franco and having been concerned with the very early stages of the transition). Suárez succeeded in building a party of the centre-right, the UCD (Union of the Democratic Centre) by bringing together a number of disparate elements in a federal organisation. However, these rapidly divided again with the result that the party had virtually disappeared by the time of the election of 1982. Yet, between 1977 and 1982, the UCD provided the basis for a stable executive. Spain had then the good fortune of exchanging a relatively stable centre-right government with a stable centre-left government after the 1982 general election. For the first time the Socialist Party (PSOE), under the charismatic leadership of Felipe Gonzales, obtained an absolute majority and the party retained an absolute (although appreciably reduced) majority at the 1986 general election.

If one judges the stability of cabinets by the duration of the Presidents of the Government in office, one could conclude that Spanish cabinets have been relatively stable (see Table 6.1). Post-Franco cabinets have covered the period for which they were appointed – that is to say have lasted the duration of a legislature – except in two cases. First, those of the pre-constitutional and pre-parliamentary second cabinet of Arias, which was replaced by the first Suárez cabinet in July 1976 before his plan for a neo-Francoist reform was accomplished. Second, the third Suárez cabinet, which ended with his resignation in February 1981 before the end of the Congress elected in 1979.

TABLE 6.1    Spanish cabinets since 1975

| | |
|---|---|
| Arias II | December 1975 – July 1976 |
| Suárez I | July 1976 – July 1977 |
| Suárez II | July 1977 – March 1979 |
| Suárez III | March 1979 – February 1981 |
| Calvo Sotelo | February 1981 – December 1982 |
| González I | December 1982 – July 1986 |
| González II | July 1986 – xxxx |

NOTES:
Glossary of Party Abbreviations
AP      *Alianza Popular*
CDS    *Centro Democrático Social*
PCE    *Patido Comunista de España*
PSOE  *Partido Socialista Obrero Español*
UCD    *Uniõn de Centro Democrático*

However, the duration of cabinets cannot be measured by that of the President only, and if we consider the ministerial composition the picture changes somewhat. Only the second Arias cabinet (December 1975 to July 1976) remained unchanged during the seven months of its existence (it was dismissed by the King). The first Suárez cabinet (July 1976 to July 1977) lasted only one year and underwent its first change only two months after it was set up (it was to undergo two further changes, in each case concerning one Minister only). The second Suárez cabinet (July 1977 to March 1979) lasted 20 months and underwent three reshuffles, the last of which, halfway through its duration, affected six ministerial offices (the other two changes each having affected only one department). The third Suárez cabinet (March 1979 to February 1981) lasted 23 months. It also underwent three reshuffles, but these were far more substantial as the first affected three departments, the second eleven, and the third fourteen (there were therefore, in practice, three different cabinets).

The Calvo-Sotelo cabinet (February 1981 to December 1982) lasted 22 months and underwent four changes, the first affecting two departments, the second ten, the third five and the last only one. On the other hand, the first González cabinet (December 1982 to July 1986) underwent only one reshuffle in its almost four years, six of the fifteen departments being affected. The second González cabinet (from July 1986) underwent no changes during its first year of existence. Thus, while cabinets lasted an average of 21.2 months, a reshuffle occurred every 6.3 months. Thus, while cabinets have been relatively stable, the 'reshuffle' rate has been high (Blondel, 1985).

## 2  CABINET STRUCTURE

Members of the government act both individually and collectively and have their own area of competence – and in this respect they can individually involve the whole government. Collectively members of the government meet in the Council of Ministers (*Consejo de Ministros*) where the most important decisions are taken – and in cabinet committees (*Comisiónes Delegadas del Gobierno*). There is also a committee of under-secretaries (*Comisión General de Subsecretarios*) and a variety of other inter-ministerial committees.

### The members of the government

The Prime Minister is formally appointed by the King, but only after having obtained the confidence of the lower house (*Congreso de los Diputados*). An absolute majority of the members is required at the first ballot, and only a relative majority at the second (Article 99 of the Constitution). Thus the King has no effective choice (Bar, 1983 and 1985b; Aguiar, 1980). The Vice President and the other Ministers are also formally appointed and removed from office by the King, but he does so on the proposal of the President of the Government. The President has therefore the effective appointment power, the power of the King being purely formal also in this respect (Article 100 of the Constitution) (Bar, 1983 and 1985c; Morell, 1980). Secretaries of State, Under Secretaries and General Secretaries are also appointed by Royal Decree: in this case the appointment is the result of a collective decision of the Council of Ministers on the proposal of the Minister concerned.

Formally, the President of the Government directs the government and coordinates the activities of its members in accordance with Article 98.2 of the Constitution. Yet, even in constitutional terms, the role of the Prime Minister is greater, as will be seen later. Formally, too, the Vice President substitutes for the President of the Government whenever necessary, although his role has changed somewhat from cabinet to cabinet. In the Socialist government of Felipe González there is only one Vice President. His main function is to participate in the overall political leadership of the cabinet together with the Prime Minister, different areas of policy being shared between them.

While the Prime Minister tends to concentrate on general political strategy and on international politics, the Vice President is in practice concerned with internal matters, institutional problems and problems of coordination. Previously, when the centre-right government of the UCD was in office, there was in one case no Vice President,[1] and in other cases there have been as many as three. Vice Presidents were deemed to coordinate specific areas of government: economy, defence, security, and so on. These Vice Presidents were then often heads of ministerial departments and a hierarchy among the Ministers was established as a result.

Ministers normally head a department. In this capacity they act as policy-makers and formulate the department's policy, being relatively autonomous and individually responsible to Parliament in this respect although they cannot be censured individually. There are currently fifteen ministerial departments which have been set up by statute.[2] However, Ministers Without Portfolio and Junior Ministers can be appointed without a new law (this was customary in the centrist UCD cabinets, both to satisfy the wish for power of each party faction and to pay heed to political areas of special and temporary concern). Moreover, it is possible to introduce a further level in the hierarchy by giving some Ministers a coordinating role in a given policy area, such as the economy, security or defence, and this has often been the case.

During the third Suárez government, as a result of the reshuffle which took place in September 1980, this form of pre-eminence was institution-alised by giving eight of the cabinet members, all heads of ministerial departments, the title of 'Ministers of State'. But the move, which was made in order to solve a number of intra-party problems, did not have the desired effect and the idea was abandoned in the next cabinet, that of Calvo-Sotelo (February 1981). When the Socialist government was reshuffled on 23 July 1986, the cabinet was organised in a simple manner and was made up of the President of the Government, one Vice President and fifteen Ministers, each of whom was given a department (Bar, 1985a).[3]

Secretaries of State are in charge of a section of a department which has some autonomy as a result of its importance. These sections are almost mini-ministries within the ministry. Secretaries of State are thus political appointees who are hierarchically immediately below the Minister. Their number has varied since the creation of these posts in 1977 and there can be more than one in any given department.[4] Occasionally, Secretaries of State do not head a section of a ministry but are merely close collaborators of the Prime Minister – as often occurred in the UCD cabinets (Bar, 1985; Guaita, 1978; Molina, 1979; Martin, 1980).

While Ministers – and also Secretaries of State – formulate and direct policy, Under Secretaries are usually administrative heads. These positions are also political: Under Secretaries are in charge of the foreign relations of the department, so to speak, as they are responsible for the coordination of the activities of the ministry with those of other ministries. There is at least one Under Secretary per department. When there is no Secretary of State, Under Secretaries rank immediately after the Minister.

Finally, General Secretaries are responsible for units within a ministry or within a Secretariat of State which, without being of sufficient importance to justify the establishment of a Secretariat of State, has to be given special attention. The number of General Secretaries is low[5] (Bar, 1985a; Guaita, 1978; Molina, 1979; Martín, 1980; de la Morena, 1966; Cortés, 1965).

### The cabinet as a collective body

The cabinet, which meets collectively as the Council of Ministers, is composed of the Prime Minister, the Deputy Prime Minister and the Ministers. Secretaries of State may attend in order to present a report when they have been specially requested to do so, but are not formal members. In broad terms, the responsibility of the Spanish Council of Ministers is similar to that of other parliamentary cabinets.

There are standing cabinet committees (*Comisiones Delegadas del Gobierno*) which include the members of the cabinet who are concerned with the specific areas of government activity (the economy, security, foreign affairs, and so on) dealt with by the committee. The main function of these committees is to coordinate, but they also take some decisions. They are presided over by the Prime Minister or the Deputy Prime Minister. The setting up and abolition of these committees is decided by the Council of Ministers.

The *Comisión General de Subsecretarios* was formally established in 1985, although it had been in existence for some time. It is composed of all the Under Secretaries and is chaired by the Deputy Prime Minister. Its function is to study and prepare the matters which the Council of Ministers will discuss. As will be seen later, however, its role is not only to coordinate and to prepare bills and decrees, but also to decide on major issues. Indeed, this role has increased in order to relieve the Council of Ministers of some of its work.

Finally, there are also many inter-ministerial committees and commissions – both formal and informal, both standing and *ad hoc* whose purpose is to coordinate and to generally facilitate the work of the government. These bodies are composed of representatives of ministerial departments generally below the rank of Minister (de Miguel, 1972; Bar, 1985a).

The Spanish cabinet is thus relatively small. It has only seventeen members and is one of the smallest in Europe (about the size of the West German, Austrian or Irish cabinet, in contrast to the 30 members of the Italian cabinet, the 26 members of the Greek cabinet, the 23 members of the French cabinet and the 21 members of the British, Swedish or Danish cabinets). Moreover, even if we include the Secretaries of State and other governmental members who do not belong to the Council of Ministers, the Spanish government had only 54 members in 1987. This is still one of the smallest governments in Europe among those which have Junior Ministers (the British and Italian cabinets had respectively 103 and 89 members).

The Spanish cabinet meets in the Council of Ministers every Friday morning for periods ranging from four to eight hours. Its meetings can be of a debating or 'decision-making' character, depending on whether formal decisions are to be adopted or not. The second type of meeting is the most frequent, whereas the meetings in which debates take place on one or more important issue, or over planning matters or political strategies, only take place every one or two months. Meetings are convened and presided over by the President of the Government. The King may attend the Council of Ministers, but only when invited by the Prime Minister and merely to be informed on affairs of State (this has only taken place twice so far, and on both occasions during the first Socialist cabinet).

The Council of Ministers' agenda is set by the President in the case of meetings which discuss, and by the *Comisión General de Subsecretarios* for the regular decision-making meetings. Ministers wishing to submit a text or a proposal to the Council of Ministers must first communicate this to all cabinet members and to the Minister Secretary of Government (*Ministro para las Relaciones con las Cortes y Secretario del Gobierno*) who, on the basis of the material received from the various Ministers, drafts the agenda which is presented to the *Comisión General de Subsecretarios* ('black index'). This committee discusses the matters submitted, which are then sent to the Council unless there is no agreement in the committee. However, if the matter on which there is no agreement is important it is also sent to the Council of Ministers.

The Council of Ministers therefore gives purely formal approval to matters on which there is already *a priori* decision or agreement between the ministries' representatives ('green index') and only discusses important issues, whether there has been a prior agreement or not – especially if the Minister concerned insists on it ('red index'). Sine 1986 the *Comisión General de Subsecretarios* has been chaired by the Vice President of the Government. This enables the Prime Minister to exercise influence over the matters which are to be presented to the Council of Ministers (see Figure 6.2).

## 3  CABINET LIFE

### Cabinet pre-eminence

The constitutional system established in Spain by the Constitution of December 1978 is parliamentary, with the integration and collaboration of powers between executive and legislature. It is, however, a 'rationalised' parliamentary system in which the government's position is pre-eminent and hegemonic, even with regard to the *Cortes Generales* (the

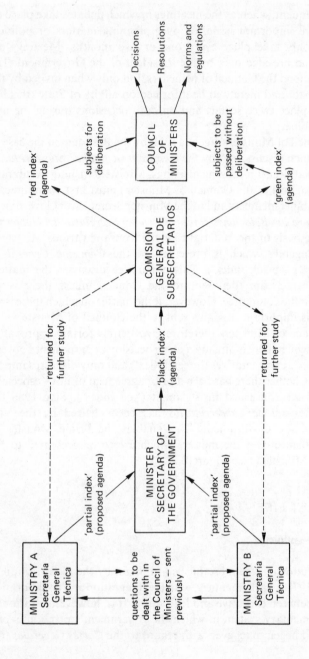

FIGURE 6.2    The decision-making process in the Spanish cabinet

Spanish bi-cameral Parliament) and to all the institutions of the state in general terms. This pre-eminence is the result of both technical-constitutional and socio-political factors.

From a constitutional point of view the cabinet only needs to enjoy the confidence and support of the Lower Chamber (*Congreso*), which only requires an ordinary majority. The Senate is not asked to give a vote of confidence to the government, and plays no significant part in the relationship between Parliament and Government. Parliament cannot defeat the government except by a formal vote of censure and this vote is organised in a very restrictive manner. In order to be passed the motion of censure has to obtain an absolute majority among the members of the House, *and* the name of an alternative candidate for the presidency of the government must be adopted in the same motion (this arrangement, which is the same as the one in force in West Germany, is known as a 'constructive motion of censure'). The system thus allows minority governments to survive, since it is virtually impossible for Parliament to defeat the cabinet.

The (rather restricted) proportional representation system in force at present thus cannot have a decisive influence on cabinet stability, as the potential incidence of the multi-party system on the duration of the government is severely reduced by the constitutional arrangements relating to the motion of censure. Moreover, the strength of the government derives both from the parliamentary support on which it can rely and, through Parliament, on the support of popular opinion. The personalisation of political activity makes the Prime Minister an acknowledged popular leader who draws his legitimacy directly from the electorate, even though he is not elected by the people as such. Members of Parliament, on the contrary, do not have the same type of links with the people. They are elected through a system of 'blocked' lists on which they are placed by their party machine. As a result they are relatively unknown and remain distant from the electorate.

Perhaps the most important aspect of the current Spanish political system, more important even than the prominent position of the cabinet – which is indeed typical of other parliamentary systems – is the part played by the President of the Government within cabinet and the political system as a whole. The President of the Government is not really a Prime (first) Minister as he is no longer a *primus inter pares* but a real President as his official title indicates. The cabinet revolves entirely around him – it is created, lives and dies with him and it acts under his direction and follows his political programme. Only he receives the vote of investiture from the Congress when he is appointed (the rest of the cabinet is appointed only once the President has been elected).

The governmental programme is drawn up by the President of the Government and is presented to the Congress when the House is asked to vote the motion of confidence. Thus, when the Ministers are appointed they find the governmental programme already drawn up. They can only accept it or turn down the post, although in practice the programme is prepared not just by the President himself, but in part at least by the party machine and by some of the future cabinet Ministers. Ministers are, moreover, appointed and removed by the President of the Government. Furthermore, although the government as a whole is responsible to Congress (there is no individual responsibility of Ministers) the most important political decisions relating to Government-Parliament relations which may threaten the cabinet's existence – such as the decision to ask for a vote of confidence, to dissolve the *Cortes* or to call a referendum – are taken by the President alone, and he is not obliged to follow advice from the rest of the cabinet (Bar, 1983).

**The cabinet and its environment**

Political conditions also play a part in this context. The Spanish experience in the post-Franco period shows that the constitutional structure becomes operative only if it is combined with personal and political leadership on the part of the President of the Government. Thus the system functions to the full when the President comes from a party which is united, which has a substantial parliamentary majority, and in which the Prime Minister is the undisputed leader with charisma and popular support. This was the case in the 1980s with Felipe González and the Socialist government, and with the second Suárez centre-right government between the 1977 and 1979 general elections. At that time, despite the absence of a large parliamentary majority and despite the fact that the party in power, the UCD, was not wholly united, Suárez played a strong role as he had popular support, charisma and because he was considered to have been primarily instrumental in dismantling the Franco regime.

Conversely, when those characteristics do not obtain, not only is the President of the Government's power markedly weakened, but elements of 'dysfunction' appear in the constitutional arrangement. This in turn leads to blockages which might endanger the stability of the political system. This occurred during the third Suárez cabinet – between the 1979 elections and February 1981 – which was a period which culminated in the unsuccessful *coup d'Etat* carried out by Colonel Tejero on 23 February 1981. At that time President Suárez' leadership began to be questioned within his own party as internal disputes arose among the different factions of the UCD. There was even a confrontation between the cabinet and its parliamentary group in Congress. This led to the resignation of Suárez.

A similar situation occurred with the Calvo–Sotelo cabinet (February 1981 to October 1982) which culminated in a second and again unsuccessful attempt at a *coup d'Etat* in October 1982, shortly before the general elections which led to the first victory of the Socialist Party. When Calvo–Sotelo was appointed Prime Minister, in February 1981, he was not the head of the UCD (he only became President of this party in November of that same year). At the moment at which the party was undergoing a major crisis which led to its disintegration, Calvo–Sotelo resigned from the UCD presidency – in July 1982 – three months before having to hand over power to the Socialist leader.

More than the electoral system, the party system has played a determining part in the way the governmental system developed. The fact that the system was new and not yet 'consolidated' led to major changes in the space occupied by individual parties on the left-right continuum. On the left, successive splits in the Communist Party (PCE) left a vacuum which was then occupied by the Socialist Party, the latter also obtaining a significant percentage of its votes from the centre-right. In the centre, the disappearance of the UCD left a large empty space, most of which was taken over by the PSOE, but which a new party, set up by Suárez and known as the CDS, has been fighting to regain in the second half of the 1980s. The right is very divided, even atomised, the *Alianza Popular* being the largest party though a substantial space is still unoccupied (Bar, 1982 and 1984; Esteban and López, 1982; Caciagli, 1986; Linz, 1986).

These political developments have had an effect on the nature and functioning of the governments. The short life of the UCD is a good example. Begun as a coalition of small heterogeneous groups – ex-Francoists, Christian Democrats, Liberals, undefined centrists and Social Democrats – it became a united party with a centrist orientation, only to disappear as it became a victim of internal tensions and of the struggle for power between the different factions (Chamorro, 1981). UCD cabinets therefore underwent frequent reshuffles in the attempt to satisfy the desires of these factions. Although the leadership of Suárez remained intact for a time, tensions soon spread which set the cabinet and its parliamentary group at loggerheads and eventually dislodged

Suárez from the Prime Ministership before destroying the party itself
(Attard, 1983; Huneeus, 1985). Conversely, the solid electoral position
of the Socialist Party following two consecutive elections (1982 and
1986) and the undisputed leadership of Felipe González have ensured
the relative stability of his cabinets.

## Coordination

The coordination of governmental activity, which is constitutionally
allocated to the Prime Minister and which is mainly carried out via the
Council of Ministers and the *Comisión General de Subsecretarios*, is also
carried out through other bodies. These are either formally established,
such as the previously mentioned *Comisiónes Delegadas del Gobierno*,
the inter-ministerial *ad hoc* committees, and commissions composed of
members below the ministerial level, or informal ones. In 1987 there were
five standing cabinet committees (*Comisiónes Delegados del Gobierno*) in
the following areas: foreign policy, state security, economic affairs,
policy with respect to the autonomous regions, educational, cultural and
scientific policy. Only the committee on economic affairs meets on a
regular basis, however. There are also informal committees such as the
meetings which the President of the Government holds regularly with
some cabinet members and which were more common during the UCD
governments.

Coordination is also achieved by the personal staffs of the members of
the government (known as ministerial *cabinets*) who help the Prime
Minister, as well as by the Ministers and the Secretaries of State. These
constitute an informal network parallel to and outside the formal
hierarchical administration structure. These *cabinets*, of which the
largest is naturally that of the President of the Government, carry out
tasks of communication and coordination among government departments. These advisers were already appointed in substantial numbers
when the UCD was in power, but the network of personal staffs was
increased and generalised after 1982 by the Socialist government.

### Ministerial personnel

The one hundred men and women who have been Minister between 1976
and 1986 have not been very mobile. Only nineteen Ministers of the 'pre-
constitutional' period immediately following Franco's death returned to
office after the Constitution came into force in December 1978.
Conversely, in this ten-year period, Ministers have been in office slightly

less than twice, or 1.84 times (see Table 6.2). Ministers have changed posts at about the same rate (1.85 posts per Minister, as shown in Table 6.3). Thus the vast majority of Ministers had only one post. On average, Ministers were in government for almost two years (22.4 months) from a maximum of 74 months in the case of Calvo–Sotelo to a minimum of two months in the case of Camuñas. The average duration of Ministers in the same post was 17.7 months, from a maximum of 55 months in the case of Suárez (as President of the Government) to two months in the case of Camuñas (as Attaché Minister for the Relations with the *Cortes*).

TABLE 6.2    Frequency in office of Spanish ministers

| No. times | No. minister | % |
|---|---|---|
| 1 | 51 | 51.0 |
| 2 | 31 | 31.0 |
| 3 | 7 | 7.0 |
| 4 | 7 | 7.0 |
| 5 | 2 | 2.0 |
| 6 | 2 | 2.0 |
| Total | 100 | 100.0 |

TABLE 6.3    Ministerial turnover in Spain

| Ministries held | No. Ministers | % |
|---|---|---|
| always the same ministry | 23 | 46.93 |
| 2 different ministries | 17 | 34.70 |
| 3 different ministries | 4 | 8.16 |
| 4 different ministries | 4 | 8.16 |
| 5 different ministries | 1 | 2.05 |
| Total | 49 | 100.00 |

Since the late 1970s Spanish Ministers have been younger than they were in the Franco regime or during the transition period. Their average age since 1978 is 46.8 years, and this age drops to 44.6 years when we consider only those cabinets formed after the approval of the 1978 Constitution. Only 21 per cent of the Ministers come from the private sector, whereas the vast majority (79 per cent) come from all branches of the public sector. Among these, university professors (24 per cent) and state lawyers (13 per cent) are the largest groups. The majority of these Ministers coming from the public sector and those coming from the private sector have been trained in law, while the others were mainly economists (7 per cent of the total) or came from other professions.

Only 19 per cent of the Ministers were appointed without having previous experience in Parliament or in a 'political' post within the administration or such as Subdirector, Director General, Secretary General or Under Secretary or Secretary of State. Thus the vast majority of Ministers (81 per cent) can be described as having followed a 'political' route to office, as they either had held political appointments in the administration (48 per cent) or had been in Parliament (18 per cent, with 15 per cent having had both backgrounds) as can be seen in Figure 6.3.

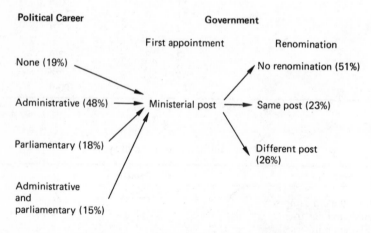

FIGURE 6.3    Ministerial careers in Spain

Members of the Spanish cabinet (and Secretaries of State) can be members of Parliament as well as Ministers. However, between 1976 and 1986, only 70 per cent of the Ministers were simultaneously members of the *Cortes* (4 per cent of whom were Senators, all of them in the same Suárez cabinet, during the period when the constitution was drafted). The high percentage of non-parliamentary members in the Spanish cabinets (30 per cent), together with the substantial proportion of Ministers who had not held political posts previously, suggests a tendency to select 'technicians' or 'specialists' alongside 'political' Ministers. These specialists have been slightly more numerous in the Socialist cabinets, in which 30 per cent were non-parliamentarians as against 26 per cent in the UCD cabinets.

## 4 CABINET DECISION-MAKING

The Spanish cabinet is, by and large, dominated by the President of the Government, although the influence of the Prime Minister is affected both by general political conditions and by personal factors. The compliance of Ministers has therefore been greater in the Socialist government which is homogeneous, is backed by a strong parliamentary majority and is based on a party of which the Prime Minister is the undisputed leader. In this way, Felipe González is a far more effective leader and coordinator of the government than were his UCD predecessors. Meetings of the Socialist cabinet have as a result been shorter and private informal meetings between the Prime Minister and cabinet members designed to facilitate the decisions of the Council of Ministers are also no longer as common. According to Felipe González, votes are not taken in the Council of Ministers and decisions are taken on a consensual basis with the President having the final word.[6] Yet it must be noted that the Council of Ministers does not have internal rules regulating or restricting debate. This situation also enhances the presidential leadership.

There are nonetheless inter-departmental conflicts in the cabinet, and these are solved in most cases through the intervention of the President of the Government. Some areas tend to be particularly conflictual, either by nature or due to the personality of the Minister concerned. During the first Socialist cabinet, for instance, the Ministers of Economy and Finance (there were two during the life of that cabinet) accounted for about a quarter of all conflicts taking place within government, followed by the Minister of Industry and the Vice President (about a sixth), the Minister of Defence (about one in eight) and the Minister of Foreign Affairs (about one in twelve).

The Spanish cabinet is thus relatively small, but it is complex and hierarchical and is somewhat more 'technical' than 'political'. Perhaps the most important of these aspects is the hierarchical character of the cabinet, which is manifest in the decision-making process. The President of the Government is the crucial element – the Constitution gives him all the necessary formal powers for his will to prevail over the Ministers, but general political factors, and the party system in particular, have further strengthened his position. Both the relative stability of the cabinets and the substantial ministerial turnover have also fostered hierarchical tendencies, although in the case of UCD cabinets factionalism and, at times, the lack of personal authority of the President of the Government have reduced the position of the leader. The somewhat technical character of cabinets, on the other hand, does not result primarily from a conscious decision on the part of Prime Ministers. It is by and large the consequence of the fact that the new Spanish political class is still small as only a decade has elapsed since the democratic system was re-established.

Thus, on balance, it seems that the current character of the Spanish cabinet owes at least as much to the context in which Spanish politics developed since the end of the Franco period as to · the formal arrangements under which it operates. However, these formal arrangements have set the scene on which the power of the Prime Minister to rule and to coordinate governmental activity could be established.

# Notes

1. The cabinet of Calvo-Sotelo, between February 1981 and December of the same year.
2. This was set up by a Law of 16 August, 1983. However, as a result of a provision of the *1985 Budget Law*, the 1986 Socialist government was organised by way of a Presidential decree.
3. The fifteen ministerial departments are: Foreign Affairs; Justice; Defence; Economy and Finance; Interior; Public Works and Urbanism; Education and Science; Labour and Social Security; Industry and Energy; Agriculture, Fisheries and Food; Public Administration; Transport, Tourism and Communication; Culture, Health and Consumer Affairs; Relationship with the *Cortes* and Secretary to the Government.
4. There were in 1987 eleven Secretaries of State covering the following areas: European Community, International Cooperation, Iberoamerica (Department of Foreign Affairs); Defence; Finance, Economy and Planning, Commerce (Department of Economy and Finance); State Security (Department of the Interior); Universities and Research (Department of Education and Science); Autonomous Communities (Department of Public Administration); Sports (Department of Culture).
5. There were in 1987 eleven General Secretaries covering the following areas: Finance, Budget and Planning, Commerce (Department of Economy and Finance); Police, *Guardia Civil* (Department of the Interior); Education (Education and Science); Energy and Mineral Resources (Department of Industry and Energy); Maritime Fishing (Department of Agriculture, Fishing and Food); Tourism, Communications (Department of Transport Tourism and Communications); Sanitary Assistance (Department of Health and Consumption).
6. Interviewed by *El Pais* (17 November 1985) pp. 13–15.

# 7 Italy: A Fragmented Government

Maurizio Cotta

## 1 CABINET SETTING

Only with the second Italian Constitution, the Republican Constitution that came into force after the Second World War and the breakdown of fascism, did the institution of government find explicit mention and regulation in the highest legal text of the country. Under the previous Constitution, the Piedmontese *Statuto Albertino* of 1848 progressively extended to cover the entire country with the process of Italian unification, the cabinet was not clearly mentioned in a constitutional text that still reflected in its inspiration the model of the constitutional monarchy.

The cabinet, a typical product of the parliamentary form of government, came into existence as a *de facto* result of the new political situation and of the new constellation of political forces triggered by the implementation of the *Statuto* rather than as a direct *de jure* consequence of this Constitution *octroyée* by the King (Rotelli, 1972). As in many other European countries, the practice of parliamentary government developed in Italy within a constitutional framework that had been conceived with another model of political regime in mind. Incidentally, it must be recalled that, in the Italian case, the same Constitution could survive another dramatic change in the configuration of the central political institutions: the rise of fascism and the transformation of government into a basis for Mussolini's dictatorial power (Aquarone, 1965).

The Constituent Assembly of 1946 attempted to define with greater stringency the position of the government *vis-à-vis* the other central political institutions in order to prevent the great swings it had experienced under the *Statuto Albertino*. But as we shall see in greater detail, the attempt to prescribe 'through' the constitutional text the position and functioning of the government within the political system and to predetermine its relative strength (or weakness) was by and large frustrated. Reality followed to a great extent its own designs. There are two major explanations for why this happened. First, the Italian constitution-makers, as often happens, were haunted by past experiences and preoccupations but could not foresee clearly the problems of the future. In particular they could not foresee the impact which the new party system would have upon the structure and functioning of the central democratic institutions they had devised. Second, on this as on most crucial points, a compromise had to be found between widely different constitutional models leading thus to formulations of the constitutional text that are not very cogent.

In order that the nature and role of government in a democratic policy be defined, a number of questions have to be answered. We will see what answers the Italian Constitution has provided and to what extent actual political life has been organised by these answers.

The first questions to be answered concern the political legitimation of government and the process through which government is formed (the two points are obviously closely connected). The second group of questions concerns the internal structure of the governmental institution, and in particular the relationship between the individual components (the Ministers), the government as a collective, global unit and the relationship between the Prime Minister and other ministers (the degree to which hierarchy prevails over equality in status or *vice versa*). The third group of questions concerns the role of the government in the policy-making process and particularly its relations with Parliament in the law-making process.

Most of the answers the Constitution of 1947 provides to these questions are somewhat ambiguous. Being the result of a compromise between conflicting constitutional projects, the Constitution does not give a clear-cut solution but instead middle-of-the-road arrangements open to different interpretations.

Concerning the first point, the Italian Constitution explicitly adopted the model of the parliamentary government. The cabinet needs a positive vote of confidence from both chambers to come to power, and the vote of no confidence of one chamber only is sufficient to bring it down. These provisions point in the direction of a strong dependence of government on Parliament (more exactly on a parliamentary majority) and leave little space for experiments in minority government.

In order to balance the power of Parliament and to reduce governmental instability, the Constitution has introduced some limitations to the presentation and discussion of motions of no confidence (Article 94). This provision, however, has proved relatively ineffective in preventing governmental instability. The point is that this Article assumed that government instability would arise from the unpredictable behaviour of individual parliamentarians and tried consequently to reduce its effect. After World War Two, however, instability has had its origins in the behaviour of parties and of party factions, against which constitutional rules could do very little. Governments have tended to resign as soon as the coalition agreement broke down and without waiting for a parliamentary vote of no confidence.

As for the internal structure of government the Constitution does not opt clearly among a collegial, a prime ministerial model, or a model of ministerial autonomy. Instead it introduces elements of each of the three (Merlini, 1982; Pitruzzella, 1986). On the one hand it assigns special status to the Prime Minister (both in the process leading to the formation of a cabinet and in the daily life of the cabinet). It is up to the Prime Minister to propose the names of Ministers to the Head of State (Article 92) and it is also stated that the Prime Minister coordinates the action of Ministers and leads the policy of the cabinet (Article 95). In practice, however, this special position does not make the Prime Minister more than a *primus inter pares* and does not contradict the collegial character of the cabinet (Article 94–95). It is the cabinet as a whole, and not the Prime Minister, who receives the vote of confidence (Article 94). This is in contrast to the solution which was adopted in other constitutions (for instance in the German *Grundgesetz*) to strengthen the role of the government leader. It may be worth mentioning that some recent proposals for constitutional reform have suggested the adoption of the German solution in order to increase the authority of the Prime Minister *vis-à-vis* the Ministers and the cabinet.

On the question of cabinet collegiality *versus* ministerial individualism, the Constitution seems at first to opt in favour of a collegial system coordinated and led by the Prime Minister (Article 95). The principle of the collective responsibility of Ministers is explicitly stated. At the same time, however, the Constitution introduces a somewhat vaguely defined individual responsibility of Ministers with respect to matters concerning their department. More importantly, the Constitution does not provide instruments for disciplining individual Ministers (in particular, there is no mention of a prime ministerial power to dismiss them).

Finally, with respect to the law-making process, the Constitution does on the one hand attribute some privileges to the government, the most relevant of which is its power to enact decrees that have the same status as acts of Parliament (though these decrees have to be approved subsequently by Parliament within 60 days or lapse).

On the other hand, with respect to bills, government and individual Members of Parliament have the same power to initiate. As in most countries, the details of the legislative process are not regulated by the Constitution but by parliamentary standing orders. Even in this respect, government does not receive a specially favourable treatment compared to ordinary members. It is not its *de jure* but its *de facto* position, resulting from its majority following among Members of Parliament, which explains the greater success of its bills compared to that of private members' bills (Di Palma, 1977).

Thus the analysis of the constitutional norms is not very rewarding for understanding the pecularities of the structure and functioning of the executive in the Italian political system. If we want to go beyond the level of generalities we must therefore look elsewhere.

In fact, most of the peculiar traits of the Italian government do not find their roots in constitutional provisions but rather in a number of political factors which, in the absence of constitutional provisions able to check and regulate them, can play a large part. The legal (and constitutional) framework can be said to be 'permissive' rather than 'channelling' or 'supportive' with respect to the political factors (actors).

Three political elements have markedly characterised the Italian government since the World War Two: the fact that coalition governments have dominated the field; that only limited alternation has taken place among the parties involved in government; and that the duration of governments has typically been short.

The first point draws its origin from the fact that no single party has ever been able to command the absolute majority in both chambers of Parliament which is required by the Constitution. The only possible solutions have therefore been the following:

1) full coalition governments with all the parties of the parliamentary majority holding posts in the cabinet;
2) single party or more rarely coalition governments with the 'external' support of other parties producing a majority in Parliament;
3) minority governments (that is, single party or coalition governments without a real majority in Parliament but able to count on the abstention of other parties);
4) caretaker governments which failed to receive a vote of confidence in Parliament.

All these possibilities have been adopted more than once (see Figure 7.1). But their relative frequency has varied over time, as the relations among the parties of the so-called 'governmental area' have changed. The first solution has been more frequent when a relatively peaceful

FIGURE 7.1    Italian governments 1946–1987

| Prime Minister | Date in | Date out | Duration (months) | Parties in Government (number of ministries) | External support | Abstention |
|---|---|---|---|---|---|---|
| — C O N S T I T U E N T   A S S E M B L Y — | | | | | | |
| De Gasperi II | 13.07.46 | 02.02.47 | 6 | DC (11) PCI (4) PSI (4) PLI (1) PRI (2) | | |
| De Gasperi III | 02.02.47 | 31.05.47 | 4 | DC (8) PCI (3) PSI (3) other (2) | | |
| De Gasperi IV | 31.05.47 | 23.05.48 | 12 | DC (15) PLI (2) | | |
| — I  L E G I S L A T U R E — | | | | | | |
| De Gasperi V | 23.05.48 | 14.01.50 | 8 | DC (12) PSDI (3) PLI (3) PRI (1) other (2) | | |
| De Gasperi VI | 27.01.50 | 19.07.51 | 6 | DC (14) PSDI (3) PRI (3) other (2) | | PLI |
| De Gasperi VII | 26.07.51 | 07.07.53 | 23 | DC (16) PRI (3) other (1) | PRI | PSDI PLI |
| De Gasperi VIII | 16.07.53 | 02.08.53 | 1 | DC (19) govt. without vote of confidence | | |
| — II  L E G I S L A T U R E — | | | | | | |
| Pella | 17.08.53 | 12.01.54 | 5 | DC (18) | PRI PLI PNM | PSDI MSI |
| Fanfani I | 18.01.54 | 08.02.54 | 1 | DC (19) govt. without vote of confidence | | |
| Scelba | 10.02.54 | 02.07.55 | 17 | DC (15) PSDI (4) PLI (3) | PRI | |
| Segni I | 06.07.55 | 15.05.57 | 22 | DC (14) PSDI (4) PLI (3) | PRI | PMP |
| Zoli | 19.05.57 | 01.07.58 | 13 | DC (22) | PNM PMP MSI | |
| — III  L E G I S L A T U R E — | | | | | | |
| Fanfani II | 01.07.58 | 15.02.59 | 8 | DC (19) PSDI (4) | PRI | |
| Segni II | 15.02.59 | 25.03.60 | 13 | DC (23) | PLI PMP PNM MSI | |
| Tambroni | 25.03.60 | 27.07.60 | 4 | DC (23) | MSI | |
| Fanfani III | 26.07.60 | 21.02.62 | 19 | DC (24) | PSDI PRI PLI MSI | |
| Fanfani IV | 21.02.62 | 21.06.63 | 16 | DC (19) PSDI (3) PRI (2) | PSI | PDI |
| — IV  L E G I S L A T U R E — | | | | | | |
| Leone I | 21.06.63 | 04.12.63 | 5 | DC (23) | PRI | |
| Moro I | 04.12.63 | 22.07.64 | 8 | DC (16) PSI (6) PSDI (3) PRI (1) | | |
| Moro II | 22.07.64 | 23.02.66 | 19 | DC (16) PSI (6) PSDI (3) PRI (1) | | |
| Moro III | 23.02.66 | 24.06.68 | 28 | DC (16) PSI (6) PSDI (3) PRI (1) | | PSI PSDI PRI |
| — V  L E G I S L A T U R E — | | | | | | |
| Leone II | 23.06.68 | 12.12.68 | 6 | DC (24) | | PSU PRI |
| Rumor I | 12.12.68 | 08.08.69 | 8 | DC (17) PSU (9) PRI (1) | | |
| Rumor II | 08.08.69 | 27.03.70 | 8 | DC (25) | PSI PSDI | PRI |
| Rumor III | 27.03.70 | 06.08.70 | 4 | DC (17) PSI (6) PSDI (3) PRI (1) | PSI PSDI | PRI |
| Colombo | 06.08.70 | 17.02.72 | 18 | DC (16) PSI (6) PSDI (4) PRI (1) | | |
| Andreotti I | 18.02.72 | 26.06.72 | 4 | DC (25) govt. without vote of confidence | | |

| Prime Minister | Date in | Date out | Duration (months) | Parties in Government | External support | Abstention |
|---|---|---|---|---|---|---|
| **VI LEGISLATURE** | | | | | | |
| Andreotti II | 26.07.72 | 07.07.73 | 11 | DC (17) PSDI (5) PLI (4) | PRI | |
| Rumor IV | 07.07.73 | 15.03.74 | 8 | DC (17) PSI (6) PSDI (4) PRI (2) | | |
| Rumor V | 15.03.74 | 20.11.74 | 8 | DC (16) PSI (6) PSDI (4) | PRI | PLI |
| Moro IV | 20.11.74 | 11.02.76 | 14 | DC (20) PRI (5) | PSI PSDI | PSI PRI PLI |
| Moro V | 11.02.76 | 29.07.76 | 5 | DC (29) other (1) | PSDI | PSI PRI PLI |
| **VII LEGISLATURE** | | | | | | |
| Andreotti III | 30.07.76 | 13.03.78 | 19 | DC (21) others (1) | | PCI PSI PSDI PRI PLI |
| Andreotti IV | 13.03.78 | 21.03.79 | 12 | DC (21) others (1) | PCI PSI PSDI PRI | |
| Andreotti V | 21.03.79 | 04.08.79 | 5 | DC (14) PSDI (5) PRI (3) govt. without vote of confidence | | |
| **VIII LEGISLATURE** | | | | | | |
| Cossiga I | 04.08.79 | 04.04.80 | 8 | DC (17) PSDI (3) PLI (2) other (2) | | PSI PRI |
| Cossiga II | 04.04.80 | 18.10.80 | 6 | DC (16) PSI (9) PRI (3) | | |
| Forlani I | 18.10.80 | 28.06.81 | 8 | DC (14) PSI (7) PSDI (3) PRI (3) | | |
| Spadolini I | 28.06.81 | 23.08.82 | 13 | PRI (2) DC (15) PSI (7) PSDI (3) PLI (1) | | |
| Spadolini II | 23.08.82 | 11.12.82 | 3 | PRI (2) DC (15) PSI (7) PSDI (3) PLI (1) | | PRI |
| Fanfani V | 11.12.82 | 03.08.83 | 8 | DC (14) PSI (7) PSDI (5) PLI (2) | | |
| **IX LEGISLATURE** | | | | | | |
| Craxi I | 04.08.83 | 01.08.86 | 24 | PSI (6) DC (16) PSDI (3) PRI (3) PLI (2) | | |
| Craxi II | 01.08.86 | 17.04.87 | 9 | PSI (6) DC (16) PSDI (3) PRI (3) PLI (2) | | |
| Fanfani VI | 17.04.87 | 28.07.87 | 3 | DC (17) others (9) govt. without vote of confidence | | |
| **X LEGISLATURE** | | | | | | |
| Goria I | 29.07.87 | 17.04.88 | 9 | DC (16) PSI (9) PSDI (3) PRI (3) PLI (1) | | |
| De Mila | 18.04.88 | | | DC (16) PSI (9) PSDI (3) PRI (3) PLI (4) | | |

*Notes*

[a] in some cases the position of the parties changed during the government life without provoking its fall; here are recorded the positions of the parties at the outset of each government.

[b] party names: DC = Christian Democratic Party; PCI = Italian Communist Party; PSI = Italian Socialist Party; PLI = Italian Liberal Party; PRI = Italian Republican Party; PNM = National Monarchist Party; PMP = People's Monarchist Party; MSI = Italian Social Movement (neo-fascist party); PDI = Italian Democratic Party (monarchist); PSDI = Social Democratic Party; PSU = United Socialist Party (a fusion of PSI and PSDI); other = independent.

[c] the first party mentioned is that of the prime minister.

[d] the party underlined holds the vice-premiership.

[e] the number of ministers may be less than the number of ministries counted here, since there are cases of a minister holding more than one department.

alliance between government parties could be built. The second and third solutions have been adopted as transitional devices when an organic and public agreement could not be reached between traditional and/or new alliance partners and some of them preferred to give less visible support to government without engaging themselves in full participation. The last situation is obviously the result of the lack of even this limited agreement.

The four situations mentioned can be seen as a sort of scale of declining agreement between the parties with a *Regierungsfähigkeit* (ability to be in government). It must be added that the last solution (caretaker government) has always taken place at election times (either when a regular election was due or in order to produce an anticipated election). The constutional legitimacy of this solution has been questioned by many, and such situations have in fact coincided with serious strains in the relations among the political forces and constitutional organs (in particular between parties and the Head of State).

The first feature of Italian governments has meant that each cabinet, if it wanted to survive and produce policies, has had to face 'coalition' problems within the cabinet itself (whenever the cabinet was a coalition cabinet). This also occurred in the parliamentary arena, when it had to count upon the 'external' support of other parties that had not accepted becoming part of the executive, but were nonetheless necessary to sustain a majority in Parliament. The only exception would be the 'true' minority governments, which by definition skip the problem of finding a majoritarian coalition. In the Italian case, at least, their purpose seems to be not so much to produce 'governmental outputs' – that is to say, policies – but rather to prepare new elections.

The second point deserving attention touches on the composition of coalitions. During the whole period considered, the governmental coalitions have been formed by adding other parties to the 'relative majority party' (Pappalardo, 1978; Marradi, 1982) – that is, the Christian Democrats. No 'alternative' coalition without that party could ever come into being or even be envisaged realistically at the national level (while at regional or lower levels of government it has often been experimented). To use the Sartorian terminology, 'peripheral turnover' instead of full alteration has characterised the government-building process in Italy (Sartori, 1976). Only relatively small parties of the centre-left or centre-right have moved in and out of the governmental coalitions.

The main reason for this situation lies in the fact that the other parties of the left and centre, which would have been necessary (and sufficient since 1976) to built an alternative government to those led by the Christian Democrats, had until now never been ready to consider the largest opposition party (the Communist Party) as a suitable government partner. In spite of all their criticisms of, and disagreements with, the Christian Democratic Party, the small parties which in local politics have been ready to form government coalitions with the Communist Party have in the end thought it less risky for the country (or for the political interests they represent or for their electoral performance) to build a coalition at the national level with the Christian Democrats. At most, as at the peak of the electoral growth of the Communist Party in the second half of the 1970s, they have asked that the Communist Party 'also' be associated with the government. This was, for instance, the request of the Socialist Party in the years preceding the so-called governments of national solidarity which received the parliamentary support of the Communist Party as well.

It must be said that a large responsibility for such a situation can be attributed to the Communist Party itself. Its lack of *Koalitionsfähigkeit* (ability to participate in coalitions) has had much to do with a deliberate choice of the successive leadership groups of that party not to put at risk the unity of the organisation's following by reorienting too drastically the line and the programmes (particularly in the most visible electoral arena) as it would be required if the Communist Party were to become a suitable government partner. The political course followed by the largest opposition party has been a mixture of overt opposition to the government and its policies combined with pragmatic deals struck in the less visible arenas such as parliamentary committees (Cazzola, 1974; Di Palma, 1977). Moreover, between the two largest government parties – Christian Democrats and the Socialist Party – the Communist Party has never clearly sought an alliance with the second, although it is the only party which, because of its position on the left, could help the Communist Party to build an alternative government coalition of some homogeneity. On the contrary, the Communist Party has constantly tried to keep bargaining options open and to play one party off against the other.

Only in the period of the so-called governments of national solidarity (1976–79) did the possibility of a relevant change from the normal government formula seem to materialise. Following a dramatic electoral leap of the Communist Party (7 per cent), a governmental alliance between the Communist Party and the Christian Democrats, together with the other traditional government parties, became (for the first time since 1947) acceptable to both sides. However, even then the Communist

Party could not achieve full governmental status (on participation in the cabinet) but only gave parliamentary support to a cabinet composed of Christian Democratic Ministers. The formula broke down before the Communist Party succeeded in participating in the cabinet.

Another aspect to be mentioned is the fact that the 'right' of the largest party (the Christian Democrats) to obtain the prime ministership was never seriously contested until 1979. Since that time the post of Prime Minister has been a matter of sharp conflict among the governmental parties (and particularly between the two largest, Christian Democrats and the Socialist Party). This new situation indicates that the dominant role of the Christian Democrats within government coalitions has declined in recent years. It may also suggest that the premiership has become a political post of greater importance (and visibility) than in the past.

The third characteristic of Italian government is the relatively short duration of cabinets. As is well-known, the definition of governmental stability is not simple given the many dimensions of the concept which applies to the stability of the cabinets themselves and also of the individual components and of the parties involved (Herman, 1975). At this point it is sufficient to stress the main aspect and note that the short duration of cabinets is a clear indicator of the high level of conflict within the governmental coalitions.

Party coalitions supporting the government are put to the test shortly after they have come into existence. The commonly mentioned point that, in spite of high cabinet instability, government personnel is relatively stable and that not infrequently a ministry is held by the same Minister in more than one cabinet, do not contradict the general impression of instability. Indeed, these remarks taken together provide important insights into the working of Italian cabinets. Stability at the individual rather than at the collective level suggests a balance of power between (individual) Ministers and the (collective) cabinet which is skewed in favour of the first.

## 2  CABINET STRUCTURE

According to the Constitution the cabinet is composed of the Prime Minister (*Presidente del consiglio*) and the Ministers. The Constitution does not even mention another group which currently forms part of governments – the group of the 'Under Secretaries'. Introduced in Italy at the end of the nineteenth century (by a law of 1888), they do not take part in the official meetings of the Council of Ministers unless summoned and in a restrictive formal sense they are not part of the government (Ruggeri, 1983).

On the other hand, from a *political* point of view the appointment of Under Secretaries is currently seen as part of the government-building process. The allocation of these posts among the parties follows more or less the same plan as that of the ministerial posts. It is part of the complex distribution of governmental positions among the parties and further among the factions existing within the parties that can satisfy all the requests only if under-secretaryships are taken into account. Moreover, Under Secretaries can substitute for their respective Minister in a number of ways, particularly in Parliament, with the outside world (interest groups, electors and so on) or within the ministry itself. In a less restrictive sense they can therefore be seen as part of the government.

Among them a special position is occupied by one of the Under Secretaries attached to the Prime Minister, who has the role of Secretary of the Council of Ministers. Alone among Under-Secretaries he takes part (but without formal voting powers) in cabinet meetings. Furthermore, he has a crucial role as the closest collaborator of the premier in preparing the work of the council. Very often he will conduct, instead of the Prime Minister, the complex negotiations among Ministers and with party representatives which precede cabinet discussions (Cassese, 1981).

We can therefore describe the government as a two-tier structure, the first tier (that of Ministers) being responsible for the collective process of decision-making and the second tier (that of Under Secretaries) being active only at the level of each department (including, as we have seen, the relations between ministries and Parliament and ministries and other external actors).

The Constitution does not determine the number of Ministers (nor of course of Under Secretaries) and can only prescribe that the number, responsibility and organisation of the ministries be regulated by law (and not merely by regulation or decree). In fact, the size of the government has grown steadily. During most of the nineteenth century we had cabinets of less than ten members (the number of departmental ministries could be a little larger, as the Prime Minister typically held also another important ministry, first the foreign affairs, or war, then more and more regularly interior). We have now reached cabinets of 25 to 30 members, while the government as a whole, including Under Secretaries, has approximately 90 members (Bartolotta, 1971; *Keesings Archives*).

The growth in the number of Ministers is only partly due to the addition of new departments. It also arises from the appointment of an increasing number of Ministers without Portfolio. A major factor responsible for this growth has been the necessity to accommodate the requests of the many parties involved in the coalitions. Evidence supporting this explanation can be derived from the fact that single-party governments have always been smaller in size than coalition governments of the same period.

The distribution of ministries among coalition partners (and subsequently among party factions within each of the parties and particularly within the largest party of the coalition) has always been a crucial question in the formation of governments. A rule of proportionality has been more or less followed. However, small parties have in general obtained a larger share of ministerial positions than their parliamentary weight would have allowed. But the largest coalition party – the Christian Democrats – has usually held control of the most important ministries of Interior, Defence, Foreign Affairs, Finance and Education (Marradi, 1982).

The problems involved in building and maintaining heterogeneous coalitions have often loomed large in the definition of the structure of cabinets. This has frequently led to the appointment of a vice-premier. He is typically a politician of high prestige belonging to the second largest party of the coalition (or even to the largest party, the Christian Democrats, when this party has had to leave the premiership to another coalition partner as during the Craxi government of 1983–1987).

Another solution often discussed but achieved for the first time in the Craxi government has been to create within the government an inner cabinet composed of the leaders of the coalition parties (or of the Minister of highest rank of a party when its chairman did not belong to the government) and of the other most important Ministers. This device has probably played a significant part in the unusual longevity of the Craxi government. It eventually failed, in part because it had not been possible to include in the government the top leader of the largest coalition party, the Christian Democrats, which had also been deprived of the premiership. The Christian Democrats were represented in this inner cabinet only by the number two in the party hierarchy and agreements reached in the inner cabinet could always be rejected by the party chairman, who had not personally taken part in them.

The coalition nature of the government and the proliferation of ministries (which as we have seen is partly a consequence of the former point and partly the result of more general trends in the contemporary world) have had another important effect on the structure of the government. Some of the most important policy areas (for instance external relations and financial and economic affairs) have been fragmented into more than one ministry and allocated to the representatives of different parties. This has meant, in the best case, that *the* policy of the government in that area has been the result of long consultations between the Ministers (and also the parties and the ministerial bureaucracies) responsible for that area. In the worst case it has meant that each Minister went his own way and that there has been more than one government policy in each area.

An institutional effort to counteract the fragmentation of ministries has been the creation of inter-ministerial committees, whereby in certain policy domains the actions of a number of ministries could be coordinated (Ciriello, 1981). To what extent these committees are in accord with the Constitution is a matter for debate, especially for those committees whose powers are not wholly confined to the government. A point often made against their constitutionality is the fact that they reduce the collegial decision of the cabinet as a whole and privilege some Ministers (and the Prime Minister who normally chairs them) over others. Indeed, it is clear that they are a departure from the principle that the government decides everything in its full collegiality.

It is not, however, only the committees which violate that principle. A much greater menace to the principle of full collegiality comes, on the one hand, from the decisions of individual Ministers (ministries) that the cabinet cannot effectively control. On the other hand, it comes from decisions taken outside the cabinet by party representatives who may or may not be members of the cabinet and which become cabinet policy without further discussion. As to the efficacy of such committees in coordinating the policy areas for which they are responsible, the Italian experience suggests that their impact has been much less than hoped or feared (Merusi, 1977). A common interpretation is that they have been more an instrument for legitimising the independent role of certain ministries *vis-à-vis* the cabinet than for effective coordination.

The weight of the Prime Minister in the real structure of the Italian government is commonly judged to be not very heavy, particularly *vis-à-vis* individual Ministers. Two main factors concur to explain this situation.

First, the Prime Minister has a very limited role in the choice of Ministers (nor has he any real power to dismiss them) because their selection is left to each party of the coalition as far as the quota of ministerial positions assigned to that party is concerned. Even the Ministers of his own party are not really the choice of the Prime

Minister, but rather of the chairman of the party (in consultation with the other top leaders). From a purely legal point of view there is some ground for arguing (although the Constitution is mute on this point) that the Prime Minister has at his disposal the strongest instrument of control – namely the power to sack his colleagues. In fact, this power has been completely taken out of his hands and there is no case of a Minister dismissed from government by the Prime Minister since World War Two. The only (real) power of a Prime Minister, if unsatisfied with his own cabinet, is to resign and thus provoke the collapse of the government.

The second factor at work pertains to the technical and organisational dimension of the government. While the individual Ministers can count on the resources of their departments, the Prime Minister does not have any comparable supporting bureaucracy at his disposal. His position is now even worse than it was in the pre-fascist period when the Prime Minister typically held a major ministerial position (the interior, finance or foreign affairs) and could therefore count upon the resources of his department to support his work as leader of the government.

In order to overcome this situation and the negative effects it has upon the quality of the policy outputs of the government, many proposals have been put forward in recent years for the reform of the organisation of the cabinet (*Quaderni Costituzionali*, 1982). All these proposals have paid special attention to the position of the Prime Minister. The proposal which was put forward by the Craxi government, which came very near to obtaining parliamentary approval before the dissolution of 1987, hinged on three fundamental points:

1) increased collegiality realised through a detailed and more extensive definition of the matters which require compulsorily collective deliberation in cabinet and cannot be decided by single Ministers;
2) better circulation of information among members of the cabinet and more stringent procedural rules to ensure that cabinet decisions are 'really', and not only formally, collective;
3) creation of an apparatus serving the cabinet as a whole and assisting the Prime Minister in particular in his leading and steering capacity.

Innovations of this type could probably prove effective in counterbalancing the forces which move towards fragmentation along departmental lines, which derive from factors of a bureaucratic character. But it is doubtful whether these changes would prove effective against the more political factors producing fragmentation, which result mainly from tensions among the different parties of coalition.

This does not mean that the Prime Minister has no influence. As can be expected in a situation of fragmentation, his greatest impact is not when he attempts to direct his Ministers and the cabinet along the lines of a predetermined programme. It is when he assumes the role of mediator (for which he is obviously in a good position) between the many actors in the governmental arena.

## 3  CABINET LIFE

The image an observer draws from looking at the functioning of the governmental institution is so full of contrasts that it verges on schizophrenia! On the one hand, there is a high instability of cabinets as measured in terms or their duration (a little less than a year being their mean length in office). On the other hand, there is the much greater continuity in the political *formulae* of party coalitions supporting the cabinets, even greater continuity of some of the parties involved and of the political elite that has manned the institution (Calise and Mannheimer, 1982 and 1986).

Up to a point, the stress placed on one aspect rather than the other depends on the observer's subjective assessment or on the viewpoint taken in the analysis. Less arguable is the explanation given for this situation. It can be traced to a number of factors – namely the fact that a more radical alternative to the successive coalitions has until now never been viable, that the electoral system has proved unable to prevent the fragmentation of the party system or to encourage a process of concentration, and that at least the largest governing party is factionalised and collegial. The lack of credible alternatives has resulted in the long-term continuity of the parties 'in' government.

This situation, combined with the internal structure of parties, has reduced the opportunities for dislodging incumbent Ministers from their positions and has fostered the growth of a strong ministerial oligarchy. Meanwhile, the heterogeneity of the coalitions and the number of the parties that have been involved in them (as many as five, for instance) has increased the level of conflict within the government itself. The terms of the coalition agreement have therefore had to be frequently renegotiated. The lack of serious political alternatives has probably had a negative effect upon the stability of governments (as a collective entity). The fact that the risk of losing power is not a real one for the members of the governing coalition has eliminated a factor of cohesion and a potential deterrent against the tendency to push conflicts too far.

The political conditions under which the government-building processes take place have produced a situation where more attention is given to the discussion and formulation of complex formulae for legitimising fierce disputes over power positions in the cabinet and for explaining small changes from one cabinet to another than to the substantial contents of policies (Pridham, 1983). The fall of cabinets can be explained more in terms of disputes over the allocation of power among the coalition parties than in terms of serious, let alone insoluble, conflicts over policies. The crisis of the long Craxi government was typical of this tendency. This was due to a conflict between the two largest coalition parties over who should lead the cabinet.

Another important factor of cabinet instability has arisen from electoral results, although the impact of elections has in fact been indirect rather than direct. Rarely have general elections resulted in the collapse of a cabinet because the parliamentary majority which supported it had disappeared and a new one had materialised. More important have been the less clear-cut psychological effects of elections. The loss of some votes by a governing party in favour of a party in opposition has often induced the former, in fear of losing its following, to rethink its participation in the government (that is, to become more uncompromising in policy matters and even to prefer to stay out of government for some time). But often it was the shifts of votes among the coalition parties that increased internal conflicts and eventually led to the request that the coalition agreement and structure of the cabinet be rediscussed. This 'sensitivity' of parties and (as a consequence) of cabinets to even small electoral shifts has meant that not only general elections but also local government elections held between general elections have been responsible for the fall of governments (and for changes in coalitional formulae).

What we have said about the role of power conflicts in provoking the collapse of cabinets does not mean that conflicts over policies have been irrelevant. Quite the contrary: they have deeply affected the policy-making process and outputs of policy-making, but they have affected the duration of cabinets only when coupled with conflicts over power. If conflicts over power were lacking, a solution could be found either by negotiating a compromise or often simply by removing the issue and postponing its solution.

## 4  CABINET DECISION-MAKING

The policy-making style of governments has been heavily affected by this situation. All the analyses of legislative outputs (Cantelli, Mortara and Movia, 1974; Di Palma, 1977; Bonanni, 1983; Motta, 1985) have shown that to the huge quantity of bills introduced by the government *corresponds to the reduction in the significance of their content*. Instead of legislating about general situations and broad interests, governments tend to meet particularistic demands and to regulate small groups. Instead of redistributing resources they tend to distribute something to everybody, and instead of choosing among conflicting interests they tend to accommodate all concerned through complex agreement mechanisms.

Among the direct consequences of this type of legislation one could mention the huge public debt (an obvious consequence of distribution exceeding redistribution). Also, the progressive balkanisation of the public administration due to the growth of disparities in economic treatment and in career requirements and to the proliferation of special categories and groupings. This is a direct effect of the prevalence of interventions at the micro level over broader-gauged legislation. Finally, the increasingly frequent need to revise pieces of legislation shortly after they have been brought into operation (a clear consequence of the poor legal formulation of texts which try to realise 'impossible' compromises between conflicting interests).

A crucial point for the understanding of the working of the Italian cabinets lies in the relations between government and parties. The Italian case is probably the one which shows the greatest divergence between the two. Except for relatively short periods, party leaders have tended to refuse cabinet positions and stayed outside the government. The proposal repeatedly made to create within the government a *directorium* of the leaders of all the coalition parties (along the lines of the first cabinets of the transition period between fascism and democracy) has always been rejected. The opposition has been particularly strong in the largest party, the Christian Democrats, where after De Gasperi the structure of the party leadership developed along directorial and collegial, rather than monocratic, lines. The proposal to concentrate governmental (and for a very long long time that would have obviously meant the premiership) and party authority in the same hands has always been considered by the other party co-leaders as an unbearable menace.

The two posts of party and government leader (and of course all other ministerial positions) have been valued prizes to be assigned in the complex factional game of the largest party (Zuckerman, 1979) and an instrument for compensating conflicting ambitions and avoiding extensive concentrations of power through a careful distribution of offices. In the smaller coalition parties the separation of ministerial and party positions has been less rigidly followed, probably because of their less articulated structure. This has more frequently enabled a single leader to become pre-eminent in the party and therefore to concentrate all the spoils in his hands.

In recent years, however, a trend toward concentrating prime ministership and party leadership has been noticeable. In the two cases in which the premiership went to a party other than the Christian Democrats, the party leader also held this position (Spadolini for the Republicans and Craxi for the Socialists). But when the prospects for a return of the leadership of the government to Christian Democratic hands were discussed, and the event did take place after the 1987 elections, the separation of the two roles seemed necessary once more.

This means that, when it touches on questions which are particularly sensitive for the image and programme of a party of the coalition, the government cannot forget that it has to take into account other crucial actors outside its ranks. The attitudes of 'external' party leaders (of the majority) towards the government have had different temperature levels which it some cases have been bordered on explicit chill. As a rule party chairmen, as guardians of the party interests and purity of the party line (and not having a personal stake in the stability of a government) have been much readier to see a governmental crisis occur than the Ministers and Prime Minister of the same party.

Even when the question of the survival of the government has not been at stake, the division of roles between party and government has required that many decisions on specific policies be taken not simply in cabinet but in a more complex decisional setting that would include also the so-called 'party experts' (that is, the party officials responsible for that specific policy area). Occasionally, for particular crucial questions which could affect the life of the cabinet, meetings of the top party leaders together with the Prime Minister have taken place (the so-called *vertice* or summit).

Another important aspect heavily affecting the policy-making role of governments has been their relationship with Parliament. It has always been more difficult to keep under control, in the parliamentary arena than at the cabinet level, the lack of homogeneity and the divisions existing in governmental coalitions. This is understandable given the factionalised nature of most of the governing parties and the highly individualistic nature of electoral campaigns. Voters are allowed to express preferences for individual candidates and the governmental majority in Parliament has therefore always been more heterogeneous than the team of its representatives sitting in cabinet. One must also add the organisational pecualiarities of the Italian Parliament, with its strong legislative committees, the limited powers given to the government in the determination of the agenda and in leading the law-making process and the role of 'secret' voting whereby parliamentarians can vote on many issues without having to disclose the way they voted (Manzella, 1977).

One should also take into account the greater cohesion of the largest opposition party (the Communist Party). It is therefore hardly surprising that in order to get its proposals through the parliamentary process the government should frequently have to agree to compromises both with dissenting sectors within the majority and with the opposition (Cazzola, 1974; Di Palma, 1977). In Italian political jargon an expression frequently used by members of the government to express this readiness is that they will accept 'improvements' (*miglioramenti*) to their legislative proposals made by Parliament. When the government is not ready to make such moves it is not uncommon to see, with the complicity of the 'secret' vote, its majority vanish and a new one appear, comprised of elements of the majority siding with the opposition.

The joint working of the factors mentioned above has produced a situation whereby the government as a collective body has perhaps been far less in control or at the centre of the policy-making process than in other European countries. It is permissible to suggest that Italy has been 'governed' not so much 'in' government (cabinet) as in other policy-making arenas. This is not to say that the government has been absent from these arenas, but it was represented there not so much as a whole as through individual governmental actors (the Prime Minister, individual Ministers or a section of the cabinet). These had to negotiate more or less on a parity level with other political actors (parliamentary, bureaucratic and party actors). The government itself has been deeply permeated by the polycentric character of the entire political system (Cotta, 1987).

# 8 Austria: Routine and Ritual

## Peter Gerlich and Wolfgang C. Müller

### 1 CABINET SETTING

The Austrian federal Constitution, which dates back to 1920, contains only very few provisions concerning the organisation, tasks and procedures of the federal government, as the collective top executive body is officially called. This is rather surprising since the political culture of the country usually places a great deal of emphasis on legality and legal regulations (Gerlich, 1981). However, the few explicit norms concerning the cabinet have been supplemented by constitutional conventions which derive from long established state practice and are therefore usually respected.

The 'silence of the Constitution' (Pfeifer, 1964), with respect to the explicit regulation of cabinet affairs, can be explained by historical precedants and circumstances at the time when the Constitution was drafted. A certain distrust of concentrating too much power in a clearly defined top executive council prevailed (Welan and Neisser, 1971). Rather than provide for a strong leadership in cabinet, the tendency was to strengthen departments (which, particularly in coalition governments, were as a rule party strongholds).

The Constitution states initially that federal Ministers (the Chancellor being considered as *primus inter pares*) are entrusted with top executive tasks. Only then does it state that all Ministers jointly form the federal government. Incidentally, the Constitution does not mention the term 'Council of Ministers' regularly used in official language. The Constitution explicitly regulates the appointment of the Chancellor (by the President) and the Ministers (by the President after a proposal by the Chancellor).

The President may dismiss the government or its members individually (in the latter case on the proposal of the Chancellor). Moreover, the political responsibility of the cabinet is also explicitly regulated. If the National Council (*Nationalrat*), the main chamber of parliament, passes a vote of no confidence, the cabinet (or individual members who have lost this confidence) must be dismissed. There are rules governing the substitution of Ministers and their rights as well as provisions allowing for the appointment of junior ministers (Secretaries of State).[1] Yet virtually no rules relate to the cabinet as such. Only a few tasks of the cabinet are explicitly, albeit incidentally, mentioned, the most important being to decide on government draft bills to be proposed to parliament and to decide on acts of delegated legislation if these have been explicitly entrusted to the cabinet. A number of more formal powers are also mentioned.[2] Moreover, it is generally acknowledged that the cabinet serves to coordinate departmental policies, but it is the individual departments rather than the cabinet which, both legally and constitutionally, hold in principle supreme executive power.

These scare constitutional provisions have in practice been supplemented by a number of conventional rules which might be summed up under three headings: Chancellor rule, the unanimity requirement and parliamentary supremacy. In a sense these rules seem more relevant for the workings of the Austrian cabinet than the more explicit provisions mentioned so far.

## Chancellor rule

Although the Constitution does not provide for the right of the Chancellor to issue binding directives to the members of the cabinet,[3] most observers agree that in fact the Chancellor's position within the cabinet is very strong – unless the political power constellation works against him.

This strength can be deduced from his power to appoint and dismiss cabinet members, from the effects of the generally respected unanimity rule, but also from the fact that he is head of an important department – the 'Chancellery' – and above all from the dominant position a Chancellor usually holds within the largest party. Some analysts even speak of prime ministerial government in Austria (Welan, 1976). However, the principle of Chancellor rule is always counter-balanced by departmental rule. In practice departments are to a great extent guaranteed autonomy from cabinet interference and individual Ministers regularly manage to maintain this relative independence to a large degree.

## Unanimity requirement

To the chagrin of many lawyers who feel that the use of majority rule would be legally correct, cabinet decisions are traditionally always taken unanimously. Although no official rules of procedure for the cabinet are known to exist, it is generally assumed that the principles of a provisional document dating from 1918, when the republican cabinet first met (Pfeifer 1964) are still applied today (Walter 1972). This document maintains that a member of the cabinet who does not agree with the others, has to offer his resignation and that in the case of lack of unanimity the Chancellor himself may decide and thus bind the whole cabinet (or enforce a resignation). This did in fact take place in 1947 when the last Communist Minister left the cabinet because of a disagreement with the Chancellor (Pfeifer 1964). It can be assumed that during the Monarchy the unanimity requirement ensured that the Emperor's government would speak only with one voice. The principle was taken over by the republican executive not least because it corresponds to the deeply ingrained need among Austrian political elites to achieve and maintain consensus (Gerlich 1986), a fact which may be overlooked by the legal critics of this rule.

## Parliamentary supremacy

There is general agreement among legal scholars that the cabinet is not only constitutionally responsible to the National Council, but also functionally subordinated to it rather than to the President. A cabinet will regularly resign after parliamentary, but not after presidential elections. Although some constitutional preconditions for a Gaullist arrangement exist in Austria and although the President is popularly elected, the office of President has always been understood to be of symbolic significance only and not to allow for active interference with executive affairs.

These three principles, together with the more explicit constitutional rules mentioned earlier, provide a broad framework for different kinds of political behaviour. Far from determining the activity or even the distribution of power within the cabinet they only provide opportunities for action, which different Chancellors and government teams have used in different ways.

Most relevant in this respect is the party composition of governments.[4] As Table 8.1 shows, three main periods of cabinet life may be distinguished. From 1945 to 1966 the dominant model was that of the Grand Coalition. During this period the two large Austrian parties comprising together close to or more than 90 per cent of parliamentary deputies formed a joint government. Thus most formal rules became less important and important decisions were in fact taken by an extra-

TABLE 8.1  Austrian cabinets since 1945

| Chancellor | Date in | Date out | Duration (% years) | Government composition | Government type |
|---|---|---|---|---|---|
| Renner | 04.45 | 12.45 | 0.6 | SPÖ ÖVP KPÖ | provisional |
| Figl I | 12.45 | 11.47 | 1.9 | SPÖ ÖVP KPÖ | grand coalition |
| Figl II | 11.47 | 11.49 | 2.0 | ÖVP SPÖ | grand coalition |
| Figl III | 11.49 | 10.52 | 3.0 | ÖVP SPÖ | grand coalition |
| Raab I | 04.53 | 06.56 | 3.2 | ÖVP SPÖ | grand coalition |
| Raab II | 06.56 | 07.59 | 3.0 | ÖVP SPÖ | grand coalition |
| Raab III | 07.59 | 04.61 | 1.7 | ÖVP SPÖ | grand coalition |
| Gorbach I | 04.61 | 03.63 | 2.0 | ÖVP SPÖ | grand coalition |
| Gorbach II | 03.63 | 04.64 | 1.0 | ÖVP SPÖ | grand coalition |
| Klaus I | 04.64 | 04.66 | 2.0 | ÖVP SPÖ | grand coalition |
| Klaus II | 04.66 | 04.70 | 4.0 | ÖVP | single-party |
| Kreisky I | 04.70 | 11.71 | 1.5 | SPÖ | single-party |
| Kreisky II | 11.71 | 10.75 | 4.0 | SPÖ | single-party |
| Kreisky III | 10.75 | 06.79 | 3.6 | SPÖ | single-party |
| Kreisky IV | 06.79 | 05.83 | 4.0 | SPÖ | single-party |
| Sinowatz | 05.83 | 06.86 | 3.0 | SPÖ FPÖ | coalition |
| Vranitzky I | 06.86 | 01.87 | 0.6 | SPÖ FPÖ | coalition |
| Vranitzky II | 01.87 | | | SPÖ ÖVP | grand coalition |

parliamentary as well as extra-cabinet coalition committee (Rudzio, 1971). Prior to 1947 there was even an all-party government including the Communists. Between 1966 and 1983 a single party, first the People's Party (ÖVP) and later the Socialist Party (SPÖ), managed to form governments by themselves. This created a different situation making the official institutions again more relevant.

From 1983 to 1987 the trend has again been that of coalition governments, first between the Socialists and the small Freedom Party (FPÖ), and in 1987 there was a return to the traditional Grand Coalition pattern. Table 8.1 also shows the length of time of governments in office. In general Austrian cabinets have been in office for relatively long periods. During the single-party area the longest possible tenure of four years was approached or even achieved. Coalition governments usually cooperate successfully for relatively short periods.

## 2  CABINET STRUCTURE

Although the founding fathers of the Austrian Republic after 1918 wanted to arrange matters quite differently from what they had been during the monarchy, they were nevertheless the heirs of a long tradition of organisation of the executive which had evolved during the nineteenth century. Thus, partly against their will, the Imperial Council of Ministers served as a model for the new republican cabinet.

Three traditions stand out: consensus, smallness and informality. Since the old Council of Ministers had always been considered an institution created by the Emperor and dependent only upon him (there was no political responsibility to parliament), it was felt only natural, as was mentioned above, that decisions within the council should be reached by unanimous vote. As the instruments of the Emperor, the ministers could speak with one voice only and could hold only one opinion (Pelinka and Welan, 1971). Ministers who disagreed were required to resign. Moreover, the Council of Ministers had always been a relatively small body, advising the Emperor and in no way a large and representative committee of parliament.

Finally, a preference for informality, an unwillingness to regulate the organisation and powers of the top executive, so as not to determine it too closely, can also be considered to be a heritage of the Monarchy (Bernatzik, 1911). This situation probably corresponded to the interests of the traditionally influential senior bureaucracy. This group preferred a small and informal political committee as its formally superior body.

This body would be too small to exercise excessive influence, while it should enjoy sufficient prestige to enable it to legitimise bureaucratic institutions and policies.

Two further factors were important during the subsequent period. One was that in terms of crisis the position of the Chancellor tended to be strengthened, and this enhanced his prestige even when the crisis was over. One could recall the strong position of the Chancellor during the Austro-fascist period, or the dominating role of Karl Renner during the provisional government of 1945.

Table 8.2 illustrates the relative smallness of the Austrian cabinet as well as its relatively slow growth. While the provisional state government had been quite large, the number of departments and other governmental positions declined thereafter.[5] This number slowly grew again in response to the expanding tasks of the modern welfare state.

It has already been stated that there are practically no formal rules establishing cabinet procedure. It is agreed that the Chancellor (or his deputy in his absence chairs cabinet meetings and that unanimity rather than majority vote is used in taking decisions. The agenda is formally determined by the Chancellor, but each member of the cabinet is entitled to ask for topics to be included. This agenda thus emerges from the suggestions of the individual ministers, while it also includes certain items automatically. This second group comprises some matters relating to the civil service (promotions and travel of civil servants), the notification of legislative acts of the various regions (as these can be voted by the cabinet) as well as communications and resolutions specifically addressed to the cabinet.

Cabinet members are entirely free to present proposals: the only formal requirement is that these proposals must be delivered in time at the cabinet office (*Ministerratsdienst*), a small branch of the Federal Chancellery. Late proposals are automatically placed on the agenda of the next meeting. In practice, however, proposals from individual ministers are only raised in cabinet if they have previously been approved informally by various bodies or have been agreed to through the formal consultative mechanism (*Begutachtungsverfahren*).

The cabinet meets as a rule once a week, except in times of crisis, when it meets more frequently. There are also a few ceremonial meetings. Cabinet meetings do not normally take place during the summer recess or around Christmas. However, official cabinet meetings are preceded by unofficial preparatory meetings. Originally, these were meetings of the individual parties represented in the Grand Coalition, but they continued to take place during the seventeen years of single-party

TABLE 8.2  Size of Austrian cabinets since 1945

| Chancellor | Government Positions | | | Government Personnel | | |
|---|---|---|---|---|---|---|
| | Departments | Non-departmental Ministerial Posts | Secretaries of State | Total | Ministers | Secretaries of State |
| Renner | 10 | 3 | 25 | 40 | 15 | 26 |
| Figl I | 11 | 2 | 2 | 22 | 18 | 4 |
| Figl II | 11 | 2 | 2 | 18 | 16 | 2 |
| Figl III | 8 | 1 | 4 | 19 | 15 | 4 |
| Raab I | 8 | 1 | 5 | 21 | 16 | 5 |
| Raab II | 9 | 1 | 6 | 20 | 14 | 7 |
| Raab III | 10 | — | 4 | 19 | 14 | 5 |
| Gorbach I | 10 | — | 4 | 16 | 12 | 4 |
| Gorbach II | 10 | — | 6 | 19 | 12 | 7 |
| Klaus I | 10 | — | 6 | 19 | 13 | 6 |
| Klaus II | 11 | — | 6 | 26 | 18 | 10 |
| Kreisky I | 12 | — | 2 | 17 | 15 | 2 |
| Kreisky II | 13 | — | 4 | 20 | 16 | 4 |
| Kreisky III | 13 | — | 4 | 23 | 18 | 7 |
| Kreisky IV | 13 | — | 9 | 28 | 18 | 10 |
| Sinowatz | 14 | 1 | 8 | 32 | 24 | 8 |
| Vranitzky I | 14 | 1 | 6 | 22 | 16 | 6 |

government. Since the return to a coalition government in 1983, both intra- and inter-party preparatory meetings are held. The length of cabinet meetings naturally varies greatly, but even if the preparatory meetings of single-party cabinets and of the more recent coalition governments are included, they rarely exceed two or three hours.

## 3 CABINET LIFE

As a rule the results of general elections decide whether a single-party government or a coalition government will be formed. In the latter case the nature of that coalition is decided only after the election in inter-party negotiations. So far, the strongest party in parliament has never been excluded from government and has therefore always been able to nominate the Chancellor.

According to the Constitution, the Federal President appoints the ministers and secretaries of state purely on the basis of a proposal of the Chancellor. In practice, however, the Chancellor's power of nomination is restricted, as one of the principles of Austrian coalition government is that each party has full autonomy in the selection of its cabinet members. Thus, for this purpose at least, the Vice Chancellor is a second Chancellor. Both, however, are also limited in their discretion by intra-party realities. All parties include factions which must be represented in the cabinet, such as the trade unionists within the Social Democratic Party, the three Leagues within the People's Party and the national and liberal wings within the Freedom Party.

Additionally, important regions which are particular strongholds of individual parties will have to be represented in government. The factions lay claim to particular portfolios. Thus, for instance, trade unionists normally take the Ministry of Social Affairs, the Farmers' League the Ministry of Agriculture and the Business League the Ministry of Trade and Commerce. The factions may either nominate one of their representatives for a given department, or the Chancellor himself (and Vice Chancellor) may nominate a minister from the corresponding faction. However, nowadays Chancellors (and Vice-Chancellors) seem to have greater room for manoeuvre with respect to the selection of ministers. This is partly as a result of the seventeen years of single-party government when the power of the party chairman was considerably increased.

In nearly all cabinets one can distinguish three types of ministers – politicians, politically-based experts and independent experts.

Politicians are those members of the cabinet who are appointed because of their position in the party. If one uses membership of the national party executive as an indicator, politicians constituted 27 per cent of all appointments between 1945 and 1987 (Müller and Philipp, 1987). Independent experts are the smallest group, being only twelve (about 7 per cent) during the same period. This type of minister is appointed to 'neutralise' politically sensitive portfolios in coalition governments (such as the Ministry of Justice) or to indicate a non-partisan approach (in particular in foreign policy, in single-party cabinets).

As a rule, both the cabinet and the cabinet members are given room for manoeuvre by the party outside parliament in the policy field. Ministers monopolise policy-making: they must be careful, however, not to run against the interests of the factions and the important component organisations of the parties. Moreover, the most important political matters are discussed in the party executives and/or negotiated between coalition parties. But these discussions and negotiations are usually prepared by proposals which comes from the appropriate government departments.

The parliamentary parties only play a marginal part in framing political objectives and in decision-making. This is particularly the case in the Socialist Party, less so in the People's Party and least of all in the Freedom Party. By and large parliamentary parties are seen primarily as machines whose *raison d'être* is to implement the will of the party or the government. This holds particularly true for single-party governments. In coalition governments MPs (who might be ministers in single-party governments) may act as negotiators for their parties with ministers of the other party. The parliamentary parties are disciplined; in virtually every case they follow the suggestions made by the intra-party decision-making machinery. MPs who nonetheless wish to break party discipline do so by absenting themselves from the chamber rather than by voting against their party (Fischer, 1974). The single-party governments of the People's and Socialist parties could rely respectively on a parliamentary majority of not more than five seats (out of a total of 165) and three or seven seats (out of 183). Yet these cabinets completed their term without ever facing a parliamentary defeat. The parties in parliament hardly constitute a problem for the government.

**Coordination**

The coordination of cabinet work is achieved in a number of ways. The fact that decisions in cabinet have to be unanimous constitutes an important element. Ministers will therefore avoid openly opposing the policies of their cabinet colleagues. Consensus in cabinet is also strengthened by more positive forms of coordination. A formal and permanent element is the procedure of consultation (*Begutachtungsverfahren*). Draft bills of individual departments are sent to other ministries (as well as to a variety of interest groups and administrative units), which comment on it and may recommend or demand revisions (Fischer, 1972). These comments are usually taken into account when preparing the final draft of the bill. Moreover, coordination is often necessary during the implementation phase. This is achieved by what is known as an 'accord', that is to say by introducing a clause (*Einvernehmens-Klausel*) which states that the ministers must agree on the administrative decisions to be taken (Barfuss, 1968).

Coexisting alongside this framework there are many informal bilateral contacts between ministers concerned. These contacts may occur at the request of these ministers or, occasionally, of the Chancellor. Issues which are prominent on the political agenda are often coordinated, not to say decided, by the Chancellor himself. Policies which require additional financial resources are coordinated by the Minister of Finance. When conflicts between ministers arise the Chancellor may act as an arbiter, though less so if the conflict occurs on party lines in coalition cabinets. In such cases the matter is often removed from the cabinet context and dealt with by inter-party negotiations.

. A more formal means of cabinet coordination is constituted by cabinet committees, but there is little available information regarding them. Since 1945, some committees have been established on a permanent or near-permanent basis, but most of them have been created *ad hoc* in connection with a particular problem. If a similar question arises at a later date, the same or a similar committee may be appointed (Welan and Neisser, 1971). In all cases, however, the final decision rests formally with the cabinet itself.

Committees may serve different purposes. They may be set up to deal with a problem; but a parallel committee composed of civil servants is then usually established to work along the same lines. It will deal with the technical aspects of the question and thus prepare the political decision, which has to be taken by the cabinet committee itself. Cabinet committees may also be involved if the civil servants do not manage to overcome their differences. The success and duration of committees varies. Some will come up with a solution after a few weeks, while others work for years without any apparent result. Finally, some committees are set up to block, but in a polite manner, a policy initiative of a cabinet member. Although the proposal is not rejected outright, no action will be taken on the matter.

The work – and the successes and failures – of cabinet committees gives a measure of the activities of the government as well as of the government's problem solving capacity. This state of affairs is best illustrated by the developments which occurred during the Grand Coalition period (up to 1966): as immobilism and the inability to act increased, the number of committees did likewise. One could usually agree to set up a committee, but one could not achieve any solution afterwards.

In the Austrian governmental system the 'spoils system' is restricted to the position of ministers and secretaries of state. Civil servants remain in their posts, regardless of whatever cabinet is in office. Ministers can appoint a few personal secretaries to the departments which they control, but these have to rely on the permanent bureaucracy. The very high degree of party organisation among civil servants means that ministers often have to cooperate with officials belonging to a different party. As a matter of fact, bureaucratic rules are likely to constitute a bigger test of the loyalty of civil servants to ministers than party affiliation, especially when it comes to ministers who are anxious to innovate (Neisser, 1974).

The relationship between ministers and their parliamentary parties poses fewer problems since these parliamentary parties have, as we have seen, a limited impact. Although ministers attend meetings of the parliamentary groups on a regular basis, this is more to inform members about proposed policies than to convince them of their content. Ministers do, however, try to help MPs with respect to their individual activities.

In a political system which has been frequently labelled corporatist (Gerlich, Grande and Müller, 1985), the relationship between cabinet members and interest groups is often of central importance. As mentioned above, in many cases interest groups play some part in the selection of ministers. These cabinet members then have a double role: they must put forward the views of the groups which they represent in the government and mobilise the support of these interest groups for the government's policy. Ministers who do not have such a background also try to establish and maintain good relations with the interest groups which are relevant to the activities of their department. In Austria, good contacts of this type is generally seen as a prerequisite for becoming a successful minister.

No other relationship of the cabinet has changed as much over the last twenty years as the relationship with the mass media (Müller, 1983). Ministers are markedly more oriented towards their public image than in the past. The number of press conferences and other media events has multiplied and the personal staff of ministers regularly includes press secretaries. The question of media performance is now a particularly relevant consideration when selecting a minister, while the political and even the private behaviour of ministers is scrutinised by investigative journalism. Indeed, a number of ministers were dismissed from the cabinet since the late 1960s as a result of misconduct brought to light by the press.

## 4 CABINET DECISION-MAKING

What takes place before the cabinet meeting has, as we saw, an enormous impact on the (formal) decision-making which takes place there. Only those topics which are expected by the minister concerned to be acceptable to the cabinet are placed, as a rule, on the agenda. All cabinet members receive the agenda and the proposals of their colleagues in advance. They, their civil servants or the members of their personal staff can therefore usually give detailed consideration to the proposals of other ministers. Specifically, they can find out whether queries which have been made (for instance during the formalised process of consultation) have been taken into consideration in preparing the final bill.

In a country with a strongly legalistic political culture, such as Austria, the cabinet is confronted with a huge amount of purely formal or routine matters. These matters take little time as they are not discussed during the meeting and are accepted on the nod. Attention is paid only to policy matters, and on these the cabinet is informed in some detail. But, even here, as long as the proposals do not create difficulties with other ministers the government member concerned has substantial room for manoeuvre. The cabinet is then only truly concerned with highly conflictual matters, though this does not mean that the principal decisions are taken by the cabinet as such.

Since the beginning of the Second Republic in 1945, this type of decision-making has tended to be shifted to smaller bodies: the Political Cabinet Council in 1945, the coalition committee during the period of the first Grand Coalition, very narrow party circles during the period of single-party governments (1966–1983) and small inter-party bodies in the post-1983 coalitions. Yet the technical preparation remains within the province of the individual departments, while the final stages are in the cabinet's province. Moreover, in the 1980s, the cabinet has acquired greater autonomy, in part because one of the major issues has been to reduce the budget deficit, which is an unpopular exercise and has naturally been left to the cabinet by all those who were or might have been concerned.

The Austrian cabinet thus manages to blend successfully the formal and the informal, leadership and consultation, political and technical requirements. By and large, this has been possible because of the relatively limited number of deep conflicts in the society itself. Yet it is a testimony to the problem-solving capacity of post-World War Two Austria that the necessary adjustments have been made and, above all, that the system has been able to develop types of arrangements which have ensured that difficulties were easily surmounted. The long period of the Grand Coalition has surely played a major part in allowing these informal developments to take place and to be accepted by all. As a result the Austrian cabinet system has acquired a specific character – it is almost an 'ideal-type' at the opposite extreme of the British or Irish system.

## Notes

1. Secretaries of State are considered to be auxiliaries of the ministers. They are not members of the cabinet but can be present at its meetings. They are entitled to stand in for their ministers in parliamentary meetings. In coalition governments they usually come from the other party and serve as instruments of control and 'internal opposition'.
2. It is interesting to note that, if no other regulation applies, the cabinet as a whole continues to exercise those powers which during the monarchy were formally reserved to the Emperor (Adamovich, 1971, 264).
3. Some legal scholars maintain that such a power is self evident and therefore needs no explicit regulation (Welan and Neisser, 1971, 122).
4. To define a cabinet the criteria 'same Chancellor', 'same party composition' and 'between parliamentary elections' were used.
5. Note that the Chancellor and Vice Chancellor have to be added to the number of ministers (during two periods, 1966 to 1968 and 1983 to 1987 a departmental minister also served as Vice Chancellor, however). Non-departmental ministers were: three quasi-Vice Chancellors in the provisional state government of 1945, one minister within the Chancellery from 1945 to 1959, as well as a minister for the civil service within the Chancellor's Office since 1983.

# 9 Federal Republic of Germany: A System of Chancellor Government

Ferdinand Müller-Rommel

## 1 CABINET SETTING

It was not before the early nineteenth century that the first Council of Ministers was established in Germany. Due to personal problems in coordinating governmental policy, the King of Prussia appointed a group of equally-ranked Ministers to discuss policy and solve inter-departmental disputes. Although the various Ministers (who formed the first cabinet) were largely independent of one another, they remained exclusively the Ministers of the Crown. They had direct access to the King and jointly advised the monarch in his policy decision-making.

This collegial principle (later referred to as the *Kabinetssprinzip*) changed with the appointment of a Minister who was solely responsible for 'the acts of the crown'. This Minister took on the role of an administrator heading the entire government. In 1867 an Imperial Chancellery was established. According to the Constitution the Chancellor was alone responsible for the policy of the empire (later referred to as the *Kanzlerprinzip*). Ministers were his administrative subordinates and cabinet no longer existed.

The situation changed somewhat with the Weimar Constitution. A cabinet was re-established and Ministers (now politicians rather than bureaucrats!) were given some autonomy in conducting departmental policy (later referred to as the *Ressortprinzip*). However, the Chancellor's primacy remained intact. He was responsible for national policy and for the appointment and dismissal of ministers. On the other hand, the Weimar Constitution gave the President of the Republic the power to appoint or dismiss the Chancellor. If a Chancellor had to deal with too many parties in Parliament and could not find a majority to vote for a government, the President could nominate a new Chancellor. This constitutional regulation allowed President Hindenburg to appoint Hitler as a Chancellor in 1933.

The Constitution of the Federal Republic of Germany adopted most of the Weimar principles with two major differences: the government was no longer dependent upon the power of the President and the link between Parliament and government was strengthened, so that the parliamentary majority has the power to dismiss a Chancellor by a so-called 'positive vote of no confidence' (*Konstruktives Mißtrauensvotum*). The executive power in Germany is shared between the Chancellor (*Kanzlerprinzip*), the cabinet government (*Kabinettsprinzip*) and the Ministers (*Ressortprinzip*). Thus the power structure in the Federal Republic is dispersed rather than hierarchically arranged. Article 65 of the Bonn Constitution begins:

> The Chancellor determines and bears responsibility for the general policy of the government. Within this policy, each Minister conducts the affairs of his department independently under his own responsibility. The government decides on differences of opinion between Ministers. The Chancellor conducts the business of the government in accordance with the rules of procedure adopted by it and approved by the President.

The government in the Federal Republic is drawn from a parliamentary majority. Ministers are politicians, not bureaucrats. They are appointed, and can be dismissed, by the Chancellor. With the exception of the Finance Minister all other ministers have equal rights in cabinet meetings (Braunthal, 1972; Dyson, 1978). The Finance Minister is in a superior position. 'He has the power to veto all decisions of financial importance, including all legislative proposals with implications for public spending, provided the Chancellor sides him' (Mayntz, 1980).

The Chancellor plays a dominant role in cabinet decision-making, in part because of his constitutional power (Ridley, 1966). He is in charge of ministerial appointments, organises the executive, and formulates general policy guidelines. He also supervises the services of the Press Office and of the Federal Intelligence Service. Besides these formal tasks the Chancellor has the power to set priorities among policy goals and to formulate directives for policy implementation. To carry out both policy aims and administrative tasks the Chancellor is aided by the Chancellor's Office, presently composed of about 300 staff.

The post-war cabinets in the Federal Republic were composed of majority coalitions. Only in 1963 and in 1982, when the Ministers of the Liberal Party withdraw from office (and consequently from cabinet), did the Federal Republic have a minority government for one month. Because of a general fear of minority coalitions strongly anchored in the

well as do not have very much on
the Netherlands, so I hope these books will
be of some interest to you.

*With the Compliments of*

P.P. Denise
*Librarian*

INSTITUTE OF PUBLIC ADMINISTRATION
57-61 Lansdowne Road, Dublin 4, Ireland. Telephone: 01 - 6686233 Fax: 01 - 6689135

TABLE 9.1   Cabinets in the Federal Republic of Germany: 1949–1987

| Chancellor | Date in | Chancellor Party | Cabinet Composition | Duration in days by cabinet | by Chancellor |
|---|---|---|---|---|---|
| Adenauer | 15.09.49 | CDU | CDU CSU FDP DP | 1120 | |
| Adenauer | 09.10.53 | CDU | CDU CSU FDP BHE DP other | 1480 | |
| Adenauer | 29.10.57 | CDU | CDU CSU DP | 1479 | |
| Adenauer | 17.11.61 | CDU | CDU CSU FDP | 728 | 4807 |
| Erhard | 16.10.63 | CDU | CDU CSU FDP | 734 | |
| Erhard | 20.10.65 | CDU | CDU CSU FDP | 406 | 1140 |
| Kiesinger | 01.12.66 | CDU | CDU CSU SPD | 1055 | 11055 |
| Brandt | 21.10.69 | SPD | SPD FDP other | 1149 | |
| Brandt | 14.12.72 | SPD | SPD FDP | 518 | 1167 |
| Schmidt | 16.05.74 | SPD | SPD FDP | 942 | |
| Schmidt | 15.12.76 | SPD | SPD FDP | 1420 | |
| Schmidt | 05.11.80 | SPD | SPD FDP | 694 | 3065 |
| Kohl | 01.10.82 | CDU | CDU CSU FDP | 180 | |
| Kohl | 29.03.83 | CDU | CDU CSU FDP | 1397 | |
| Kohl | 25.01.87 | CDU | CDU CSU FDP | in office | 1157 |

BHE = Block der Heimatvertriebenen und Entrechteten
CDU = Christlich Demokratische Union Deutschland
CSU = Christlich-Soziale Partei
DP = Deutsche Partei
FDP = Freie Demokratische Partei
SPD = Sozialdemokratische Partei Deutschlands

political culture, West German political parties try to coalesce with their immediate neighbours (for example, CDU with CSU) and add other adjacent parties until a majority government is formed. In post-war Germany, there were five different types of majority cabinet systems (see Table 9.1):

● Multi-party coalition cabinet (1949–1957)
● three party coalition cabinet (1961–1966 and 1982–1987)
● dominant coalition cabinet (1957–1961)
● grand coalition cabinet (1966–1969)
● two party coalition cabinet (1969–1982)

## 2  CABINET STRUCTURE

The formal structure and the political composition of the centre of government in the Federal Republic can at best be described by examining cabinet size and party strength in cabinet, the preparation of cabinet proposals and the professional experience and duration of Ministers.

### Cabinet size and party strength in cabinet

Since 1949 West Germany has had fourteen cabinets. Besides the Chancellor, all Ministers together with the State and Parliamentary Secretaries to the Chancellor's Office, and the Federal Press Office, belong to the cabinet. In addition the Chief of the President's Office, the Personal Secretary of the Chancellor, and the keeper of the minutes attend cabinet meetings. In the absence of the relevant Minister, the Parliamentary State Secretary will participate in cabinet meetings. Departmental State Secretaries and Heads of Divisions at the Chancellor's Office (*Abteilungsleiter*) participate by invitation. Only the Chancellor and the Ministers are entitled to vote on policy decisions.

The size of the cabinet has varied over the years. During the consolidation period it was rather low and increased markedly in the 1960s. In 1969 Chancellor Brandt decreased the number of cabinet positions but increased the number of posts of State and Parliamentary Secretaries. While the Secretary of State – as a career civil servant – is responsible for the continuity of the departmental administration, the Parliamentary Secretary – as a Member of Parliament – is concerned

TABLE 9.2  Cabinet size in Federal Republic of Germany

| Chancellor<br>Party<br>Period | Adenauer<br>CDU<br>49–63 | | | | Erhard<br>CDU<br>63–66 | | Kiesinger<br>CDU<br>66–69 | Brandt<br>SPD<br>69–74 | | Schmidt<br>SPD<br>74–82 | | | Kohl<br>CDU<br>82–87 | |
|---|---|---|---|---|---|---|---|---|---|---|---|---|---|---|
| Legislature | I<br>49–53 | II<br>53–57 | III<br>57–61 | IV<br>61–63 | IVa<br>63–65 | V<br>65–66 | Va<br>66–69 | VI<br>69–72 | VII<br>72–74 | VIIa<br>74–76 | VIII<br>76–80 | IX<br>80–82 | IXa<br>82–83 | X<br>83–87 |
| Ministries (1) | 14 | 18 | 17 | 20 | 22 | 21 | 19 | 15 | 17 | 15 | 15 | 16 | 16 | 17 |
| Chancellor's office: secretaries of state | 1 | 1 | 2 | 3 | 3 | 3 | 3 | 2 | 2 | 4 | 4 | 4 | 4 | 4 |
| parliamentary secretaries | — | — | — | — | — | — | — | — | — | — | — | — | — | — |
| Total cabinet | 15 | 19 | 19 | 23 | 25 | 24 | 23 | 18 | 20 | 20 | 20 | 21 | 23 | 24 |

NOTE:
(1)  The Chancellor is excluded; add 'one' to the total cabinet size when including the Chancellor.

with relations and communications between the ministries on the one hand and Parliament and party groups on the other. The Parliamentary Secretary is expected to keep closer contacts with the various party groups than the Minister himself.

Although the number of ministries has been fairly stable over more than ten legislatures, the total number of persons who have significant influence on cabinet decision-making has increased (see Table 9.2). Interestingly enough, since 1969, the size of the administrative and top-political elite of ministries has tended to be twice as large as that of cabinet. This suggests two things. First, the political influence of top civil servants (*Staatssekretäre*) and of top parliamentary party elite (*Parlamentarische Staatssekretäre*) has grown, presumably because of the increasing number of activities of the modern state and the declining role of Parliament. Second, cabinet decision-making has become increasingly dependent on a consensual bargaining process of a political-administrative character. To constantly integrate the demands of bureaucrats (that is, will a policy be acceptable?) seems to be one of the most important problems a contemporary German cabinet has to deal with.

The number and the relative strength of parties in cabinet is another central aspect in the study of cabinet government. A government exclusively composed of one party is more likely to be 'hierarchical' or 'oligarchical' than collective.

In West Germany, the Liberal Party has been longest in government. The FDP has taken part in 31 of the 38 years of post-war cabinet government. This is despite the fact that the numerical strength of party representation was low in relation to that of the Christian Democrats, followed by the Social Democrats.

It has often been claimed that the Schmidt cabinet was similar to the Adenauer cabinet in that both were very hierarchical. Although the personality of the Chancellor might partially explain this phenomenon, the structural conditions of party strength in the cabinet under both Chancellors should also be considered (see Table 9.3). Helmut Schmidt and Konrad Adenauer (as well as Willy Brandt in his first cabinet) had a comfortable party majority in the cabinet, while Helmut Kohl, Ludwig Erhard and in particular Kurt Georg Kiesinger have presided over cabinets in which the strength of their party was rather low. Consequently, the decision-making process under those Chancellors needed to be more collective as opposed to hierarchical or oligarchical as was the case under Adenauer, Schmidt or Brandt.

## TABLE 9.3  Party strength in cabinet (%) (1)

| Chancellor | Adenauer | | | | Erhard Kiesinger | | | Brandt | | Schmidt | | | Kohl | | Mean | |
|---|---|---|---|---|---|---|---|---|---|---|---|---|---|---|---|---|
| Party Period | CDU 49–63 | | | | CDU 63–66 | CDU 66–69 | | SPD 69–74 | | SPD 74–82 | | | CDU 82–87 | | | % |
| Legislature | I 49–53 | II 53–57 | III 57–61 | IV 61–63 | IVa 63–65 | V 65–66 | Va 66–69 | VI 69–72 | VII 72–74 | VIIa 74–76 | VIII 76–80 | IX 80–82 | IXa 82–83 | X 83–87 | | |
| CDU | 36 | 55 | 88 | 65 | 59 | 62 | 42 | 0 | 0 | 0 | 0 | 0 | 50 | 53 | 37 | 25 |
| CSU | 21 | 21 | 12 | 20 | 18 | 19 | 10 | 0 | 0 | 0 | 0 | 0 | 25 | 29 | 14 | 25 |
| SPD | 0 | 0 | 0 | 0 | 0 | 0 | 48 | 80 | 71 | 73 | 73 | 75 | 0 | 0 | 28 | 16 |
| FDP | 29 | 18 | 0 | 15 | 23 | 19 | 0 | 20 | 29 | 27 | 27 | 25 | 25 | 18 | 20 | 31 |
| Other | 14 | 6 | 0 | 0 | 0 | 0 | 0 | 0 | 0 | 0 | 0 | 0 | 0 | 0 | 1 | 8 |
| total ministries | 14 | 18 | 17 | 20 | 22 | 21 | 19 | 15 | 17 | 15 | 15 | 16 | 16 | 17 | 242 | |

(1) Party strength in cabinet measured by average percentage of seats which a party had in cabinet.

**Preparation of cabinet proposals**

Cabinet decisions may be prepared in three different ways – politically, administratively or in a hybrid fashion. The *political way* for the preparation of proposals runs through bilateral communications between the Chancellor and various Ministers who may come from different parties. Much reliance is placed on these informal, *ad hoc* meetings of Ministers and the Chancellor, where proposals are discussed and then sent to the officials of the departments for implementation. The informal meetings may be only between the Chancellor and one Minister. However, most take place between the Chancellor, some of his personal advisers and one or two Ministers. Under the Schmidt government a small group of four executive leaders (the *Kleeblatt*) met frequently to prepare policy proposals. During the same period the Liberal cabinet members regularly had breakfast together before each cabinet meeting.

The *administrative way* involves communications between civil servants at the Chancellor's Office and those in departmental ministries to discuss policy proposals. The agenda of cabinet meetings is supervised by the Chancellor's Office. It sets dates and deadlines for the submission of proposals from different departmental ministries. Over the last 38 years the Office has become a key institution for the Chancellor. In the early 1950s the Chancellor's Office was purely responsible for the security of Adenauer. In the 1960s it developed into a letter box for passing proposals to the cabinet. Under *Brandt*, the office became an institutional watchdog over the ministries and a clearing house for bills submitted by ministries to cabinet (Dyson, 1974).

Today, the office supplies the Chancellor 'with advice and information for the consideration of policy issues, and link him with Ministers and their departments' (Johnson, 1983). In general, the Chancellor's Office had a mjaor part to play in structuring cabinet decisions along the Chancellor's line. However, the Office is by no means a Cabinet Secretariat: the cabinet as such is without an administrative infrastructure.

Although Ministers are free to initiate policy proposals, they depend on cabinet approval for their implementation. But while cabinet may reject ministerial proposals, it cannot 'give orders' in the sphere of ministerial jurisdiction. Civil servants from the Chancellor's Office and from the ministries bring together facts and knowledge about particular proposals and try to formulate compromises. Usually the agreement among civil servants is accepted by the Minister and the Chancellor and submitted for cabinet approval. As a result, new views on particular issues seldom emerge in the cabinet meeting.

The *hybrid way* is through cabinet committees. Although these are formally chaired by the Chancellor, they are often taken over by the Minister responsible for the issue under discussion. Sometimes, the Minister sends a deputy who is often a senior civil servant from the department. In contrast to England, cabinet committees do not play an important role in Germany. In fact, one should not refer to a 'system of cabinet committees' in the Federal Republic, as the cabinet makes only limited use of committees as decision-taking and coordinating bodies. While in the mid-1960s there were only two cabinet committees in operation (Economics and Defence), a few *ad hoc* committees for special subjects emerged in the late 1970s. For the period of 1982–1985 Mackie and Hogwood found 16 cabinet committees in the Federal Republic (1985). These committees only met occasionally, however, and played no major role in cabinet decision-making.

### Professional experience and duration of Ministers

In so far as cabinet decisions matter, cabinet members do, too. Studies on the social composition of cabinets in the Federal Republic from 1945 to 1987 found that the majority of the Council of Ministers were male and university-educated, and had been lawyers before entering Parliament – particularly in CDU and FDP governments (Armingeon, 1986; Müller-Rommel and Sprengel, 1986). Although the social background of Ministers illustrates the social conditions of the political selection process, it is not relevant to the analysis of decision-making in cabinet. In this respect it seems more appropriate to identify the political, technical and managerial experience and expertise of cabinet members.

One might reasonably assume that Ministers who have (as Member of Parliament) specialised in certain policy fields may well be inclined to 'look after' these issues in cabinet. In addition, Ministers who are former chairmen of their party's or parliamentary faction's committees are more competent to deal with certain issues than Ministers without 'committee experiences'. Furthermore, those Ministers in the Federal Republic who have served as junior ministers (*Parlamentarische Staatssekretäre*) had more managerial training than the others (Müller-Rommel, 1981).

In the Federal Republic we can identify four types of cabinet members with partially different experiences:

*the amateur*: who has neither the technical knowledge about the policies discussed in his ministry, nor has the long-lasting experiences in so-called parliamentary management.

*the administrative professional*: who has either parliamentary or minis-terial experience. This group includes the cabinet members who are former chairmen of party or parliamentary committees. Sometimes they were even former Parliamentary Secretaries or departmental Secretaries of State.

*the technical professional*: who knows the subject of his ministry because of his occupational background.

*the administrative and technical professional*: who has expertise in both respects.

Table 9.4 shows that in the SPD/FDP coalition cabinets tended to be administrative and technical, whereas since 1982 and before 1969 Christian Democratic cabinets were composed of administrative profes-sionals. In the Brandt and Schmidt era between 20 to 30 per cent of Ministers had simultaneously administrative and technical experience. Cabinets from 1969–1982 were indeed composed of Ministers with multiple experience. This might explain why governing under Brandt and Schmidt was on the one hand easy (because of the high competence of most Ministers), and on the other politically more difficult and sensitive (because of the political skills of most Ministers). In spite of differences among post-war cabinets, the administrative professional has been the dominant type among Ministers in the Federal Republic.

Much research has been conducted on the duration of Ministers in cabinet (Blondel, 1985). It has been argued that cabinet systems with long-standing Ministers (long duration of Ministers) would have a pronounced 'hierarchical' or 'oligarchical' structure, whereas systems in which the duration of Ministers is low tend to be more 'collective' in character. In the Federal Republic there were 242 ministerial positions across the 14 legislatures (1949–1987). Overall, 122 different individuals occupied a ministerial position at one time or another – and occasionally more than once. With the exception of the 1961–1963 Adenauer cabinet, the duration of Ministers increased with the duration of the Chancellors in office. (Müller-Rommel, 1988). This finding indicates that cabinet under one Chancellor tends to move from a 'collective' to a 'hierarchical' or 'oligarchical' structure.

TABLE 9.4   Professional experience of ministers (%) prior to first ministerial post

|  | Adenauer | Erhard | Kiesinger | Brandt | Schmidt | Kohl | Mean |
|---|---|---|---|---|---|---|---|
| Political amateur | 32 | 10 | 28 | 14 | 9 | 14 | 18 |
| Administrative professional | 40 | 66 | 52 | 42 | 43 | 53 | 49 |
| technical professional | 18 | 9 | 16 | 24 | 14 | 9 | 15 |
| administrative and technical professional | 10 | 15 | 4 | 20 | 34 | 24 | 18 |
| Total (1) | 88 | 46 | 25 | 35 | 60 | 37 |  |

(1) Total number of ministers in cabinet for more than three months (including multiple affiliations of ministers in different legislatures). For more details on the distribution of ministers' professions in the post-war legislatures, see Müller-Rommel (1988).

## 3   CABINET LIFE

### The leadership style of the Chancellor

As was pointed out earlier, the Chancellor plays an important role in cabinet government. According to the Constitution the Chancellor *determines* – among other things – the general policy of the Federal Republic. Although the authority to formulate policy guidelines has been used by all Chancellors, most of them have devoted themselves to some selective policy fields. Adenauer and Brandt had a special interest in foreign policy, the first directed to the West and the second to the Eastern bloc. Erhard and Schmidt had a similar interest in economic questions.

The way in which the six Federal Chancellors have implemented policy has depended upon both their individual leadership style and the specific institutional setting within which they operated. Naturally, both factors are strongly interrelated. The leadership style of a Chancellor is determined by the operating system of the cabinet and by the support he receives from his party, his parliamentary group, his coalition partner(s) and by his public image. The latter is particularly important for *coming* to office, while support from the party and coalition partners is more significant for *staying* in office (von Beyme, 1983).

Interestingly enough, intra-party opposition or opposition from the coalition partner was the initial reason for the resignation of *all* Federal Chancellors.

## Konrad Adenauer

Since the operating system of cabinet has changed over time, the leadership styles of the various Chancellors has differed markedly. Adenauer has often been labelled the strongest Chancellor of the Federal Republic (Küpper, 1985). He used his institutional powers to the full and at times demonstrated an authoritarian tendency. He viewed his Ministers as legal subordinates who were asked to manage their departments along the Chancellor's broad policy lines. Often Adenauer decided on policy issues himself without even consulting the cabinet, which he regarded as a board of experts who should assist him only at his request. In addition, he received political advice from independent research committees which he had established for his personal use. Every time Adenauer presented bills to cabinet, he would have the weight of the independent research committees on his side.

Adenauer exercised his power cleverly and tactically. On the one hand he claimed autonomy in foreign policy, and on the other he asked his parliamentary party and the heads of the Federal Government to deal with domestic policy issues. Adenauer, together with his politically important personal adviser Globke, also succeeded in recruiting those civil service administrators who strongly supported the Chancellor's policy. In doing so, Adenauer was surrounded by loyal followers among Ministers and civil servants for over ten years. He created a governmental nucleus within which there was hardly any opposition against his policy goals.

## Ludwig Erhard

Adenauer's immediate successor, Ludwig Erhard, did not prove to be a strong Chancellor.

Due to the fact that Adenauer remained the party leader and openly proclaimed that Erhard was less able than himself, Erhard was unable to develop a clear leadership style. He was more collegially-minded and consulted the Council of Ministers more often on policy matters. However, he also gave the public the impression of being unable to understand practical politics. He experienced problems in leading the cabinet, in formulating clear policies, in integrating the administration for the preparation of policy proposals and in using the media for his own purposes. He was consequently unable to deal with the economic recession of the early 1960s (a rather tragic outcome as he had been very successful as Minister of Economics under Adenauer).

## Kurt Georg Kiesinger

The third CDU Chancellor, Kurt Georg Kiesinger, who formed the 'grand coalition', could not – for a number of institutional and political reasons – establish an efficient leadership style.

First, the weight of the Chancellor's party in cabinet was low. It was the first time that the CDU had to share power with another large party in cabinet, and Kiesinger often had to negotiate between the two rival parties in order to maintain the coalition. His aim was constantly to seek compromises and this partly explains why he could not develop a strong leadership style.

Second, with Willy Brandt and Karl Schiller the SPD had the Vice Chancellorship, the Foreign Office and the Ministry of Economics. Kiesinger had to deal with the fact that the former policy domains of the conservatives (foreign and economic affairs) were now in the hands of Social Democrats.

Third, the SPD displayed political competence in both fields: Willy Brandt proclaimed the *Ostpolitik* and Karl Schiller successfully managed to take the country out of the economic crisis.

Fourth, Kiesinger came to office by an external route. Prior to becoming Chancellor he was head of the regional government in Baden-Würtemberg. As such, he had no strong personal followers at the national party level.

Finally, the grand coalition created a pattern of policy-making that was characterised by less power within the cabinet and more political influence being held by small informal groups of politicians. At the time of the grand coalition, the political elites from both coalition parties met regularly as the *Kressbronner Kreis*, and became a more effective decision-making body than the Council of Ministers (Haungs, 1986).

## Willy Brandt

The leadership style of the first Social Democratic Chancellor, Willy Brandt, was different in his first and his second term in office. From 1969 to 1972 Brandt was seen as a strong, though non-authoritarian Chancellor.

From the very beginning he was primarily interested in foreign policy issues, especially with respect to Eastern Europe. He expected the relevant Ministers to look after domestic issues. In contrast to all CDU Chancellors, Brandt reached cabinet decisions in a more collective manner. However, after his political success in establishing *Ostpolitik* and after he was awarded the Nobel Peace Prize in 1971, Brandt was more and more accused of providing a weak leadership (*Führungs-schwäche*).

In Brandt's second term as a Chancellor (1972–1974) he was no longer willing or able to achieve political decisions in cabinet, and discussions in cabinet were viewed as 'increasingly pointless' (Mayntz, 1980). Some of his colleagues used the 'spy affair' (the fact that one of his close associates proved to be a spy) to force his resignation.

### Helmut Schmidt

Among these colleagues was Helmut Schmidt, Brandt's successor as Chancellor. Although the leadership style of Schmidt was similar to that of Adenauer, he achieved the reputation of being a short-term crisis manager rather than a politician concerned with the long-term.

Schmidt was well known for being frank both in cabinet and in public and for using all his influence to bring cabinet and Parliament into line with his policy goals (often without consulting other Ministers). He recruited Ministers who were loyal to him personally although they were sometimes ineffective. His leadership style in cabinet was pragmatic: he was always very well prepared for cabinet meetings and expected the same of his Ministers. He was willing to listen to arguments but expected his Ministers to agree with his conclusions. He has sometimes treated his cabinet in much the same way as an American President, while also using de Gaulle's tactic of threatening to resign unless the party followed his policy. It is widely accepted that Schmidt had by far the most effective leadership style since Adenauer (Paterson, 1981).

### Helmut Kohl

His successor, Helmut Kohl, is different from Schmidt in almost every way. His leadership style is based on decentralisation. His Ministers have greater opportunities to formulate their own policies and their own political image. Consequently, some cabinet members have had a better reputation in the public than the Chancellor himself.

Kohl is a generalist who is not very interested in the details, which most of his Ministers understand better than him. During cabinet meetings Ministers – rather than the Chancellor – pick out weak points and the implications of proposals. Kohl expects his Ministers to agree among themselves before they come to cabinet. In contrast to Schmidt, Kohl is markedly concerned with his party. He is still its leader and remains keenly aware of the need to bring to the top those politicians who would succeed him. Kohl is not a charismatic leader but he is close to public thinking (*volkstümlich*), which explains most of his success.

As a summary, Kohl and Schmidt might thus be labelled Chancellors with a 'policy managing style', while Brandt and Adenauer can be characterised as Chancellors with a 'policy innovating style'. Kiesinger and Erhard were only 'interim' Chancellors who did not supply significant political leadership.

## 4  CABINET DECISION-MAKING

The analysis of cabinet style usually gives rise to a dilemma. An exclusive concentration on formal aspects of decision-making may provide 'hard' facts, but the interpretation of these facts may well be difficult as the real working style of a cabinet can differ widely from what the formal provisions were intended to guarantee. As has frequently been pointed out, reliable quantitative indicators on cabinet decision-making in the Federal Republic are rare, and from a formal point of view perhaps impossible to discover.

Basically, cabinet work consists of discussions on current political matters and on policy proposals submitted by different ministries. Formally, these proposals must be approved by the cabinet before going before Parliament. In general, all important cabinet decisions are taken while Parliament is in session (when the cabinet meets once a week). In the parliamentary summer recess the cabinet meets only once or twice a month, depending on problems which have to be debated and the policy proposals to be approved.

In most cases, however, cabinet decisions on proposals are a mere formality, as these proposals are approved on the nod. This is mainly due to two reasons. Firstly, most proposals which appear on the cabinet agenda have already been agreed on, either through negotiations between civil servants in the Chancellor's Office and their colleagues in the departments, or by informal discussions between top executives and the Chancellor – as was mentioned earlier.

Second, cabinet Ministers in the Federal Republic enjoy a wide range of autonomy in decision-making which they do not wish to forego. In fact, 'the political system's capacity for active policy-making is largely a capacity of its ministerial bureaucracy' (Mayntz and Scharpf, 1975). Federal Ministers have to rely on the expert knowledge of their civil servants, who have to provide them with solid and lucid information. Because ministers are usually deemed to be successful or unsuccessful by the way they manage their departments, those who are respected (not only by civil servants but also by their fellow Ministers and by the Chancellor) are those who are able to handle their departments and see to it that the cabinet approves the policy proposals and financial requests formulated by their departments. To achieve consensus in cabinet, however, every Minister has to ensure that there is inter-departmental coordination prior to cabinet meetings, especially when policy issues affect more than one department.

Consequently, in cabinet meetings Ministers avoid raising matters which have not been initiated by, or which can affect, their own department. All Ministers have a vested interest in not interfering with, or in not criticizing, the proposals of fellow Ministers and in this way they protect their own autonomy. They can also expect colleagues to behave in the same way when proposals for their own department come to cabinet. Thus policy issues create conflicts among cabinet members only very rarely. In such cases the Chancellor usually formulates what he perceives to be the majority view. If no cabinet member opposes, the Chancellor's suggestion becomes the cabinet decision. Formal voting in cabinet is very rare.

To sum up, the cabinet of the Federal Republic cannot be defined as a 'working cabinet'. Basically, its role is limited to a final political check on the general lines of governmental policy. Decisions are approved, rather than made by, the cabinet. The role of the leader and the desire of Ministers to maintain the autonomy of their departments (and thus to achieve higher status in the government and in the nation) give the cabinet as such, on the whole, a rather low profile. It is more a loose board of managers than the kind of political committee which was once felt to epitomise the nature of government in the parliamentary system.

# 10 Denmark

## Tove Lise Schou

### 1 CABINET SETTING

Parliamentarism developed from a monarchical foundation, both historically and in the sense that the power of cabinet is based on the royal prerogative. The fact that the highest position in the State is hereditary in societies in which political authority derives directly or indirectly from elections is therefore not surprising.

In this respect, Denmark is not an exception. It is a parliamentary monarchy and the authority which the constitution formally gives to the King or Queen is exercised by ministers responsible to parliament. The King or Queen has few independent functions – he or she ensures continuity and is the symbol of the unity of the kingdom. The monarch is thus above politics and is consequently not politically responsible (the ministers being answerable for the conduct of the government). The Danish constitution states this explicitly.

The responsibility of the ministers is exercised through the formal requirement of the 'countersignature' – the signature of the monarch on bills or on governmental documents is valid only when one or more ministers have also signed. These ministers thereby become politically responsible. As a matter of fact, the 1964 Act on Ministerial Responsibility has extended this responsibility to all the ministers who participated in the decision, regardless of whether or not they signed the document.

The Danish constitution also states who is empowered to charge ministers and which court can try them. Before 1953 this power was held by a special court, the *Rigsret*, which consisted of the members of the Supreme Court and of the same number of members of the lower chamber elected by the Chamber itself. When the second chamber was abolished in 1953, the membership of the *Rigsret* stood at a maximum of fifteen members of the Supreme Court and of the same number of persons elected by the *Folketing*, the Danish parliament, on a party proportional basis but from outside its members. Appointment to the *Rigsret* is for six years. Because of its original composition, the *Rigsret* never had the influence of a second chamber in other constitutional monarchies and in the early period it could be expected to be in opposition to the majority of the parliament. It was therefore pointless for this majority to prosecute a minister in the *Rigsret*, as is shown by the analysis made by E. Rasmussen of attempts made in 1877.[1]

Since parliamentarism was fully established in Denmark in 1901, there have been only two cases of ministers prosecuted in the *Rigsret* – I.C. Christensen and S. Berg in 1909–1910. There were suggestions, both immediately after the Liberation in 1945 and in 1959–60, that the procedure might be used, although it was not. It might still play some part in the future, but it has lost its political importance. Its main function is now administrative and is related to the ministers' responsibility in running their departments, although administrative and political responsibilities cannot of course by fully separated.[2]

Both the Danish cabinet collectively and the ministers individually are politically responsible to the *Folketing*. According to the constitution, a minister must resign if there is a vote of no confidence in the *Folketing* against him or her. If there is a vote of no confidence against the Prime Minister, he or she demands the resignation of the cabinet unless a writ for an election is issued. A minister may have to resign and the cabinet still remain in office, but normally the Prime Minister declares that the cabinet supports the minister who is under attack and the collective responsibility of the government comes into play.

Previously, the cabinet would also resign if an important governmental proposal was rejected by the *Folketing* but, more recently, a new practice has emerged with the Schlüter four-party coalition of 1982 (the so-called 'four-leaf clover') composed of Conservatives, Agrarian Liberals, Centre Democrats and members of the Christian People's Party. Although the majority of the *Folketing* has opposed governmental policy on a number of occasions, the cabinet did not subsequently resign. This occurred in particular over foreign policy matters, and this state of affairs is reflected in the fact that there is often an asterix alongside the Danish position in documents of the European Community and of other international organisations. This indicates that the Danish government has had to make reservations.

Prime Minister Schlüter has stated that the composition of the *Folketing* is decided by the electorate and that it is the duty of the cabinet to conduct a foreign policy approved by the majority. In the opinion of the government, Denmark has such serious economic problems that it cannot afford frequent elections. The Prime Minister thus does not wish too often to use the right of dissolution of the four-year *Folketing*, despite the fact that the constitution gives him this power.

From 1950 to 1987 Denmark had 22 governments, as shown in Table

10.1. This relatively large number does not indicate real instability. To begin with, four changes of Social Democratic Prime Ministers occurred for reasons of death (H. Hedtoft and H.C. Hansen), illness (V. Kampmann) or for other personal reasons (J.O. Krag). In the last case, however, there was a political element as well. The referendum on Common Market membership, which had just taken place, had split the Social Democratic Party into two nearly equal groups (the majority of the General Workers' Union was against Market membership). It was felt that the unity of the party might be restored if the leader of the union, A. Jörgensen, became Prime Minister instead of J.O. Krag, who had been a strong advocate of membership. Overall, an element of continuity has been assured by the Social Democrats. Sixteen of the 22 governments were formed by their party alone or in coalition, and of the ten coalitions, five included the Social Democrats.


## 2  CABINET STRUCTURE

The Danish constitution gives the monarch the right to choose the ministers, but any government not acceptable to the majority of the *Folketing* would be short-lived. In practice, party leaders advise the King or Queen as to which of them should lead the process of cabinet formation, and the monarch acts on this advice. If the party leader who is asked first fails in the task another is called, the process being repeated until a government, is formed. Given the conditions of party politics in Denmark, the role of the monarch is not insignificant in the process of government formation.

Formal cooperation between monarch and ministers takes place in the State Council, the *Statsrad*, of which the heir to the throne is also a member when he or she comes of age. The King or Queen chairs the deliberations. This development stems from the long history of Danish governmental practice. In the very early period, Denmark had a mixture of hereditary and elective monarchy. The King was then only the first among a group of chiefs coming from various parts of the country, as stated in *Jyske Lov*. In 1282, King Erik Klipping had to sign a coronation charter which can be viewed as the first constitution of the kingdom, and a parliament was established. Coronation charters became more comprehensive in the course of time, and the one signed by Frederik III in 1648 gave the *Rigsrad* powers to oppose the King's decisions.

TABLE 10.1  Cabinets in Denmark: 1945–1987

| PM | Date in | Party Composition of Government |
|---|---|---|
| Buhl | 05.05.45 | Communist, Social Democrats, Venstre, Radikale, Venstre, Conservatives, Liberation Movement |
| Kristensen | 07.11.45 | Venstre |
| Hedtoft I | 13.11.47 | Social Democrats |
| Eriksen | 27.10.50 | Venstre, Conservatives |
| Hedtoft II | 30.09.53 | Social Democrats |
| Hansen I | 01.02.55 | Social Democrats |
| Hansen | 27.05.57 | Social Democrats, Radikale Venstre, Retsforbundet |
| Kampmann I | 19.02.60 | Social Democrats, Radikale Venstre, Retsforbundet |
| Kampmann II | 18.11.60 | Social Democrats, Retsforbundet |
| Krag I | 29.08.62 | Social Democrats, Retsforbundet |
| Krag II | 26.09.64 | Social Democrats |
| Baunsgaard | 01.02.68 | Venstre, Radikale Venstre, Conservatives |
| Krag III | 09.10.71 | Social Democrats |
| Jörgensen I | 05.10.72 | Social Democrats |
| Hartling | 17.12.73 | Venstre |
| Jörgensen II | 13.02.74 | Social Democrats |
| Jörgensen III | 30.08.78 | Social Democrats, Venstre |
| Jörgensen IV | 26.10.79 | Social Democrats |
| Schlüter | 10.09.82 | Venstre, Radikale Venstre, Conservatives, Christian |

Pressure for a strong central power designed to control the nobility came from the clergy and the citizens of Copenhagen. This led to the establishment of an absolute monarchy in 1660, the coronation charter being returned to Frederik III. The absolute monarchy was legalised by a *Kongelov*. During the period of the absolute monarchy which lasted until 1848, the King was assisted by a collective group of senior civil servants who had a considerable influence on the country's development. There were, for instance, reforms of the status of the peasantry which in effect amounted to a peaceful revolution (*Reventlow*).[3] But the country still had no representative organ, either of the mass of the population or even of the nobility.

The influence of the French Revolution of 1789 and of the principle of the separation of powers was gradually felt in the early part of the nineteenth century and, in 1831, Frederik VI set up advisory provincial assemblies of the Estates of the Realm on the basis of a North German model. The assemblies were introduced at the same time in the Duchies of Holstein and Schleswig and in Denmark.[4] Pressure for real representation continued to grow, however, and in 1848 Frederik VII formed a cabinet and called for elections for a Constituent Assembly.

The constitution of June 1849 set up a *Rigsdag* with two chambers – the *Folketing* and the *Landsting*. The second chamber was intended to be a conservative protection against the *Folketing*, which was expected to press for reforms. Amendments to the constitution were passed in 1866, and these strengthened the position of the *Landsting* in relation to the *Folketing*. In 1873, however, the majority of the *Folketing* insisted that the government be acceptable to the majority of the lower chamber and should in no way depend on either the *Landsting* or on the King. Christian IX maintained, on the other hand, that the King was free to choose his ministers. The bitter struggle which ensued ended only in 1901, when the principle of parliamentary government was eventually recognised *de facto*.

In 1919 this principle was formally recognised by the monarch although, in 1920, during the so-called 'Easter Crisis', Christian X dismissed the Zahle cabinet when the opposition demanded an election over the question of the return to Denmark of the areas to the South of the country which had been lost after World War One. The parliament did not insist. Parliamentarism was fully recognised by the constitutional amendment of 1953 which also abolished the second chamber. As a matter of fact, the constitution still has remnants of the absolute monarchy as it states that the monarch is the 'highest authority over all affairs of the kingdom' and that he or she 'exercises this authority through the ministers'.

Cabinet government has thus a long tradition in Denmark, although or perhaps because, it emerged gradually and informally; it can be said to date back to 1848 and has been able to adjust to changes in society. Responsiveness also characterised the reactions of the monarchs and in particular Frederik VII who, after much hesitation, decided to accept the decisions of the Constituent Assembly in 1849. This responsiveness accounts for the calm development of the Danish cabinet system. There has been scope for change within the existing framework. This no doubt contributed to the effective functioning of the system whose fundamental characteristics never had to be altered.

One of the first tasks of the first Danish cabinet of 1848 was to undertake a reform of the administration (this was implemented by the end of that year). Parliament had no say in the reform, but the cabinet was guided by public debates and newspaper criticisms. In fact, the issue had indeed already been discussed in the assemblies of the Estates of the Realm.[5] The old system, which was based on a collegial rather than a hierarchical structure, was criticised with respect to financial matters for which several units were responsible. It was almost impossible to obtain an overall picture of the country's finances as a result. The reform of the administration streamlined this aspect of the public sector, while the administrative structure was also rationalised in a general manner. Matters which were considered to be closely related to each other were henceforth placed under the responsibility of a single minister.

The King agreed that the cabinet formed in 1848 would be in charge of the government of the country. However, this cabinet was led by a Prime Minister who was not formally above his colleagues, as his task was only to chair cabinet meetings. There were no rules of procedure nor was there any listing of the matters pertaining to the cabinet. Questions were passed from the cabinet to the State Council according to the ministers' own judgement (for instance, if an issue was important or might cause conflict). Questions which affected more than one minister and even more those which involved overall governmental policy were also sent from the cabinet to the State Council.

In the State Council, decisions were normally made on a unanimity basis, although votes were occasionally taken. The ministers did not form a collective body, as at the time only those who had counter-signed a document were legally bound by it. In the course of time the State Council became increasingly formal, decisions being increasingly taken by the cabinet. However, it was never abolished and it stills meets under the chairmanship of the King or Queen.

During the period of the absolute monarchy, administrative authority was not delegated generally to one civil servant only. Decisions were taken by collegial bodies, although in the case of foreign affairs the department was ruled directly by the minister. The introduction of the ministerial system had the indirect effect of leading to the abolition of the collegial system and to its replacement by a strict hierarchy. Previously the King had been the superior of the civil servants and could be viewed as being as 'permanent' as them and in a sense above politics. The 1849 situation introduced a layer of political ministers between the civil servants and the monarch. It was then decided that the most senior civil servant in each department would be its *departementschef* (permanent secretary) who represented continuity while ministers often changed.

At the same time the central administration was divided into seven areas, an arrangement which was inspired from abroad. There were thus ministries covering Foreign Affairs, War, the Navy, Justice, Cultural Affairs, Finance and the Interior. This organisation remained essentially unchanged until the 1890s, and even after that date the reforms which were introduced took place within the framework of the 1848 arrangements.

The constitution of 1849 did not lay down rules about the powers of public bodies. In 1855, however, a 'common' constitution for Denmark and the Duchies stated that the King had the right to decide on the number of departments and on the allocation of functions among them. This rule is still in operation.[6] It was also stated in 1855 that there had to be a regular budget and that this budget could only be changed by Act of Parliament. But the *Folketing* could not affect the structure of the government, even by means of the budget. A conflict arose in 1872, but the opposition did not, in the end, try to limit the royal prerogative in this respect. With the advent of parliamentary government, however, a majority in the *Folketing* might of course have decided on any issue concerning the structure of the government if that issue was turned into a question of confidence (but this did not occur).[7] Until the 1890s the number of ministries remained unchanged, but the establishment of the Ministry of Public Works in 1894 started a process of expansion, and in the 1965–85 period there have been on average eighteen cabinet ministers.

Despite the many parties and the many coalitions, the political personnel has remained relatively stable. Only about 3 per cent of Danish ministers have been in office for less than a year, although 1 per cent was truly long-standing and were in the cabinet for ten years or more (all of whom belonged to the Social Democratic Party). The 'normal' ministerial career is thus appreciably less than a decade.

Moreover, cabinet-holders move fairly frequently from post to post, as Prime Ministers are prone to reshuffle their governments. Overall, Denmark is about average among Western European countries, both from the point of view of overall duration and from the point of view of the number of posts held by each minister.[8]

Cabinet government in Denmark is essentially based on the idea of representation, although administrative skills are also important. Civil servants are naturally anxious to see their departments headed by ministers who carry weight in cabinet, who can succeed in pushing through policy proposals and are able to defend the interests of their departments. Yet the representative principle dominates: the process of government formation is markedly constrained by pressures from the party in power or from the various parties of the coalition. The party leader may select ministers outside the parties themselves, but these normally join a party immediately after their appointment to the government and they stand as parliamentary candidates at the next election.

Well-known examples of ministers who were not members of the *Folketing* before taking office are the Minister of Cultural Affairs, H. Sølvhøj (1964), who was managing director of Denmark's broadcasting service, the Minister without Portfolio with special responsibility to foreign affairs L. Østergaard (1978), who was professor of psychology at the University of Copenhagen, the Minister of Industry, N. Wilhjelm (1987), who was director of the Federation of Danish Industries and the Minister of Cultural Affairs, H.P. Clausen, who was a Professor of Political Science at the University of Aarhus.

Ministerial departments vary markedly in size. The distribution of departmental responsibilities normally coincides with the minister's area of competence but, in most governments, some office-holders run more than one department. In such cases, the two ministries are independent of each other. Conversely, there are also cases where one department is divided between two ministers, but the structure of the department remains unchanged. From the middle of the 1960s, this formula was adopted to relieve the minister of Foreign Affairs, next to whom a minister for European Affairs was appointed. Although there was no administrative split within the department, the arrangement suggested the establishment of new priorities (the European Community issue was then hotly debated in Denmark). Since the end of the 1970s, however, Denmark's attitude towards the European Community has been more positive and there ceased to be a need for two ministers at the head of the Department of Foreign Affairs.

The distribution of policy fields among the departments can be used as a political instrument to give priority to some fields (for example, the setting up of a new department and the abolition of another). The Department of the Environment is an example of a department established in response to the emergence of a new salient policy area: it was set up in 1973 in A. Jörgensen's social democratic government. A Department of Health was established in 1987 in P. Schlüter's four party bourgeois coalition as public expenditure on health had risen to such a level that major controversies arose about priorities in this field.

Ministerial departments have a varied organisation. Some are centralised, while others are composed of autonomous divisions. Indeed, there are differences in organisation from one part of the department to another.[9] It is from the departments that proposals for new legislation and government regulations emerge, as well as the draft budgetary demands which are then sent to the Ministry of Finance.[10]

## 3 CABINET LIFE

The proportional representation system, with a low threshold (2 per cent of the votes), has given rise to a multi-party system. Five to eleven parties are represented in the *Folketing*, yet despite increasing fractionalisation, the system can still be described as 'a working multi-party system'.[11] The relationship between government and parliament has evolved from a separation of powers system to a parliamentary system in which the *Folketing* cooperates closely with the government. The influence of the *Folketing* takes place in many informal ways, in particular by means of party groups. The various minority governments have had to find different majorities in parliament and therefore to negotiate with their parliamentary representatives.

A characteristic feature of the style of Danish government from the second half of the 1960s has been a series of agreements on economic matters between the government and some of the opposition parties. State intervention with respect to collective bargaining in employer-labour relations has also been large, often on the basis of a broad agreement made in the *Folketing*. Thus, governmental policies had often to be compromises involving at least parties of the moderate right, of the centre and of the moderate left.

Two different left-right conflict dimensions exist in Danish politics, as shown in a study of election manifestos and election literature.[12] The first leads to the opposition between orthodox left and orthodox right, with the left being opposed to conservative economics and supporting labour groups. The left is also concerned with more democracy, and with peace. The second dimension is overwhelmingly concerned with welfare policies connected with peace through internationalism.

There is near-consensus on the welfare state in the country. However, in the 1980s, the expansion of the social services has been questioned. The Danish public sector is large and corresponded in 1982 to 61 per cent of the national product, and more than one quarter of the labour force is in public employment.[13]

While the Social Democratic Party has been the dominant party in Danish politics, it is not as strong as in Sweden or Norway. It peaked at about 40 per cent of the vote then declined – and was even reduced to a quarter of the vote at the 'earthquake' election of 1973 when new 'protest' parties entered the *Folketing*. Consequently, coalition and even minority governments have been frequent. These have to achieve compromises with respect to public expenditure, to social policy and to incomes policy. Demands for increased public ownership are now very limited. Thus, while Denmark is as a welfare state to the left of many other states, it has a liberal economy with less state intervention and less publicly-owned companies than many other countries.

A number of coalitions have been across the left-right divide, and these have more than occasionally been successful. Governments of this type were formed between 1957 and 1964 in the form of majority coalitions composed of the Social Democrats, the Radical Liberals and the Justice Party (to which a Greenland minister was later added). Denmark then experienced economic growth and major social change. This period was known as that of 'the second industrial revolution'. Danish industry became the most important export sector in Denmark, a role hitherto played by Danish agriculture.

A number of important decisions were taken at the time. An agreement on defence was made between the coalition government and the two non-socialist parties in opposition – the Conservatives and the Agrarian Liberals. This agreement, remarkably enough, was accepted both by Radical Liberals in the coalition and by the Conservatives outside it (an outcome which had never previously taken place). The Radical Liberals showed themselves prepared to see Denmark participate in the integrated defence system of NATO. During the same period an Economic Council was set up consisting of representatives of the major economic organisations of the country. A third important innovation of the period related to profit and incomes.[14]

A second type of coalition cutting across the left-right divide was that of Social Democrats and Agrarian Liberals in 1978–1979. It was a historical but short-lived event. The two main adversaries in Danish politics had reached agreement, but cooperation lasted only until a conflict arose over collective bargaining between employers and workers. The organisations on both sides were dissatisfied, and demanded that the government introduce legislation designed to compensate their members for the losses they had incurred. Distance between the two coalition partners became large and the government collapsed. An election followed in October 1979.[15]

Other types of coalitions were formed by the non-socialist parties and were alternatives to Social Democratic governments. The Agrarian Liberal-Conservative government of 1950–1953 was important in that, hitherto, the rivalry between these two parties had been an obstacle to cooperation. A non-socialist majority coalition government was formed by the Radical Liberals, the Conservatives and the Agrarian Liberals in 1968. In fact, its policy statement to the *Folketing* was to the left of the Social Democratic government which had preceeded it.[16] Its policies were of 'the middle' and the public sector grew appreciably and taxes were raised.

Finally, the non-socialist parties formed a government in 1982, under the Prime Ministership of P. Schlüter, composed of the Conservative, Agrarian Liberal, Centre Democratic and Christian People's parties – the so-called 'four-leaf clover'. Being a minority government, it had to cooperate closely with others willing to support governmental policies on specific issues. It even had to implement policies forced upon it by a majority outside the government, for instance in foreign affairs. This government can thus be described as having been of the 'middle'.

Parliament and the electorate thus impose constraints on the government. Parties also impose some constraints, though these are generally stronger on the left than on the right.[17] Party organisations do not affect the composition of the cabinet, which is made by the Prime Minister designate, but executive committees of parties must endorse any decision of parliamentary parties to form a government alone or in coalition. Moreover, the statutes of the Socialist People's Party state that decisions relating to governmental participation as well as relating to all important matters have to be endorsed by the executive committee. As the Socialist People's Party has not yet taken part in government, the question remains somewhat academic. Moreover, although discussions have taken place about a possible Social Democratic-Socialist People's Party coalition, the two parties are so far apart, especially on foreign policy issues, that this is probably not a realistic alternative.

Discipline is high in nearly all Danish parliamentary parties, although the Constitution of the Centre Democratic Party states that its members in the *Folketing* are bound only by their conscience (this provision has had no impact on coalitions).

Constraints within the cabinet arise primarily from the fact that the government is a party government. The individual minister is responsible for the management of his or her department. In a single-party cabinet all ministers will be subjected to the same party constraints derived from the party organisation and the coordination of cabinet work will be influenced by the priorities of the party programme. In a coalition, parties will be bound to some extent by the overall governmental agreement: negotiations leading to the coalition relate both to policies and to the distribution of portfolios. The government is then deemed to be collective and to present a united front to parliament.[18]

Some problems of coordination among the departments are solved in advance by the way in which policy areas are distributed and by attempts made to ensure that the same minister be responsible for politically connected questions. Nonetheless, some issue areas cut across the fields of two or more departments. Moreover, some departments work in close cooperation with organised interests, and these push the departments in somewhat different directions.

Conflicts about the distribution of scarce resources among the departments must also be solved through inter-departmental coordination. This can take place through committees or by departments which have responsibilities cutting across several fields. Overall coordination is undertaken by the cabinet meeting, while the Minister for Economic Coordination is also expected to take on a function of overall economic coordination.[19] More specific coordination is achieved by *ad hoc* meetings of ministers and *ad hoc* committees of ministers or of civil servants, and in some cases by ministers or departments whose responsibilities extend beyond their department.

Coordination also takes place by more informal means, but the organisational structure is such that its operation is very flexible. There are, for instance, a number of committees concerned with the coordination of European Community Affairs with special committees relating to every department involved. There is also a committee of top civil servants and a Common Market Committee of ministers. Special committees first deal with matters and pass them to the Committee of top civil servants, from which they go to the ministerial committee. This structure reflects the Danish attitude to European integration which is both centralised *and* decentralised, and is based on a functionalist conception because Denmark is strongly opposed to institutional developments towards supranationality. Conflictual matters are put before the committee of ministers for decision at the highest political level, in order to allow for overall cooperation among the governments.

Ministers cooperate closely with the permanent Under-Secretary in their department and there are no political Under-Secretaries. It is occasionally alleged that a civil servant has been appointed on political grounds, but this is exceptional and even in such cases the administrative merits of the incumbent are not disputed.[20] It has sometimes been suggested that Denmark should adopt the Swedish or Norwegian system of political Under-Secretaries, but this has been rejected as Danish civil servants prefer not to have political links with ministers.

The principle of the political neutrality of civil servants is strong, with top officials willing to follow the direction of ministers though they of course can influence decisions because of their long experince while the minister is often an amateur. Indeed, even if ministers acquired experience in parliamentary committees as party spokesmen for instance, they spend so much time keeping in contact with parliamentary parties, coalition partners and the media that they have to rely on the civil servants. There is a long-standing tradition for civil servants to work in close consultation with interest organisations while preparing and implementing political decisions. Ministers also often have meetings with representatives of interest organisations when a conflict arises about a decision involving the interests of these organisations.

Cabinet life has thus many aspects. It is conditioned by the constitution and a tradition dating back to the establishment of the ministerial system of 1848. The structural conditions for cabinet life are the object of continuous evolution as various actors, political and bureaucratic, try to influence changes in arrangements in order to adapt the central administration to social, economic and political conditions. The equilibrium between representativeness and administrative efficiency in the cabinet[21] is achieved in Denmark by a division of labour between representative ministers and the politically well informed and neutral top civil servants. These civil servants have managerial skills, although it does not follow that ministers are without managerial skills and top civil servants without political influence.

## 4 CABINET DECISION-MAKING

The overall equilibrium is markedly dependent on the leadership of the Prime Minister, who carries considerable weight. He or she can appoint and dismiss ministers and call an election at any time. He or she chairs the weekly cabinet meetings. The agenda, which must be circulated seven days in advance, is prepared by the Prime Minister's Department, but the Prime Minister often agrees to extra items being discussed at the meeting. The cabinet does not discuss routine matters, which are dealt with below ministerial level with each director having decision-making powers formally delegated to him or her by the minister. On more important questions, however, the cabinet does often become genuinely involved. These issues are usually selected by interdepartmental committees which are sensitive to problems which raise serious political conflicts on matters of policy.

As a result of the reforms of the 1960s and the 1970s, legislation has moved appreciably from being detailed to having an enabling character. More comprehensive planning is therefore required. Each information department has a planning staff and there are suggestions that interdepartmental planning bodies should be set up. Ministers are more closely involved than in the past in these matters.[22] The cabinet also discusses planning matters as well as consequential problems of coordination.

There is no voting at cabinet meetings. If a conflict arises between two ministers, the Prime Minister asks his department to draw up a compromise. If the conflict is still not settled, the Prime Minister takes the decision. A recent case was that of a conflict between the Minister of Agriculture and the Minister of the Environment about the use of fertilisers.

The Minister of Finance has a prominent position in cabinet. Before the presentation of the budget, each ministry sends its proposals to the Ministry of Finance which examines the proposals and makes changes in consultation with the ministry concerned. But permanent committees of the *Folketing* exercise control over the ministers and their departments, in particular in relation to bills. Committees also evaluate the administration of a policy field. The Common Market Relations Committee give specific political mandates to ministers before a negotiation in the EEC. To this must be added the role of the Ombudsman through whom the supervision of the administration can and does take place. There is thus a comprehensive system of control of the decisions of the cabinet and the departments, both political and administrative.

**Conclusion**

The Danish cabinet is thus a flexible compromise between various elements. The fact that it originated from the King's Council and developed only slowly accounts for the combination of leadership and collective action which has typically characterised it in recent years. It is this flexibility which has made it possible for the cabinet system to be maintained, at a time when the parties were numerous and had a high tendency towards fractionalisation.

It is indeed remarkable that there should be at the same time acceptance of a moderate level of leadership by the Prime Minister and cognition by the Prime Minister and the cabinet of the overall supremacy of parliament on many issues. It seems therefore that the Danish system of parliamentary government has adjusted to a situation in which parties are numerous and where very strong leadership would not be truly feasible. Perhaps, however, the fact that Denmark is a small country has made it possible for compromises to be maintained and for the cabinet to be relatively stable in a context of political forces which, in other countries, has tended to result in greater instability.

## Notes

1.  Rasmussen, E. (1972) *Komparative Politik* (Copenhagen: Glydendal) no. 2, pp. 207–212.
2.  Ibid., p. 213.
3.  Lassen, A. and Karup Pedersen, O. (1962) *Folkestyrets midler* (Copenhagen: Munksgaards Forlag) pp. 21–34.
4.  Ibid., pp. 52–53.
5.  Petersen, N. (1962) 'Oversight over centraladministrationens udvikling siden 1848', *Betænkning*, no. 320, pp. 29–100.
6.  Ibid., p. 37.
7.  Ibid.
8.  Blondel, J. 'Ministerial Careers and the Nature of Parliamentary Government: the Cases of Austria and Belgium', EUI Working Paper, No. 87/274.
9.  Christensen, J.G. (1980) *Centraladministrationen: organisation og politisk placering* (Copenhagen: Samfundsvidenskabeligt Forlag) pp. 207–209.
10. Bogason, P. (1988) 'Denmark', in D. Rowat (ed.) *Public Administration in the Western World* (New York: Marcel Dekker) p. 135.
11. Pedersen, M.N. (1983) 'The Defeat of all parties: The Danish *Folketing* Election of 1973' (Odense University Papers, Occasional Paper) no. 10, Department of Public Finance and Policy.
12. Holmstedt, M. and Schou, T.L. (1987) 'Sweden and Denmark 1945–1982: Election Programmes and the Scandinavian Setting', in I. Budge, D. Robertson and D. Hearl (eds) *Ideology, Strategy and Party Change:*

*spatial analyses of post-war election programmes in nineteen democracies* (Cambridge: Cambridge University Press).

13.	Bogason, P. (1988) p. 134.
14.	Bille, L. (1980) *Danmark 1945–1980* (Copenhagen: Berg Forlag Aps) pp. 48–67.
15.	Ibid., pp. 117–119.
16.	Schou, T.L., and Hearl, D. (forthcoming) 'Denmark', in M. Laver, I. Budge and D. Hearl (eds), *Party Policy and Coalition Government*.
17.	Sjöblom, G. (1968) *Party Strategies in a Multi-party System* (Lund: Studentlitteratur).
18.	Christensen, J. (1980) p. 125.
19.	Ibid., p. 127.
20.	Bogason, P. (1988) p. 139.
21.	Blondel, J.(1986) 'The Analysis of Cabinet Structures and Decision-Making', EUI Working Paper.
22.	Bogason, P. (1988) p. 141.

# 11 Norway: Ministerial Autonomy and Collective Responsibility

Svein Eriksen

## 1 CABINET SETTING

The origins of cabinet government in Norway go back to 1814, when the union with Denmark was dissolved and the Norwegian Constitution was adopted. In the tradition of the age the functions of government were separated into the legislature, the judiciary and the executive. Cabinet government, however, in the sense of *parliamentary government*, first emerged in 1884 when it was established as constitutional practice that the cabinet is responsible to Parliament and can only survive as long as it can muster a parliamentary majority.

'The cabinet' is, however, in a strictly formal sense a constitutionally unknown concept. The Constitution gives executive leadership to the King, or more accurately to the 'King in Council'. According to the Constitution the King is required to select a 'Council of Norwegian Citizens' and to take his major decisions in the presence of the Council after having heard the advice of the relevant counsellors.

After the introduction of parliamentary government in 1884, the role of the monarchy in political life has become wholly symbolic. *Formally*, a number of conventions are adhered to with respect to the role of the monarch:

- When cabinets change, the King, on the advice of the outgoing Prime Minister, selects a new Prime Minister designate.
- All formal, legally-binding decisions of the cabinet are made in the name of the King, in the form of so-called Royal Resolutions.
- Every Friday the cabinet or rather the Council of the State meets with the King in a formal session at the Royal Palace. At this meeting the King gives his approval to the cabinet's decisions in matters which require that approval.

## 2  CABINET STRUCTURE

**The size of the cabinet**

Generally all Norwegian ministers (apart from the Prime Minister) are departmental ministers. Only occasionally have there been non-departmental ministers, or Ministers Without Portfolio. All ministers, and only they, are members of the cabinet. It is a constitutional requirement that the Council of State shall consist of one Prime Minister and at least seven other counsellors.

The so-called Cabinet Statute (*Regjeringsinstruksen*) of 1909 fixed the 'preliminary' number of departments at nine. Though the number of departments, and hence of cabinet members, has increased, the size of cabinet has remained quite stable considering the vast increase in government work. In 1945 there were twelve departments, in 1956 fourteen and in 1988 sixteen. The corresponding numbers of cabinet members were fifteen in 1945 (Gerhardsen, I), fifteen in 1956 and seventeen in 1987.

Several factors have tended to lead to an increase in the size of cabinets. The scope of public activity has expanded and given ministers a heavy workload. The pressure on ministers has often been mentioned as a motive for the establishment of new departments (for instance, the Ministry of Local Government in 1948). New issues come onto the political agenda, such as environmental protection and oil production. The existence of these 'new' policy areas brought about by the setting up of separate departments in 1972 and 1978 respectively.

Political factors are also at work. The establishment of new departments may be a way to satisfy political groups. For instance, the establishment of the Ministry of Fisheries in 1946 has been seen as a concession to sectoral interests. Furthermore, an increased number of departmental portfolios facilitates the efforts of Prime Ministers to reward political friends or to silence critics by giving them ministerial office. On the whole, however, Norwegian Prime Ministers and other political leaders have balanced these pressures efficiently with the more or less explicit goal to preserve the stability of the departmental structure (*St. meld*, no. 44, 1982–1983).

In the post-war years Norway has had ten Prime Ministers. These Prime Ministers headed sixteen cabinets of various kinds: national (a coalition of the major political parties immediately after World War Two), majority Labour, minority Labour, majority non-Socialist coalition, minority non-Socialist coalition and minority Conservative (see Table 11.1).

Political life in the post-war era has been dominated by the Labour Party. The heyday of Labour government were the years 1945 to 1961, when there was a succession of majority Labour cabinets. Only eleven to twelve years have seen non-Socialist cabinets. The parliamentary situation became more difficult and changes of cabinet are more frequent in the 1970s and 1980s than in the previous post-war years. This is mainly due to the decline in electoral support for the Labour Party and the failure of the non-socialist parties to form stable coalitions.

TABLE 11.1   Cabinets in Norway: 1945–1987

| Prime Minister | Date in | Party Composition of Government |
|----------------|---------|-------------------------------|
| Gerhardsen I | 25.06.45 | National coalition cabinet, Communist, Socialist, Agrarian, Liberal, Conservative |
| Gerhardsen II | 05.11.45 | Socialist |
| Torp | 19.11.51 | Socialist |
| Gerhardsen III | 22.01.55 | Socialist |
| Lyng | 28.08.63 | Agrarian, Liberal, Conservative, Christian |
| Gerhardsen IV | 25.09.63 | Socialist |
| Borten | 12.10.65 | Agrarian, Liberal, Conservative, Christian |
| Bratteli I | 17.03.71 | Socialist |
| Korvald | 18.10.72 | Agrarian, Liberal, Christian |
| Bratteli II | 16.10.73 | Socialist |
| Nordli | 15.01.76 | Socialist |
| Brundtland I | 04.02.81 | Socialist |
| Willoch | 14.10.81 | Conservative. On 08.06.83 the Agrarians and the Christians were included in the Cabinet. |
| Brundtland II | 09.05.86 | Socialist |

The Norwegian government consists of some 60 political appointees. In each ministry there normally is a minister, an Under-Secretary, and a personal political secretary. The minister holds full responsibility for all matters concerning his ministry and this responsibility cannot be delegated. The under-Secretary is second in command to the minister and is authorised to take decisions on behalf of the minister. The personal political secretary is deemed to be the personal assistant to the minister and to take care of that part of the minister's agenda which is not primarily related to the ministry. The personal political secretary has no decision-making authority. In practice, however, there are wide

variations in the division of labour between the three political appointees. In some cases the personal political secretary operates on an equal
footing with the Under-Secretary, although he is nominally his junior.
All the political appointees leave office when there is a change of
government.

## Coordination in the central administration

The size, complexity and diversity of the central administration make
coordination important, but the problems involved are considerable.
Various departments frequently have responsibility for closely related
policies. Sometimes these policies are not compatible. Frequently
recurring conflicts are those between the spending departments and the
Treasury and those between the various departments with responsibility
for land use planning.

Although the cabinet has the ultimate responsibility for central
administration coordination, the bulk of interdepartmental coordination takes place outside the cabinet itself. In most cases the cabinet's role
is to provide a final check on the course of departmental policies.

There are several mechanisms for interdepartmental coordination at
the sub-cabinet level. These include:

### Procedures for consultation

As a regular part of the departmental decision-making process the
parties likely to be affected by a policy proposal (for example, other
departments or interest organisations) are formally consulted before the
proposal is submitted to the cabinet.

### Interdepartmental committees

In the Norwegian central administration there are some 900 interdepartmental committees. Several of these consist of representatives of bodies
outside the civil service in addition to public officials. Some committees
are *ad hoc*, whereas others are permanent. In particular, the *ad hoc*
committees set up to look into specific issues are important instruments
for policy formulation.

### Coordinating departments

Several departments are responsible for coordinating activities cutting
across various administrative sectors. For instance the Treasury is

responsible for coordinating fiscal policy and the Department of the Environment for coordinating physical planning. The Treasury is considered as the leading department.

Among other things it examines all departmental proposals for new policies before they are submitted to the cabinet. The coordinating departments have, however, no powers of direction and often meet resistance from the departments they are supposed to coordinate.

The influence of the coordinating departments varies with political and economic circumstances. The words of the Budget Division of Treasury probably carry more weight in times of fiscal austerity than in times of affluence.

### Committees of under-secretaries of state

The under-secretaries of state play an important part in the relations between the departments. The Brundtland cabinet of 1986 established six committees of Under-Secretaries on taking office. The previous Willoch cabinet had nine such committees. The committees of Under-Secretaries are staffed by civil servants.

In addition to the use of these formal arrangements coordination is also achieved in more informal ways. The Norwegian central administration is comparatively small and most departments are located in the same district in Oslo. There is a common grading system throughout the civil service and a special telephone directory for the departments. The transparency of the system facilitates coordination. Generally it is not difficult for a civil servant to know who his opposite numbers in other departments are and to anticipate their points of view.

### 3  CABINET LIFE

The business of the cabinet can be divided into two main categories (Bloch, 1963). First, there are the formal and legally binding decisions of the cabinet or, strictly speaking, of the King in Council. All submissions to Parliament (*Storting*) such as white papers and bills are formally approved by cabinet (that is, the King in Council) before they are presented to the *Storting*. In many matters the cabinet (that is, the King in Council) has the final and formal decision-making authority. For instance, all appointments to senior positions in the civil service are formally approved by the King in Council. To some extent the

Constitution and ordinary legislation spell out the matters which fall
into this category.

Second, some matters are discussed informally by the cabinet, in the
sense that no legally binding decisions are taken although conclusions
arrived at may be of political importance. This category includes:

● The discussion of cabinet or ministerial statements in press conferences or in the *Storting*.

● The discussion of matters which fall within the departmental
responsibility of a single minister, but which for any reason this
minister wants to bring before his colleagues.

● Briefings to the cabinet by one of the ministers, specially typically by
the Foreign Minister on the international situation.

For the period 1974–1978 the number of matters brought to the
cabinet's attention, as well as the amount of immediate cabinet business
increased (Olsen, 1981). Four major environmental influences seem to
account for these developments: the expansion of government activity
(in the oil sector, for example); the economic recession which brought
about a number of microinterventions in business and trade; the
extensive media coverage of political life which no doubt influences the
cabinet debate and the increased activity of pressure groups.

It has been suggested that ministers are so preoccupied with *ad hoc*
business that they can be said to 'misallocate' their time (Olsen, 1981). In
Norway ministers are under constitutional obligation to give priority to
major matters (*St. meld*, no. 84, 1962–1963). However, what should be
considered as 'major matters' is not clear. Several ministers will no doubt
be disinclined to define the importance of an issue in a rational manner.
Moreover, the cabinet has to live in an environment in which problems
are ill-defined and have vague boundaries. Priorities are unclear and
usually determined by forces outside the cabinet. It may therefore be
largely a waste of time to devote much attention to the preparation of
comprehensive long-term plans. It has been argued that the only
practical way for politicians to be influential is to address themselves to
the steady stream of more or less *ad hoc* business (see Bratbak *et al.*).

The cabinet usually meets three times a week on Mondays, Thursdays
and Fridays. The Friday meetings are the purely formal sessions with the
King at the Royal Palace (that is, the Council of State). Real policy
discussions of the cabinet take place on Mondays and Thursdays. These
meetings last some three hours. Extra cabinet meetings are often

called in the initial and final stages of the preparation of the budget or when special issues arise. In February each year the cabinet sets aside a couple of days to fix the main outlines of next year's budget, which is submitted to the *Storting* in October. The cabinet also has a luncheon of some 30 minutes duration before every cabinet meeting and a somewhat longer luncheon (approximately an hour) after the meetings of the Council of State on Fridays. Coalition cabinets often need more time and hence more meetings to arrive at conclusions than single-party governments (Solstad, 1969; Berggrav, 1985).

Cabinet meetings are attended by the ministers, the Prime Minister's Press Officer (an Under-Secretary of State) and the Permanent Secretary to the Prime Minister's Office. Civil servants are called in from time to time when the subject matter requires it. During the non-socialist cabinet of Prime Minister Per Borten, from 1965 to 1971, Under-Secretaries of State were regularly present at cabinet meetings when their ministers were unable to attend. This practice has not been continued by subsequent cabinets, though Under-Secretaries may occasionally attend to assist their ministers.

During the Conservative government of Prime Minister Kaare Willoch, from 1981 until 1983, the leader of the Conservative Parliamentary Party regularly attended cabinet meetings. When the Christian People's Party and the Agrarian Party entered Willoch's cabinet in 1983, the parliamentary leaders of the three coalition parties joined the cabinet for the initial budget discussions and the preparation of the cabinet's programme.

The cabinet agenda is prepared, though mainly in a technical sense, by the Prime Minister's Office. The agenda is also circulated by his office. Topics for cabinet discussion are submitted by the departments. The departments also produce and circulate two-page memoranda, or cabinet notes, for cabinet discussion. Each minister receives two to six copies of each cabinet note.

Generally the Prime Minister's Office plays an *administrative* role in the preparation of cabinet meetings and it receives and distributes material which is drafted elsewhere. However, the extent to which the Prime Minister wants to influence the content of the material placed before the cabinet varies. While departmental proposals were listed directly on the cabinet agenda in the past, Prime Minister Willoch introduced the practice that some kinds of departmental proposals (for instance draft bills) should be submitted to the Prime Minister's Office.

During Willoch's coalition government, from 1983 until 1986, a so-called sub-committee of the cabinet was set up. This committee consisted of the Prime Minister and the chairman of the two other coalition parties (that is, the Minister of Transport and the Minister of Ecclesiastical Affairs) considered politically sensitive issues before they were brought before the full cabinet. Apart from this arrangement there has not been much discussion over the idea of setting up an inner cabinet, nor is the idea likely to be given much support (Bloch, 1963; Nordli, 1978). The main reason is probably that Norwegian cabinets are not considered too large for efficient decision-making (Bloch, 1963).

Immediately after World War Two cabinet committees were set up, partly to keep the cabinet agenda free from minor issues and partly to improve interdepartmental coordination. The number and composition of these committees vary from one cabinet to another. The cabinet committees are advisory, and their recommendations must be formally approved by the King in Council or by the relevant department. The point has been made that the committees have become less crucial over the last two decades (Olsen, 1980).

When Harlem Brundtland's cabinet took office in 1986, five cabinet committees were established. These covered Security Affairs, Local Government Affairs and Health Policy, Polar Affairs, Economic Affairs and Research Affairs. The Prime Minister chaired the first three committees mentioned.

During the preceding Willoch government there were seven cabinet committees. Four of these had the same terms of reference as the committees for Security Affairs, Economic Affairs, Polar Affairs, and Research Affairs mentioned above. In addition, the Willoch government had a so-called sub-committee for the preliminary consideration of complicated issues, as well as committees for Labour Market Affairs and Oil Affairs. Willoch presided over four of these committees. Mr Willoch headed the Committee for Economic Affairs, whereas Mrs Brundtland has left that job to her Minister of Finance.

The brief cabinet notes, or more precisely their concluding recommendations, are the basis upon which cabinet decisions are made. The cabinet notes are solely for the cabinet's own use and are not made public.

There is a ground rule not to take issues to cabinet prematurely. When there is a conflict between two or more departments, it is not expected to be referred to cabinet until all other means of resolving it have been exhausted. Proposals which involve public expenditure are to be discussed with the Treasury and, if they have major administrative consequences, with the Ministry of Consumer Affairs and Government Administration.

If conflicts are not resolved during the consultation process which precedes the cabinet meeting, and if agreement is not reached during the meeting itself, various courses of action are open (Olsen, 1980):

- The minister submitting the disputed proposal is asked to reconsider the matter and to return with a new solution.
- The ministers involved in the conflict are asked to make another attempt to find a compromise.
- The issue may be referred to a committee of Under-Secretaries of State or civil servants.
- The issue is considered by a group of ministers including the ministers concerned and a couple of senior ministers, often including the Prime Minister.

It very rarely happens that a vote is taken in cabinet, but it does occur. All the ministers are collectively responsible for the decisions reached by the cabinet. In order to avoid responsibility for a cabinet decision a minister has to dissent formally in the Council of State.

## 4 CABINET DECISION-MAKING

### The role of the Prime Minister

The Prime Minister is the head of the cabinet. His constitutional role is, however, vaguely described. To be valid all decisions by the King in Council have to be counter-signed by the Prime Minister. He has an additional vote in the very rare occasions when the King is absent from the Council of State. The Prime Minister has few formal powers *vis-à-vis* his other colleagues. He or she can require any piece of information from colleagues, but is not empowered to issue instructions. He or she cannot dissolve the *Storting*, call elections, establish or abolish ministries or reshuffle their jurisdictions. Like other ministers he or she is subject to the final, collective authority of the cabinet.

The Prime Minister is not in a position to appoint a cabinet of his or her choosing. But the degree to which Prime Ministers control the selection process has varied. Einar Gerhardsen, Labour Prime Minister from 1945 until 1951 and from 1955 until 1965, is generally considered to have exerted considerable influence in the composition of his cabinets although he was not in a position to make appointments wholly on his own. His proposals were considered by a small group of Labour and trade union leaders. Labour Prime Ministers of the 1970s and 1980s

have faced a more complicated process of cabinet making, their freedom
of choice being constrained by the various strands of party opinion. For
instance, when Bratteli formed his second cabinet in 1973 he was
compelled to renounce some of his own choices and to accept persons
whom he was reluctant to have in his cabinet (Andersen, 1984).

In coalition governments the Prime Ministers' freedom of choice is
even more restricted, since their word carries little weight outside their
own party. In coalition governments it is also difficult for the Prime
Minister to dismiss ministers not belonging to his own party without
disrupting the often fragile compromises underlying the cabinet formation (Solstad, 1969).

The Norwegian Prime Minister has modest staff resources. Until the
outbreak of World War Two he combined the office of Prime Minister
with that of being departmental minister. Thus Johan Nygaardsvold,
who was Prime Minister from 1935 until 1945, was also Minister of
Public Works in the period from 1935 until 1939. The Prime Minister's
Secretariat has been gradually strengthened during the post-war years.
In 1956 the Prime Minister's Office was established with three Under-
Secretaries of State and three senior civil servants. There are currently
five political appointees and nineteen civil servants in the Prime
Minister's Office.

Although the Prime Ministers' constitutional and administrative
resources are restricted, they are not without influence in the cabinet.
They preside over cabinet meetings and may to some extent control the
formulation of the cabinet's agenda (Berggrav, 1985). Of course, Prime
Ministers are unable to supervise the mass of policy matters dealt with in
the departments. Their involvement is selective, but may be decisive on
the outcome of the issues they engage in. They may play an important
part as coordinators. Without departmental responsibilities, but with
access to all ministers, they are probably in a better position than any of
their colleagues to see inter-relationships and inconsistencies in the
cabinet's policies, and hence to propose adjustments in the way issues
are handled by individual ministers.

The influence of Prime Ministers is dependent upon the support they
get from their party, the *Storting* and powerful interest organisations. It
also depends on whether they head a single-party or a coalition
government. Popular support is also important for Prime Ministers.
Those who win elections will probably be less dependent on party
organisations. There is no necessary correlation between the popularity
of Prime Ministers and the support they have from other political
leaders, however, Per Borten resigned as Prime Minister in 1971 partly

after pressure from members of his own government, although more people wanted Borten to stay than to leave (Olsen, 1980). In the post-war years Norway has had ten Prime Ministers. Of these six have left office without having lost an election or a vote of confidence in the *Storting* – Nygaardsvold in 1945, Gerhardsen in 1951, Torp in 1955, Borten in 1971, Bratteli in 1976 and Nordli in 1981. In all of these cases, perhaps with the exception of Gerhardsen in 1951 who said he retired because he was tired, the change of Prime Minister (and in 1971 the change of the whole government) was related to leadership problems in the cabinet and in the party or parties in office. This is perhaps an indication of a general and probably natural trend for Prime Ministers to experience a decline in their authority, because they become burnt out or because their power base disintegrates (or both).

### The role of departmental ministers

Norwegian ministers wear two hats: they are members of the cabinet as well as departmental heads. It is often argued that Norwegian ministers attach more importance to their departmental leadership role than to their cabinet role, and hence that the cabinet should be considered more of a group of departmental champions than as a body of like-minded political friends.

Several factors account for the tendency of ministers to give priority to their departmental work and to advance departmental goals. First, most policy proposals are prepared and given nearly final form by the sponsoring department. Second, ministers are advised as departmental heads and not as members of cabinet. Their view of cabinet business tends to be biased by the perspective they are given from within their department. Unless the policy initiatives of a minister affect the interests of one or more colleagues, they are not likely to be challenged by the cabinet provided, of course, that they are not incompatible with the core of party ideology.

Norwegian departments, or at least their functional sub-units, tend to develop their peculiar outlook and loyalties. Through their education and occupational experience several ministers are familiar with and tend to share the departmental points of view (Olsen, 1980). That ministers are expected to be 'specialists', rather than 'generalists' or 'amateurs', is also indicated by the fact that members of the *Storting* who are appointed ministers have to vacate their parliamentary seat when they take office. Finally, there is probably a tacit understanding among ministers that they should, as far as possible, refrain from interfering in each other's business (Olsen, 1980): 'If you don't criticize my programme, I will not criticize yours.'

However, some ministers tend to take a broader outlook than others and are more concerned about the affairs of the government as a whole. This may be due to their seniority in the party, the nature of their departmental portfolio or their personal inclination. For instance, Ministers of Finance and Ministers of Local Government and Employment are regularly involved in the business of other ministers. But this involvement is not necessarily the product of the ministers' dedication to the totality of the government's policies. A number of their interventions may be regarded as aiming at defending more or less parochial departmental interests.

The question which arises is: to what extent is the 'structural' disposition of ministers to be passive in cabinet meetings expected to be offset by other factors? It may be hypothesised that the potential for collective decision-making is greater in coalition cabinets then in single-party cabinets – the coalition partners are ideologically distinct. More views have to be reconciled and probably more ministers want to speak before the cabinet reaches its conclusion. Thus it is hardly surprising when a former Prime Minister in a coalition government described his job as 'carrying sprawling fenceposts'. Moreover, there seems to be a tendency for coalition cabinets to call cabinet meetings more frequently than single-party governments (Berggrav, 1985; Solstad 1969). It has been pointed out that a great number of the members of the Borten cabinet were former members of the *Storting*, and that this influenced the working habits of the cabinet in the sense that its negotiations resembled those of a parliamentary committee (Solstad, 1969).

However, in coalition cabinets there are constraints on the extent of discussion and of disagreements. To keep the work of the cabinet under control, several potentially controversial issues may not be on the government's agenda at all (or they may be solved outside the cabinet). Some examples illustrate this:

● During the Borten cabinet from 1965 to 1971 the deputy secretaries of state were accorded a large role in the preparation of the cabinet's policies – they had probably more influence than in any other cabinet. Matters which were considered too conflictual to be brought directly before the cabinet were referred to committees of under-secretaries, who were charged with the task of working out basic inter-party compromises (Solstad, 1969).

● Internal conflicts in the cabinet have occasionally resulted in a lack of precision in the cabinet's proposals to the *Storting*. Thus the cabinet has left it to the *Storting* to produce the necessary compromises (Solstad, 1969).

● During Willcoch's coalition cabinet politically tricky issues were not submitted to cabinet until they had been discussed by the Prime Minister and the chairmen of the other two coalition parties.

● Normally the greatest political differences are straightened out, often through protracted negotiations, before a coalition government is set up. For instance the joint statement of the three non-Socialist parties, in response to the Long-Term Programme of the 1981 Labour cabinet of Harlem Brundtland, was to some extent the political basis of the cabinet which these three parties formed in 1983.

The leadership style of the Prime Minister influences the decision-making behaviour of the cabinet. Some Prime Ministers urge the cabinet, the *entire* cabinet that is, to participate in the discussion of policy proposals. The late Labour Prime Minister Trygve Bratteli has been particularly associated with a decision-making style in which broad participation was emphasised (Andersen, 1984).

Other Prime Ministers have been more inclined to keep difficult issues outside cabinet. In the Labour Party, especially in the first post-war decade, vital decisions were often made within a small group of top leaders in the party and the trade union movement. 'Some of us have talked things over' was a saying often used to describe the decision-making mode. It has been argued that Einar Gerhardsen, the undisputed leader of the Labour Party from 1945 to 1965, was a major exponent of such a leadership style (Andersen, 1984). Arguably this also character-ised the way he led his cabinets.

Prime Minister Odvar Nordli, who headed the minority Labour cabinet from 1976 until 1981, said that he found it useful to discuss conflictual topics with a small group of ministers rather than in the full cabinet. This way of operating was chosen to spare the cabinet detailed and protracted discussions, and to keep conflicts between departmental ministers from becoming unnecessarily heated (Nordli, 1978).

The Norwegian cabinet is based on a structure which denies the Prime Minister a major part and which helps to establish individual ministers in their departmental affairs. To this extent it is not a cabinet which fits very closely with the Westminster model. The practice has modified the situation to an extent, but only to an extent. As a matter of fact, Norway has really experienced a little of both models, with some senior ministers exercising considerable influence while others tended to be arbiters in situations of minority or coalition government. To this extent, the Norwegian pattern is located at some distance from the model of the prime ministerial leadership. It is at a halfway point, and it has been able to oscillate in a flexible manner and take into account what have sometimes been difficult political situations.

# 12 Sweden: The New Constitution – An Old Practice Adjusted

Torbjörn Larsson

## 1 CABINET SETTING

Since 1975 Sweden has been living and working with a new Constitution. That year marked the end of an era as well as the end of a long struggle, for one of the world's oldest written Constitutions was transformed into a modern one.

One of the major alterations was the replacement of a two-chamber Parliament by a unicameral system. The members of the new Parliament are now elected by direct suffrage for a period of three years. The proportional representation electoral system was kept, but an electoral threshold was introduced to keep the smallest parties out of Parliament (4 per cent of the total votes or 12 per cent of the votes in one constituency). Another change was the introduction of simultaneous elections. All elections, not only elections to Parliament but also elections to local and regional councils, now take place on the same day (the third Sunday in September).

For the first time in Swedish history the principle of parliamentarism was written into the Constitution, although in reality Sweden had had a parliamentary system since 1917. The principle of power-sharing between King and Parliament in legislative matters was abolished. Parliament is now the supreme legislative body and the cabinet is deemed to execute the decisions of Parliament.

The King is still formally Head of State although his functions are merely symbolic or ceremonial and his former powers have largely been taken over by the cabinet and by the Speaker of Parliament. It is the Speaker who selects a candidate for the post of Prime Minister and presents him to Parliament, which then castes a vote. The Prime Minister afterwards selects the members of the cabinet and can also dismiss the Ministers.

Some old and specifically Swedish ways of organising the cabinet and the central bureaucracy were not changed, however. The cabinet is backed up by a large administrative apparatus (not, however, as large as in most other Western European countries) to help interpret, formulate and implement its political goals. The responsibility for this administrative apparatus is, both formally and in practice, divided among the Ministers, each of whom is in charge of a policy area. Ministers thus have a double role: they act as spokesmen for a policy area in the cabinet and they are held collectively responsible for overall cabinet policy.

Sweden is not unique in this respect but, in Sweden, the principle of collective responsibility is explicitly mentioned in the Constitution and is applicable to almost all the matters which a Minister has to deal with, the major exceptions being related to defence and foreign affairs.[1]

Sweden also differs from other countries in the way the work of the central bureaucracy is organised. Ministries are small: for example, only a few hundred people work in the Ministry of Finance which is the second largest ministry after Foreign Affairs. In other countries the implementation of government policy is traditionally carried out by the ministries, whereas in Sweden this work is assigned to autonomous boards and agencies. The central administration is thus divided into two parts – ministries, on the one hand, and boards and agencies on the other. The former are deemed to *direct* the latter by way of general guidelines, but *not to rule them in detail*. According to the Constitution, agencies or boards are responsible to the cabinet as a whole, not to individual Ministers.

The cabinet issues instructions as to how parliamentary bills are to be interpreted, but if a Minister attempts to influence a board or agency in the exercise of its powers in individual cases this is seen as a violation of the Constitution and the Minister may have to resign. A Minister who is too eager to influence an agency or who meddles too often in the business of the boards may find himself in difficulty. From time to time protests are made about Ministers who are thought to have exceeded their authority by attempting to enforce their will on a board or agency. Rarely, however, have such problems led to resignations.

Swedish ministries are also small because much of the preparatory work for government bills is carried out by royal commissions rather than within the departments.[2] These commissions are organisationally separate from the ministries. They do not normally work independently of cabinet, but are guided by relatively detailed written instructions describing their goals or the problems to be solved. The cabinet also determines the duration, budget and membership of royal commissions. Interest group representatives are often invited to sit on Royal Commissions, as are politicians from the opposition. The commissions also act as coordinating bodies, as they represent a cross-section of opinion as well as civil servants, who act as experts. Since nearly every proposal for change is prepared by at least one Royal Commission, the latter contribute significantly to the consensual character of Swedish politics.[3]

Royal commission proposals are subsequently distributed to the different groups and authorities which the cabinet consider have an interest in the matter. This method of collecting support and criticism for proposed governmental policy is called a *remiss*. In this way everyone, including ordinary citizens, can express their opinions before the cabinet reaches a decision. Ministers who are considering major changes in policy must take into account not only the recommendations of the royal commissions, but also the *remiss* answers which they receive.[4]

There is a rationale for the small size of the departments. All the departments should function as a single 'staff organisation' for the cabinet. Ministries are often described as *regeringskansliet* or *kanslihuset*. These terms date back to when most ministries were situated in the same building. It is difficult to find an adequate English equivalent for this idea, as the term 'government' is too broad since the Swedish ministries form only a small part of the administration. The term 'cabinet' is, on the other hand, too narrow as it only includes Ministers and not the 2000 to 3000 civil servants working in the ministries. The expression 'government office' is sometimes used, but this term is also misleading as it suggests that Sweden does not have any ministries at all. An expression such as 'the Ministries' with a capital 'M' might give a clearer impression of the Swedish ministries as a unified structure.

## 2  CABINET STRUCTURE

Sweden has had very stable governments for more than 50 years (see Table 12.1). The Social Democratic Party was in power for 44 years – with the exception of a few months in 1936 – from 1932 until 1976, although during part of that period it was in coalition with the Agrarian Party.

During World War Two all the parties represented in Parliament, except the Communist Party, were at some time represented in cabinet. When governing alone, the Social Democratic Party normally did not have an absolute majority in Parliament and relied on the (at least) passive support of other parties. This support frequently came from the

Communist Party, which has never joined with the non-Socialist parties against a Social Democratic cabinet in a vote of confidence.

TABLE 12.1    Swedish cabinets since 1945

| Year of formation | PM Name | PM Party | Participating party/parties |
|---|---|---|---|
| 1945 | Hansson IV | Social Democrat | Social Democrats |
| 1946 | Erlander I | Social Democrat | Social Democrats |
| 1951 | Erlander II | Social Democrat | Social Democrats, Argrarians |
| 1957 | Erlander III | Social Democrat | Social Democrats |
| 1969 | Palme I | Social Democrat | Social Democrats |
| 1976 | Fälldin I | Agrarian | Agrarians Liberals Conservatives |
| 1978 | Ullsten | Liberal | Liberals |
| 1979 | Fälldin II | Agrarian | Agrarians Liberals Conservatives |
| 1981 | Fälldin III | Agrarian | Agrarians, Liberals |
| 1982 | Palme II | Social Democrat | Social Democrats |
| 1986 | Carlsson | Social Democrat | Social Democrats |

At the 1976 election the three non-Socialist parties obtained a parliamentary majority and formed a coalition government. Due to conflicts over nuclear energy policy, the cabinet fell in 1978 and was succeeded by a Liberal minority government. At the 1979 election the three non-Socialist parties again obtained a parliamentary majority, but of one seat only. A new three-party coalition was set up, and for a second time did not last the full three-year period. For the remainder of the period (about a year) a non-Socialist minority government was formed by Liberals and Agrarians, unofficially supported by the Conservatives. At the 1982 election the Social Democratic Party was returned to power after six years in opposition.

Elections and cabinet formation from the late 1960s may be described as a struggle between the Socialist and non-Socialist blocs. The non-Socialist bloc comprises the three 'bourgeois' parties, and the other bloc includes Social Democrats and Communists.

The Communist Party has never held posts in government. Indeed, in the 1960s and 1970s, it was even common for the Social Democratic government to disregard Communist proposals made in Parliament. After their return to power in 1982, however, the Social Democrats have had to pay more attention to the Communist Party in order to ensure the passage of their legislation.

When the bourgeois parties are in power the Prime Minister is Liberal or Agrarian, provided these two parties have more seats in Parliament than the Conservative Party. The Office of Prime Minister has not been held by a Conservative since the 1920s.

In the period 1976–1982 the parties were allocated posts in coalition cabinets roughly in proportion to their size in Parliament. The leading members of the party or parties in power will normally sit in cabinet, with the exception of the Party Secretary. As a result, the party policy tends to be formulated by the cabinet, especially in a single-party government.

The modern Swedish cabinet dates back to the reform of 1840. Before that date the Ministers were not heads of departments. But in 1840 it was decided that, out of ten Ministers, seven should be heads of ministries. The other three – known as Consultative Ministers or Ministers Without Portfolio – were given competences in legislative matters which cut across ministerial boundaries. This meant that most Ministers were given a greater responsibility for the preparation of questions decided by the 'King in Council' (that is, the formal cabinet. The expression 'King in Council' refers to the way in which questions were decided – that is, the King and his Ministers reached decisions together).

The King was regarded as the ultimate decision-maker, but in most cases he was not allowed to take decisions without previously consulting his Ministers. Ministers were not only heads of ministries, they were also collectively responsible for the advice they gave to the King. This led – even prior to 1840 – to regular but informal meetings during which Ministers discussed matters of importance before they met the 'King in Council'. These informal meetings were called *Statsrådsberedningen* and, at least during the nineteenth century, these meetings could be regarded as the real cabinet.

Normally, the King was also briefed on sensitive matters by the Minister in charge before the formal cabinet meeting. This procedure soon led to a situation in which 'King in Council' simply meant the formal approval of decisions already made by the *Statsrådsberedningen*. Both the Ministers of Justice and the Minister of Foreign Affairs took the title of Prime Minister, but neither was explicitly superior to the other Ministers although the Minister of Justice was often regarded as the chairman of the cabinet. In 1876 the Ministers of Justice and Foreign Affairs lost their Prime Ministerial status and a separate post of Prime Minister was created. Initially, the Prime Minister did not have a ministry or an office of his own, but held a departmental post. In most cases he was a Consultative Minister. Not until 1965 did he have a substantial staff.

The names of the ministries and the number of Ministers were set out in the Constitution of 1840. Consequently, changes in cabinet structure have been rare. Sixty years went by before a new ministry was established. A major change then occurred about once every twenty years, until the end of the 1960s. During the nineteenth century the rules restricting the number of ministries and Ministers were gradually relaxed. After 1975 more rapid changes affected the organisation of the cabinet. In the 1980s the number of ministries and Ministers has only varied slightly from one cabinet to another.

During the late 1970s and early 1980s the cabinet normally comprised about twenty Ministers distributed over twelve to fourteen ministries (not counting the Office of the Prime Minister). Some ministries have been divided between two Ministers – one being appointed Minister and the other being a Consultative Minister – though both have full responsibility for their separate fields of competence and have equal status within the cabinet. Meanwhile, the practice of appointing Ministers without Portfolio or Ministers with responsibilities which cut across departmental boundaries in legislative matters has stopped. Finally, and most importantly, Swedish Ministers are members of the cabinet, have equal status and are formally equally responsible for the vast majority of governmental decisions.

Today the cabinet as a collective body usually meets once a week in a 'formal Government meeting' (*regeringssammanträde*) to discuss and decide on current issues. The meeting is primarily a means of giving formal approval to decisions which Ministers have already taken individually in the name of the cabinet as a whole. All important decisions which result from elaborate discussions taken by the government in other forms must also be formally approved at a *regeringssammanträde*.

Normally, the meetings have a rather ritualistic character, but proposals have occasionally been withdrawn for various reasons. The meeting resembles the old 'King in Council' – abolished under the 1975 Constitution – though the term is still used when, about twice a year, the cabinet meets the King in order to keep him informed about the various aspects of cabinet policy. The quorum for the *regeringssammanträde* is five, a figure which often corresponds to reality in the summer. Any Minister disagreeing with the general view in the *regeringssammanträde* can have this difference of opinion recorded in the minutes, but this rarely occurs.

One consequence of collective cabinet responsibility is that a very large number of decisions, about 25 000 to 30 000 every year, are taken at 'formal Government meetings'. Every Minister and ministry will provide in advance an agenda for these meetings. Only the title or a short summary of the questions being raised is mentioned in the agenda.[5]

The Prime Minister's Office (*statsrådsberedningen*) consists of two elements. First, 'non-political' civil servants who ensure that proposals and decisions are legal and constitutional. Second, civil servants with mostly political tasks (for example, to assist the Prime Minister with his speeches and in his public relations in general, and to monitor the activities of the departments). Under the coalition governments in the 1970s, this second element of the Prime Minister's Office was paralleled by similar bodies around each of the other party leaders in the coalition.

## 3  CABINET LIFE

The life and role of a Minister depends to a large extent on the relationships which he or she has with other political actors. In the first instance, he or she has to establish a relationship with Parliament.

Party discipline is very strong in Sweden. The role in the Parliament of parties supporting the cabinet consists to a large extent in defending governmental policy against the opposition. The freedom of individual MPs is therefore limited when their party is in power. The leadership of the parliamentary party group checks the proposals of individual MPs in order to avoid deviations from the official party line. When the party is in opposition this control is of course more limited.

During the long period of Social Democratic rule, this situation was sometimes heavily criticised. It was sometimes said that the ruling party in Parliament was a 'transportation company' for government bills. This changed slightly after the 1973 elections, when the Socialist and bourgeois blocs obtained exactly the same number of seats. The influence of the standing parliamentary committees on governmental policy increased. In fact, because many issues were decided by drawing lots, the number of parliamentary seats was altered and is now uneven. In the 1980s the influence of the ruling parliamentary group has reverted to the pre-1973 situation, although many observers claim that the Social Democratic cabinet has been forced to pay more attention to Parliament than in the past.[6]

The introduction of the unicameral system in 1970 changed the context of cabinet-parliamentary contracts. The main reason for this is that, since 1971, MPs appointed to government are substituted in Parliament by other candidates from the same party. Before 1971 most Ministers were also MPs: this ensured the frequent presence of Ministers in Parliament as their votes were needed to ensure the passage of government bills. This in turn led to the practice of holding many cabinet meetings in the Parliament building, with the result that Ministers were widely accessible to backbenchers. The ordinary MP never had any difficulty in reaching any or all the members of the cabinet. Under the new system, Ministers only come to Parliament when an issue which concerns them is debated, and many MPs feel that their contacts with Ministers are no longer as frequent and informal as they once were.

Ministers must also have a good relationship with their department. The internal organisation of ministries is based on a reform of 1965 (see Figure 12.1). Two basic aims governed the new arrangements. One was to achieve maximum legal protection for citizens and that proposed bills

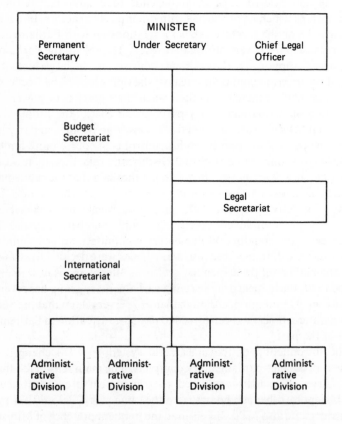

FIGURE 12.1  Organisation of a Swedish ministry

and regulations should not conflict with the Constitution and that individual cases should be dealt with fairly. The other aim was to improve the integration of policy-making and implementation. Before 1965 policy-making was handled by the Under Secretary, while implementation was carried out by the Permanent Secretary (*expeditionschef*) and departments were accordingly divided into two parts. Since 1965 these two aspects of departmental work have been placed within a common organisation.

The Minister's closest collaborators are his Under Secretary, the Chief Legal Officer and the Permanent Secretary. The Under Secretary (the Secretary of State) is the Minister's top political advisor and is responsible for running the ministry. The Chief Legal Officer is a legal counsellor who scrutinises proposals for new laws and assists in their formulation. The Permanent Secretary, unlike his British counterpart, is first and foremost a legal expert. He or she deals with the application of existing legislation to individual cases. the compatibility of government decisions with the Constitution and the existing body of legislation.

The three top advisers are assisted by three Secretariats. The Legal Secretariat is responsible for the legal formulation of ministerial policy. The Secretariat for Planning and Budget Affairs (PBS) is in charge of the formal aspects of the budgetary process and of personnel matters. The International Secretariat coordinates the international contacts of the ministry. In principle, these three secretariats supply relevant technical knowledge to facilitate the work of the top ministerial advisers, but the part played by the secretariats varies greatly in practice. There are differences in the extent to which these secretariats are used and the personality of those working in the secretariats also plays a part.

The real responsibility for drafting the policy proposals of the cabinet rests with the administrative divisions, which correspond to different subject areas. The number of divisions varies from ministry to ministry, but there are usually between three and eight of them, staffed by between five and 30 civil servants and headed by a general director. The administrative divisions deal with policy-making and with implementation, but the pre-1965 distinction sometimes reappears (some civil servants tend to specialise in policy-making, for instance). Finally, departments have a Secretary for Information, appointed to maintain media contacts and who often act as the Minister's political adviser.

A ministry is not an extended hierarchical structure. Discussions on the content of policies in different areas is carried out in most cases between the top level (the Minister and the Under Secretary) and the administrative divisions. In fact, Ministers are normally acquainted with every civil servant working in the administrative divisions.

There are few political appointments. The only two clear cases are those of Under Secretary and Secretary for Information, apart from the Minister himself. Indeed, some 'non-political' persons have been appointed to the post of Under Secretary, but it is always assumed that Under Secretaries will be in general agreement with the Minister's political aims. Before 1976 and since 1982, however, the Social Democratic Party has occasionally recruited more advisers with clearly defined political skills. This was felt even more strongly because of the degree of suspicion which the bourgeois parties had in the period 1976–1982 *vis-à-vis* the administration.

Among the most important relationships Ministers must build on are contacts with the civil servants in their own and in other ministries. These relationships are to an extent dependent upon each other. A Minister who wins his battles in cabinet, or generally has the upper hand in dealing with other Ministers, is regarded as a strong Minister and consequently becomes popular in his own ministry (as civil servants naturally like to see their proposals become cabinet policy). A Minister's potentially greatest opponent is normally the Minister of Finance, and victories over this Minister are particularly important for the prestige of cabinet members.

In the Swedish cabinet coordination is achieved in several ways. It is done through informal meetings, two to three-day meetings once or twice a year involving the entire cabinet to discuss future policy and (in coalition governments) by regular meetings between the party leaders.

Cabinet committees as such do not exist in Sweden, but at the beginning of the 1970s a special group, sometimes called the *Trojka*, was set up by the Social Democratic government to analyse industrial and employment issues. The group was chaired by the Minister of Finance and included the Minister of Industry and the Minister of Labour (all three were assisted by their Under Secretaries). Unlike a cabinet committee in the strict sense, the group included the head and deputy head of the National Labour Market Board and his deputy chief (both of them are civil servants). In this group all the participants had equal status. This group was not resuscitated after the return to power of the Social Democrats in 1982.

Lower level coordination revolves around the Under Secretaries, all of whom have lunch together once a week. Other groups of civil servants from different ministries regularly have lunch together – about once a month. Much inter-ministerial coordination takes place through informal and *ad hoc* contacts between Ministers and civil servants. These contacts are called 'joint meetings' (*gemensam beredning*). Some written instructions specify that a joint meeting must take place before the cabinet can decide on a particular issue (for example, before decisions which have economic or structural consequences are taken joint meetings must be held with representatives from the Ministry of Finance).

Civil servants often sit on inter-ministerial committees or groups. In an answer to a questionnaire put to 105 senior civil servants in 1980, 66 per cent stated that they had been members of at least one such group, only a proportion of which have a permanent character (39 per cent only stated that they had been members of a permament group.[7] In many cases it is difficult to distinguish between informal and formal meetings.

Informal coordination tends to be followed up by formal means of coordination, sometimes by way of joint meetings and in other cases by what is called 'sharing' (*delningsförfarande*). Sharing means that all directives to Royal Commissions, parliamentary proposals or answers to questions put in Parliament are distributed to the ministries for comments. The other ministries have to give a unanimous 'go-ahead' before action can be taken on these matters.

Conflicts between ministries are appreciably more common than conflicts within ministries, but the total extent of interaction is relatively low (except with the Ministry of Finance). This lack of interaction might suggest a lack of coordination. In reality, however, the departmental officials usually know the opinion which other ministries hold in advance. Consequently they either avoid taking up matters which are outside their specific domain, or attempt to minimise conflict by adapting their proposals to the expected reactions of other departments.

When the non-Socialist government came to power in 1976, it had to develop ways of achieving day-to-day coordination among the three coalition partners. The solution was to set up small staffs (*cabinets*) of political appointees around each party leader. The members of these three *cabinets* met whenever necessary to çoordinate policies or solve conflicts. These units soon provided the ministries with a means of by-passing the Ministry of Finance and, in a few cases, even the cabinet. As a result the power of the Ministry of Finance was temporarily reduced.

Much coordination takes place, regardless of the type of government in power, via the Ministry of Finance, but this type of (primarily economic) interdepartmental coordination typically blocks other forms of coordination. The Ministry of Finance coordinates by juxtaposing the departments' interests, not through true cooperation designed to find optimum solutions to interdepartmental problems.

The relationship between Ministers and civil servants is formally hierarchical. In practice, however, it can seldom be characterised in terms of issuing and obeying orders. Key concepts in this connection are rather anticipation, loyalty, trust, personality and informal discussion. In this respect, we should distinguish between two types of situation.

The first relates to appeals against previous decisions taken at lower administrative levels. Swedish Ministers take many minor decisions – indeed the large majority of decisions taken by the cabinet fall into this category. These decisions are based on the advice of higher civil servants which Ministers may accept or reject, but which they normally accept. In giving advice, civil servants typically anticipate the Minister's reaction. They often know the Minister's opinions and preferences, even in the case of a newly appointed Minister, since most cabinet members were previously Members of Parliament whose views are on record.

Ministers, on the other hand, base their judgements not only on the facts and figures presented to them, but also on their opinion of the civil servants who provide the advice. Civil servants whom Ministers trust thus have some room for manoeuvre, while those not in favour will see their proposals scrutinised and questioned. On the other hand, new problems and policies have to be dealt with differently, since one cannot fall back on precedents. The decision-making process then takes the form of a 'sounding out'.[8] The Minister and his immediate advisers discuss the matter frankly with their civil servants, thereby avoiding or reducing the risk of conflict within the department.

The Under Secretary can play a leading part within a department and the Minister may be merely an 'ambassador'. This was particularly the case before 1976. Meanwhile, during the same long period of Social Democratic rule, the distinction between administrators and political appointees was blurred. This changed in 1976, when the distinction between the two groups was once again marked. Many Ministers wished to have more direct contact with their departmental officials although, at the same time, problems stemming from the existence of the coalition contributed to some degree of frustration on the part of these officials.

The question of the relationship between Ministers, political appointees and 'regular' officials is thus not fully resolved. A key link in this respect is provided by the general directors of administrative divisions, who are not political appointees and are involved in the detailed drafting of the policy proposals of the departments. This is why it has sometimes been suggested that they become political appointees. This has not occurred, however, but it has been suggested that they have been able to achieve their task successfully because the turnover of these officials has been low, even when governments changed.

The division of the central administration into ministries and agencies raises a further problem – that of the influence which Ministers can exercise on agencies. Formally, Ministers can do little, but the informal situation may be different. The Constitution stipulates that the cabinet should give the agencies general guidelines, but in practice the relationship is more one of mutual dependency. The ministries have the funds and the agencies know how to implement policy. They need each other if they are to function effectively. Heads of agencies are therefore eager to discover plans and proposals well in advance, as the views of new Ministers are consequently closely examined by representatives of agencies.

The Swedish cabinet and the Swedish policy process are rather open. Ministers have many outside contacts and receive information from other sources than that of the civil service rank-and-file. Ministers may have close links with interest groups. A Minister who does not pay sufficient attention to the views of these bodies will soon experience difficulties when his or her proposals come before Parliament or during the implementation phase.

The mass media also play a substantial role: this is indicated by the presence of a Press Secretary in each department. Finally, an important sounding-board for Ministers is the public at large. Representing the country or party at the opening of new factories, the launching of ships, and so on is of symbolic and real political importance, while visits abroad help to ensure that the external aspects of governmental policies are satisfactorily perceived.

Of course, the broad nature of these roles suggests that Ministers have different profiles. Some Ministers prefer to work inside their department or at cabinet level, while others are happier to act as the representative or 'ambassador' of their department. But, apart from personal idiosyncrasies, the nature of the department and the nature of the problems which have to be dealt with impose constraints which force Ministers to fulfil, to some extent at least, all these roles simultaneously.

## 4 CABINET DECISION-MAKING

There are several types of cabinet meetings, both formal and informal. One type of cabinet meeting is the 'general meeting' (*allmän beredning*), which takes place at least once a week when Parliament is in session. Issues of political importance are discussed in depth and differences of opinion between Ministers are settled during these meetings if bilateral or other negotiations have failed. Officials are occasionally asked to introduce matters and to answer questions, but they have to retire for the discussion. The only 'outsider' present at this point would be the Under Secretary to the Prime Minister or, if a coalition government is in power, the Under Secretaries of each party leader. No minutes are kept and votes are seldom taken. Discussions usually end with the Prime Minister making a summary and interpreting the decision. Only about 1 per cent of the 25 000 cabinet decisions made in 1982/1983 had been discussed in general meetings.[9]

Another form of meeting is the 'lunch meeting' (*lunchberedningen*). Ministers have lunch together each weekday and the level of attendance is very high. They then discuss matters of relatively limited substance but which might be politically significant, and they also consider interdepartmental questions. The topics raised during these lunches is affected by public pressure and media attention. The main aim of these meetings is to inform and to provide an opportunity to decide whether a question needs to be brought up at a general meeting. The Prime Minister chairs both types of meeting. In his absence the Deputy Prime Minister or the most senior Minister present chair the meetings. In order to put an issue on the agenda for a general meeting, Ministers must notify the Prime Minister or his office well in advance and the agenda is then circulated. Lunch meetings have no pre-determined agenda.

By and large, collective responsibility is achieved by means of informal discussions, by the fact that Ministers are well acquainted with each other and by the preparatory work done by officials (who also know each other and adjust their policies to ensure that cooperation is maximised). Thus, the level of conflict in cabinet is low. It is therefore possible for Ministers to take many decisions individually without creating problems for the government. This was especially true during the long period of Social Democratic rule.

Ministers often remained at the head of the same department for many years and often became experts in their field. Therefore, hardly anybody outside their department wold challenge their suggestions. Only the Minister of Finance ventured outside his own departmental affairs. His position has traditionally been strong in Social Democratic governments and he is typically supported by the Prime Minister in cabinet (the Prime Minister in turn being mainly concerned with the 'external' relations of the government).

The situation has sometimes been compared to a company, in which the Prime Minister is the President and the Minister of Finance is the Vice-President.[10] This means that conflicts between the Minister of Finance and other cabinet members are more frequent. Technically, the

Minister of Finance does not have any special powers but, in practice, the relationship is rather hierarchical. Officials of the Ministry of Finance tend to give orders to officials of other departments or to veto proposals from other departments. The same cannot be said of the Prime Minister's Office, as it is too small to take on such a task on a regular basis. The Ministry of Finance had a less dominant role during the 1976–1982 coalition period. The tendency was then to bring fewer issues to cabinet, but conflicts on those issues which were brought up were higher. Coalition partners tended to meet separately before regular cabinet meetings, thus conflicts were often solved by smaller groups of Ministers.

The role of the Minister of Finance was reduced as a result, especially between 1976 and 1978, but this was an exceptional situation. Whether practices would alter if the Social Democratic party were no longer to dominate Swedish politics is a matter which can only be an object of speculation.

By and large, and perhaps because of the long period of Social Democratic rule, the Swedish cabinet has tended to be composed of men and women who knew each other well and who operated on the basis of a desire to minimise conflict by anticipating the reactions of colleagues, civil servants, Parliament, interest groups and the population at large. This system functions on the basis of many unwritten understandings and modes of behaviour. Leadership exists, but it is modified by respect for the views of colleagues and other interested parties.

The key word is cooperation, achieved by discussion and the prior examination of proposals. How far this is the result of the long experience acquired by single party government, by the relatively small size of the country or by the specific characteristics of Swedish political life is a matter which cannot easily be decided.

## Notes

1.  Elder, N. (1970). *Government in Sweden. The Executive at Work*, (Oxford: Pergamon Press) pp. 45–46.
2.  These commissions are still called Royal Commissions although they are no longer appointed by the 'King in Council'.
3.  Premfors, R., 'Governmental Commissions in Sweden', *American Behavioral Scientist*, vol. 26, no. 5.
4.  Board, J.B. Jr. (1970). *The Government and Politics of Sweden*, (Boston: Houghton Mifflin Company) pp. 146–147.

212    *Sweden*

5.   Vinde, P. and Petri, G. (1978). *Swedish Government Administration. An Introduction*, (Lund: Prisma/The Swedish Institute) pp. 30–35.
6.   Isberg, M. (1982). *The First Decade of the Unicameral Riksdag. The Role of the Swedish Parliament in the 1970s* (Stockholm: University of Stockholm, Department of Political Science, Research report).
7.   Larsson, T., *The Cabinet and its Ministries. Coordination and Bureaucracy in the Political Center of Power* (Lund: Studentlitteratur) p. 127, 1986.
8.   Olsen, J.P. (1980). 'Governing Norway: Segmentation, anticipation and consensus formation', in *Presidents and Prime Ministers*, (Washington, D.C.) p. 253.
9.   Larsson, T. (1986). p. 235.
10.  Ruin, O. (1986). *I välfärdsstatens tjänst. Tage Erlander 1946–69*, (Kristianstad: Tiden). Forthcoming version in English.

# 13 Finland

## Jaakko Nousiainen

### 1 CABINET SETTING

Seen in broad terms, the position of the State Council (as the cabinet is officially known) within the Finnish political system is governed by three constraints – namely the prominent position occupied by the President of the Republic, the strong bureaucratic tradition typical of the country's central administration and Finland's fragmented multi-party system.

Of these factors, the first determines the basis for the cabinet's formal constitutional role. The second determines the nature of its links with the rest of government, together with the type and style of its decision-making, The third determines its 'political complexion' in terms of its relations with Parliament, the political parties and other collective bodies. Article 2 of the Constitution states that:

> Supreme executive power is vested in the President of the Republic. In addition to the President there shall be, for the general government of the State, a State Council consisting of a Prime Minister and the necessary number of Ministers.

An American style presidentially-led government, however, was never envisaged. Instead, the relationship between the Head of State and the cabinet is based on a carefully and clearly defined division of responsibility. The President enjoys a number of important and specific prerogative powers, while the everyday running of executive politics is in the hands of the State Council. This division is not complete, however, as the cabinet also deals with various matters more strictly within the competence of the President.

The complete lack of a separate presidential administrative department also means that the preliminary drafting of presidential rulings and judgements must be done in the ministries and the cabinet. Presidential decisions are taken in cabinet in the presence of the Ministers of the government of the day and their execution is the responsibility of the cabinet. This arrangement is sufficient in the majority of cases to bind the President to the government's policy position.

Within this framework, the Finnish system of semi-presidential rule places a number of significant limits on the range of actions available to the cabinet.

- The President's dominant role in the area of foreign policy is undisputed. He is responsible for taking strategic foreign policy decisions and government follows his lead.
- In the area of domestic politics, the President is entitled to be kept informed of the most important issues of the moment and has the right to make his own policy initiatives and, in exceptional cases, the right to use his power of veto.
- In a multi-party system such as Finland's, the President is often in a position to nominate Prime Ministers from amongst what can sometimes be a wide field of possible contenders, and is thereby able to influence the composition of the eventual coalition which comes to make up a government. He can also, in exceptional circumstances, end a government's term of office by dissolving Parliament and ordering new elections.
- As a result of the principle of hierarchical dualism, the Prime Minister can never assume the role of a national leader in the same way as his colleagues are able to in a true cabinet system. Instead, his role tends to be restricted to something of a supervisory one, responsible for the handling of day-to-day politics. Rather than the Prime Minister, it is the President who is seen to exercise direct personal power and it is to him that popular emotional feelings attach themselves (Paige, 1977).

The bureaucratic tradition makes itself felt in the fact that the cabinet is primarily considered in Finland as a college of Ministers, with a pronounced egalitarian structure, acting as the forum for all major decision-making and its activities being governed by detailed legal provisions. Progress towards seeing an expansion in the Prime Minister's potential to take on more of a leadership role, and an acceptance of the concept of individual ministerial responsibility, has been relatively slow to emerge. Something of the same sort of development may also be evident in the cabinet's comparatively loose links with Parliament, at least compared to those found in the Westminster model of parliamentarism, although Ministers are required (this being specifically mentioned in the provisions of the Constitution) to have the confidence of Parliament.

Two of the most obvious consequences resulting from Finland's multi-party system have been the high turnover of governments and the continuing shifts which have taken place in the composition of coalitions, both of which have been typical features of the country's political life. Table 13.1 details the 34 cabinets which have held office between 1950 and 1987. The average term of office of these governments amounts to about a year. Of the 34 cabinets in question, 19 have been majority and 8 minority administrations, while the remaining 7 have been caretaker cabinets lacking any direct party political backing.

The majority of the coalitions holding office over the period in question were built around the Social Democratic Party and the Agrarian/Centre Party, in government either together or alternately. The formation of grand coalitions has required the inclusion of a third major party, either from the right (the Conservatives) or the left (the Communists). The consensus-oriented trend evident in Finnish politics goes some way to explaining why many of the majority governments have been oversized. Minimal winning coalitions have, in comparison, been rare (Lijphart, 1984).


## 2  CABINET STRUCTURE

The historical origins of the State Council go back to the central organ of domestic civil administration, known as the Senate, which was introduced during the nineteenth century. The small autonomous Finnish Grand-Duchy was administered by extremely simple means. The executive was initially divided into only five departments with the decision-making responsibility being exercised by a college of senators, which also served as the supreme court. Members of the Senate were usually appointed for successive three-year terms of office. The Diet had no means of influencing the Senate and the impact of party politics was only felt in the composition of its membership at the beginning of the twentieth century.

The nineteenth century Senate was not therefore a political cabinet, nor was it headed by a Prime Minister. Its outward status remained unchanged until the period between 1917 and 1919, when it experienced a radical transformation as part of the country's adoption of a parliamentary form of government. As a consequence of the new necessity for them to enjoy parliamentary confidence, cabinets became tied to the party political system and the previous continuity that had been the Senate's hallmark was replaced by continual change and flux. In terms of its internal relations and workings, however, the Senate was

TABLE 13.1  Governments in Finland: 1950–1987

| Prime Minister | PM Party | Date in | Duration years | Party Composition of Government | Parliamentary Support % |
|---|---|---|---|---|---|
| Kekkonen I | AGR | 17.03.50 | 0.8 | 3,4,5, | 37.5 |
| Kekkonen II | AGR | 17.01.51 | 0.7 | 2,3,4,5, | 64.5 |
| Kekkonen III | AGR | 20.09.51 | 1.8 | 2,3,5, | 59.5 |
| Kekkonen IV | AGR | 09.07.53 | 0.3 | 3,5, | 33.0 |
| Tuomioja | — | 17.11.53 | 0.5 | 4,5,7, | — |
| Törngren | SWE | 05.05.54 | 0.4 | 2,3,5, | 60.0 |
| Kekkonen V | AGR | 20.10.54 | 1.4 | 2,3, | 53.5 |
| Fagerholm II | SDP | 03.03.56 | 1.2 | 2,3,4,5, | 66.5 |
| Sukselainen I | AGR | 27.05.57 | 0.5 | 3,4,5, | 39.5 |
| Von Fieandt | — | 29.11.57 | 0.4 | 0, | — |
| Kuuskoski | — | 26.04.58 | 0.3 | 0, | — |
| Fagerholm III | SDP | 29.08.58 | 0.4 | 2,3,4,5,7, | 73.5 |
| Sukselainen II | AGR | 13.01.59 | 2.5 | 3,5, | 31.0 |
| Miettunen I | AGR | 14.07.61 | 0.7 | 3, | 24.0 |
| Karjalainen I | AGR | 13.04.62 | 1.7 | 3,4,5,7, | 54.0 |
| Lehto | — | 18.12.63 | 0.7 | 0, | — |
| Virolainen | AGR | 12.09.64 | 1.7 | 3,4,5,7, | 56.0 |
| Paasio I | SDP | 27.05.66 | 1.8 | 1,2,3, | 76.0 |
| Koivisto I | SDP | 22.03.68 | 2.1 | 1,2,3,5, | 82.0 |

| | | | | | |
|---|---|---|---|---|---|
| Aura I | LIB | 14.05.70 | 0.2 | 0, | — |
| Karjalainen IIa | AGR | 15.07.70 | 0.7 | 1,2,3,4,5, | 72.0 |
| Karjalainen IIb | AGR | 26.03.71 | 0.6 | 2,3,4,5, | 54.0 |
| Aura II | LIB | 29.10.71 | 0.3 | 0, | — |
| Paasio II | SDP | 23.02.72 | 0.5 | 2, | 27.5 |
| Sorsa I | SDP | 04.09.72 | 2.8 | 2,3,4,5, | 53.5 |
| Liinamaa | SDP | 13.06.75 | 0.5 | 2,3,4,5,7, | — |
| Miettunen II | AGR | 30.11.75 | 0.8 | 1,2,3,4,5, | 76.0 |
| Miettunen III | AGR | 29.09.76 | 0.6 | 3,4,5, | 29.0 |
| Sorsa IIa | SDP | 15.05.77 | 0.7 | 1,2,3,4,5, | 76.0 |
| Sorsa IIb | SDP | 02.03.78 | 1.2 | 1,2,3,4, | 71.0 |
| Koivisto II | SDP | 25.05.79 | 2.6 | 1,2,3,5, | 66.5 |
| Sorsa IIIa | SDP | 19.02.82 | 0.9 | 1,2,3,5, | 66.5 |
| Sorsa IIIb | SDP | 31.12.82 | 0.3 | 2,3,5, | 49.0 |
| Sorsa IV | SDP | 06.05.83 | 4.0 | 2,3,5,6, | 61.5 |

0 = non partisan
1 = communists and radical socialists
2 = Social Democratic Party
3 = Agrarian/Centre Party
4 = Liberal Party
5 = Swedish People's Party
6 = Finnish Rural Party (populists)
7 = national Coalition party (conservatives)

SOURCE: Nousiainen (1985b); Paloheimo (1984).

transformed into the new State Council largely in name only, and the bureaucratic tradition inherited from the nineteenth century continued to colour the activities of the new body for long into the future.

The formal structure of the State Council is uncomplicated and straightforward, comprising the Prime Minister and a group of Ministers of equal rank. Its precise size can vary, only the maximum number of members being prescribed by law (there are currently seventeen Ministers alongside the Prime Minister). During the inter-war years, the number of cabinet Ministers typically ranged from between ten and twelve, subsequently it has varied from thirteen to eighteen. No ministerial hierarchy exists in Finland, as there are no Deputy Prime Ministers, no junior Ministers, no political Secretaries of State and no distinction is made between the cabinet and the wider government.

There are not, it is true, enough departments for all the Ministers, as there are only twelve of them. It has become established practice to appoint two Ministers to the most important ministries and to agree on their division of responsibilities at the time of the formation of each new administration. Although one of the Ministers concerned is formally considered as the head of the entire ministerial unit, the 'second Minister', as he or she is called, is not hierarchically subordinated to the other. Instead, both are treated as having independent charge over their individual areas of responsibility. Over the last few decades, two Ministers have been typically appointed to handle the portfolios of Foreign Affairs, Finance, Trade and Industry, Education and Culture, and Social Affairs and Health. Ministers Without Portfolio, who only take part in decision-making at cabinet meetings without being responsible for any specific area of government, have not been appointed since the 1950s.

The egalitarian nature of the State Council is also reflected in the position accorded to the Prime Minister. From a formal point of view, his primary role is to chair cabinet meetings. He does of course have other special duties, such as the right to appoint cabinet members to ministerial committees and to serve as the President's substitute when necessary, but these functions are of secondary importance. The Constitution makes no reference to the Prime Minister's right or duty to direct the work of the cabinet and government policy, nor does it include any requirement that he be responsible for its general policy with respect to Parliament.

In presidential cabinet meetings the role of Prime Minister is virtually equivalent to that of any rank-and-file Minister. His vote carries no special weight in ordinary cabinet meetings. Only in cases where votes are equally divided for and against a proposal does the chairman have a casting vote. The Prime Minister is not even responsible for determining the official agenda of cabinet meetings, which instead take shape on the basis of proposals submitted for discussion by the ministries themselves. Seen against this background, the position which a Prime Minister is able to achieve for himself as leader of the cabinet is essentially dependent on the structure of the coalition in power and on his own personal experience and dynamism.

One Minister is appointed to serve as the Prime Minister's deputy, as and when the situation demands. Since the Minister in question is usually head of a ministry (a function not affected by this appointment) and only assumes Prime Ministerial responsibilities if the Prime Minister is unable to do so, it would be misleading to consider him as having effectively the status of a Deputy Prime Minister.

The personal staffs of Ministers are small. Each Minister is provided with a Political Secretary, while the Prime Minister can call upon three or four special advisers, who serve as Political Secretary and aides dealing with foreign policy, economic policy and parliamentary questions. The office attached to the State Council is also subordinated to him but this is, in essence, a fully-fledged government department comparable to a ministry and responsible for handling specific administrative matters.

As a result of the country's history, Finland's central government is characterised by formal structures and procedures based on Weberian principles, as well as by a great respect for legal norms. These principles are reflected in the careful documentation of draft proposals and of final decisions, which is standard practice, as well as in the right of public access to these decisions. These procedures are indeed reinforced by inter-party competition. These practices contrast sharply with the less rigid as well as more secretive style of operation found in the workings of the cabinets of many other countries.

The details of the division of authority existing between the President, the cabinet, individual Ministers and other central organs of government and officials at the regional and local levels, are regulated by a multitude of statutes. Within the ministries too, the delegation of authority from Ministers to civil servants is also prescribed in a similar way. Everyone in the executive is left in no doubt as to the matters which lie within their area of responsibility and on which issues they may take a decision independently from officials or bodies which are hierarchically above them. It is generally accepted that the vertical division of responsibilities cannot be modified *in casu* through the ruling of a superior official.

Before World War Two, this arrangement led to an institutionalised segmentation of responsibility wholly at odds with the principle of collective responsibility which was relatively undeveloped. The Prime Minister and the government as a whole often had little say in matters which were the acknowledged responsibility of an individual ministry. As a result, Ministers were not unknown to sometimes surprise their colleagues by taking decision independently from the rest of the cabinet on important issues. Subsequently, various informal coordinatory mechanisms have been developed in order to prevent this type of situation from occurring.

Writing in his memoirs on the question of Finland's entry into the war, K-A. Fagerholm, the then Minister of Social Affairs, commented:

> I did not know about it then and I still do not know how it happened. One thing is certain: the government did not know anything. By the government I mean the whole government – some Ministers were obviously aware of what was going on. The President, the Prime Minister, the Defence Minister and perhaps a couple of other Ministers as well must have known. (Fagerholm, 1977).

While political leadership typically becomes concentrated in the hands of a small inner circle in times of crisis, in a segmented system such as Finland's this is further emphasised by the fact that foreign policy is deemed to be the specific responsibility of the Ministers mentioned by Fagerholm, together with the cabinet's Foreign Affairs Committee. Fagerholm and the other members of the cabinet left outside this grouping had to be content with administering their own ministries, making little or no effort to penetrate the inner circle.

It would be misleading, however, to suggest that the cabinet does not take a leading role in decision-making – at present some 4500 to 5000 matters are handled annually by the cabinet during its official meetings. While cabinet decisions are centralised and taken collectively, the formal drafting and preparation of proposals is wholly devolved to lower-ranking bodies. Proposals are generally drafted in the departments and offices of the respective ministries. *The rapporteur* system in use in Finland is based on the principle that the drafting of a matter for consideration by the cabinet is the responsibility of a single civil servant. He or she assembles the background information, prepares a memorandum and a draft proposal and attends the relevant cabinet meeting to provide further information orally as required. Depending on the nature of the question, the issue has been discussed with immediate superiors and the relevant Minister.

It is not necessary, however, for the Minister and the civil servant to agree on a proposal, although this is usually the case. Civil servants are ultimately entitled to present issues as they see fit. A Minister can append his or her view on the relevant documents and naturally attempts to argue his or her case in cabinet. While what has just been described concerns routine administrative affairs, issues of wider significance, together with politically sensitive questions, are understandably less closely tied to this system of civil servant based drafting. These issues find themselves the subject of argument and discussion in the wider political arena, within the parties, the ministerial committees and elsewhere.

The drawing up of the agenda for an official cabinet meeting is not the responsibility of any single individual. Agendas take shape virtually independently of any coordinating hand on the basis of the various issues under discussion within the ministries at any particular time.

> Prior to a matter being brought before a general meeting of the cabinet, the civil servant responsible for a particular proposal in the relevant ministry distributes an agenda drawn up according to standardized practice. The distribution of an agenda requires the approval of the Minister concerned. (*Ministerin käsikirja*, 1987).

Individual Ministers are therefore in a key position. They have the right to block some issues and accelerate the progress of others. Only since 1985 has it been possible to require a Minister to bring an issue before the State Council, although such a move cannot be decided upon by the Prime Minister alone but must be decided by the whole cabinet.

This procedure has led to a clear division between formal and informal business in the work of the cabinet. All decisions having legal implications have to be taken, following an established procedural pattern, in official sittings, where it is not possible to discuss general government policy, developments in Parliament or similar questions. The latter are dealt with in a variety of separate discussion arenas, of which the most central are the cabinet's regular unofficial evening meetings, known as the government's 'evening school'. The standing ministerial committees act as a link between these two forums, the Foreign Affairs Committee, the Finance Committee and the Economic Policy Committee being statutory bodies. They are responsible for drafting specific proposals. Smaller, more informal groupings give Ministers the chance to discuss problems more freely, decide on future arrangements and resolve their political differences.

The nature of the issues at stake thus determines whether they progress along the 'formal administrative' or the 'political' route. Routine administrative business is usually processed through the first of these channels, while the more politically sensitive questions follow the more informal route, only returning to the official machinery for the ratification of a formal decision which might have been taken.

Official cabinet meetings, together with the cabinet's informal evening sessions and presidential sittings, at which the whole cabinet is present, are held on a regular basis once a week. Taken together with the regular committee meetings, the framework of the government's weekly schedule is as follows:

Tuesday – Economic Policy Committee
Wednesday – Finance Committee, preparatory and official sessions, unofficial cabinet meeting
Thursday – Official cabinet meeting, lasting about 1 hour, typically 30 to 50 items on the agenda
Friday – Economic Policy Committee
Presidential session, about 30 minutes, 20 to 30 items

## 3  CABINET LIFE

### General political background

The multi-party nature of the Finnish parliamentary system is the central characteristic accounting for the way in which this system operates. Parliament is typically composed of seven to eight politically relevant parties. There is no majority or dominant party, as even the largest parties secure only about a quarter of the seats in Parliament. Political opinion is not strongly polarised, a fact reflected in the popularity of broad centre-based coalitions and the absence of any fundamental opposition between Right and Left (von Beyme, 1985).

During the period under discussion the parties were divided, in terms of their parliamentary position, into three main groupings. The Social. Democrats and the Agrarians were the major governmental forces in governments over the period (as Table 13.1 indicates) acting as the senior coalition partners and holding office either jointly or alternately. The small centre parties, such as the Liberals and the Swedish People's Party, provided support to governments and thus allowed the creation of broader-based administrations when required. The Conservatives and the Communists formed the opposition, which tended to be weak and divided during most of the period. If the last two groups entered the government, they had to do so on the centre's terms and had to sacrifice some of their ideological objectives to obtain ministerial portfolios.

Despite its limitations, this arrangement proved adequate to provide a range of alternative coalitions which never remained exactly the same when a new government came to office; in two cases out of three a significant change of coalition partners affected at least one major party. Sixteen different men served as Prime Minister between 1950 and 1986.

Under the Finnish system the President appoints the members of a new government independently of Parliament and no formal expression or parliamentary confidence is required before a government takes office. Before any government can be formed, however, the parties have first to agree to take part in it and come to a compromise on the division of ministerial portfolios. Attitudes within the parties to this question have varied. The autonomy of the parliamentary party on these matters has been traditionally stressed on the Right, while on the Left the importance of the party organisation have been emphasised. These differences have, however, declined over the years and party policy on the shape of a new administration is currently generally decided in joint discussions between parliamentary groups and party executives.

The scope which the Prime Minister has to influence developments at the time of the formation of a new government is limited by the fact that he cannot personally select those of his ministerial colleagues who are to be drawn from outside his own party. The other coalition parties nominate their own appointees to the ministerial positions that have been allocated to them, with the exception of the post of foreign Minister, who is selected in agreement with the President.

Parties in Finland's fragmented political system are comparatively homogeneous, in both social and ideological terms, and questions of relationships between Ministers, parliamentary parties and party organisation do not usually raise major problems. Group cohesion and consensus are usually very high in the parliamentary parties and, through the judicious use of party discipline, parties are able to oversee the behaviour of their MPs.

There are, nonetheless, sources of friction or conflict. One of the characteristic features of coalition-type parliamentarism is that no one party is ever in a position to dictate government policy and, as a result, all the parties in the coalition find themselves a little at odds with this policy. The greatest difficulties in this area are likely to occur when parties do not nominate their top leaders for cabinet posts, and instead select second-ranking politicians. In some extreme situations it has been known for a party to disavow any share in government responsibility despite the fact that some of its members held ministerial office. About a third of Ministers are drawn on average from outside Parliament and these are most often criticised for not keeping their party group informed of developments (von Bonsdorff, 1982).

Finland would be unlikely to adopt the Swedish procedure according to which the Prime Minister is also chairman of his parliamentary party (Ruin, 1986). From the 1970s onwards, the attendance of Prime Ministers and Ministers at parliamentary sittings has perceptibly diminished. There have even been two years during which the Prime Minister of the day did not address MPs once in the course of a parliamentary session. To counter this tendency attempts have been made to improve informal links, by granting the leaders of the parliamentary groups of the coalition parties the opportunity to attend informal meetings of the cabinet (Nousiainen, 1985).

## Coordination mechanisms used by cabinet

The cabinet faces a number of problems in coordinating its political and administrative activities. In the political arena, difficulties are created by the fact that the parties wish, on the one hand, to oversee the running of the ministries which they control independently from the cabinet. On the other, they wish to keep a close watch on the activities of the ministries which their competitors control. Administrative problems can be caused when proposals being drafted at the technical level affect areas handled by a number of different ministries, or have to be fitted into the overall budget framework.

Reference has already been made to the rigid division of authority between the cabinet and the individual Ministers. This has traditionally allowed Ministers to act freely within their own spheres of influence. Ministers, however, are seldom in a position to take wide-ranging policy decisions independently, as all the most important questions affecting legislation, the budget and important appointments have to be raised in cabinet for final approval. The essence of political coordination lies in ensuring that issues are brought to the cabinet at a sufficently early stage, so that the Minister in question cannot exercise sole control over the proposal and thus surprise the government with suggestions more in line with his own personal views than those of the government as a whole.

Table 13.2 lists, in summarised form, the means of coordination –

formal and informal, permanent and temporary, – which are available at cabinet level (Larsson, 1986). Of these means the most important are the three permanent cabinet committees which were already mentioned. The Finance Committee and the Economic Policy Committee, in their regular weekly meetings, exercise coordination in both the political and administrative fields and constitute preliminary forums for matters subsequently to be decided in cabinet and in the individual ministries. In many cases, ministries are required to secure formal authorisation from the Finance Committee before embarking on expensive projects. The Economic Policy Committee, which meets twice a week, acts as the cabinet's general policy-drafting body, and as a result it sometimes acquires the character of an inner cabinet.

TABLE 13.2    Cabinet coordination mechanisms in Finland

|          | *Permanent*                              | *Temporary*                       |
| -------- | ---------------------------------------- | --------------------------------- |
| Formal   | permanent committees reports and memoranda | *ad hoc* committees joint preparation |
| Informal | 'the evening school' party groups        | project groups                    |

The cabinet's weekly unofficial evening meeting plays a prominent part in policy fomulation and political coordination. The agenda of these meetings is decided by the Prime Minister and usually includes proposals which are still at the drafting stage. A secondary function of these meetings is to provide an opportunity, outside the unwanted attentions of the media, for reaching last-minute agreements. The cabinet can then avoid having to vote in its official session which need not be marked by long and contentious debates. The ministerial group of the various government parties also contribute in some manner to coordination. Inter-party conflicts are discussed in joint meetings held between the leaders of these groups before the government policy becomes final.

It is difficult to draw a precise line between temporary cabinet committees and unofficial project groups. As the name indicates, the latter are usually responsible for preliminary work on a single issue, while an officially appointed cabinet committee can develop into a semi-permanent policy planning body responsible for a specific sector of government strategy. On a rough estimate, some twenty ministerial committees are established annually, a proportion of which are semi-permanent and cover an aspect of government policy. At the beginning of 1986 there were four such committees, devoted to mass communication, social security, labour questions and environmental issues (*Virallinen lehti*, no. 10, October 1986).

Administrative coordination is handled by means of various committees and working groups of civil servants from two or more ministries, and by means of requests for formal appraisals from other ministries. The latter procedure is primarily intended to assist in coordinating the implementation of budgetary legislation, the integration of the international relations of individual ministries with the country's overall foreign policy strategy and work on drafting new legislation.

## Ministerial style

The well-known phrase familiar from the early French republics – 'governments change but Ministers remain' – does not apply in Finland. Compared to many other Western European countries, the average length of time in office of Ministers in Finland is one of the shortest (under three years) and the number of Ministers holding office for only a single term one of the highest (Blondel, 1985). This relatively large turnover of Ministers, together with the broad base of many coalitions, tends to favour nominal democracy rather than administrative efficiency and amateurism rather than specialisation. Parties are not in a position to select their ministerial portfolios freely and the few which they have filled have tended to be allocated more on the basis of party achievements than on candidate competence or suitability.

Since the 1960s there have been changes in attitudes towards ministerial office. The massive expansion in the public sector and its role in directing social developments has brought with it a new set of challenges for Ministers. They have increasingly disengaged themselves from collective government, acquiring their own political authority and becoming political stars in their own right. Parties can no longer distribute portfolios merely as prizes for loyal party services or long parliamentary careers. The personal ability of Ministers has risen. Many present-day Ministers show a greater desire than their predecessors to present themselves in a forceful way to the media – they wish to appear in charge. Yet the parliamentary amateur has not been replaced by administrative or technical specialists, but by skilful politicians. Currently, a Minister is not likely to master the technical details of the matters dealt with by his department, but he is likely to identify with the goals which are pursued and will use political experience, dynamism and determination to direct the specialist manpower at his disposal.

In this context, the Prime Minister has to assert his pre-eminence and prevent the disintegration of the cabinet into a number of 'governments within governments'. But we already noted there are restrictions on the Prime Minister's room for manoeuvre, in particular as a result of the powers of the President. The Prime Minister can scarcely become charismatic and develop a creative style of national leadership. His role is more to fulfil certain tasks and especially to be dealt with everyday issues. Only the most determined Prime Ministers have been able to innovate, Urho Kekkonen being one of them during the 1950s. At the administrative level the Prime Minister's role is that of a coordinator, whereas in the political arena he is an arbiter.

In domestic politics, the role of the Prime Minister as an arbiter has become increasingly important. Given that the President is primarily responsible for foreign affairs, the Prime Minister concentrates his attention on home affairs and, above all, on economic policy. He unofficially determines the strategic policy of the cabinet and chairs the permanent cabinet committees. For the last twenty years he has played a central part in the negotiations on national incomes policy which have become a feature of Finnish life, and he also guarantees the implementation of agreements. In the 1970s the department directly subordinate to the Prime Minister was made responsible for checking the implementation of government programmes.

Within this framework personality and experience are the qualities which determine the influence of Prime Ministers. Their style has of course been different. Urho Kekkonen and K-A. Fagerholm have been described as representing two opposite extremes on their approach to the job. Fagerholm was well-known for carefully following cabinet discussions, taking notes as they moved along and throwing the field open for suggestions. Kekkonen, in contrast, often put forward his own proposal at the outset and, after listening to his Ministers' reactions, often concluded the discussion by suggesting that the government should follow his initial proposal. Ralf Törngren, a member of the small centre Swedish People's Party who was Prime Minister briefly in the mid-1950s, kept a list of how many times he supported the Agrarians and how many times he supported the Social Democrats. If the figures were equal, he considered that he had acted fairly and maintained the balance of power between the two largest parties (Virolainen, 1969).

The Prime Minister cannot appoint or dismiss Ministers, nor is he the sole government policy spokesman. The experience of the Socialist

Kalevi Sorsa, Prime Minister between 1972 and 1975, 1977 and 1979, and 1982 and 1987, shows the range of potential the office can offer to the respected leader of a large party during a time of relative parliamentary stability.

## 4 CABINET DECISION-MAKING

### Operational rules and techniques

The nature of the cabinet's decision-making apparatus varies substantially depending on whether reference is made to its official or unofficial operations. At the cabinet's formal meetings, the procedure used and the decisions taken on proposals are all based on written documentation. The submissions drawn up by the ministries and presented to the cabinet contain at least a brief resumé of the questions at issue, together with the solution suggested by the relevant department. They also often include extensive background information.

Documents relating to proposed new legislation must be distributed to all Ministers two days before the meeting at which they will be discussed, and other documents at least one day in advance. Only in exceptional circumstances, and with the Prime Minister's express permission, can an issue be brought before cabinet directly. Ministers are therefore informed in advance about the issues to be put to cabinet, and are entitled to request the postponement of discussion of a specific case for a few days to allow them more time to study it in detail.

Meetings follow a set pattern. Issues are brought up for discussion ministry by ministry. The presentation of a question is normally restricted to a reference to the documents previously distributed to those attending. A discussion on the question at hand follows, after which a decision is taken and recorded in the minutes by the Prime Minister in his capacity as chairman. In cases where discussion fails to disagreements, a vote is taken following a carefully stipulated set of rules. In practice, it is up to the Prime Minister to decide whether he allows a vote (the results are made public) or whether he decides to postpone a decision in the hope that there will be an eventual agreement.

As the bulk of politically sensitive matters is handled outside formal sessions, dozens of matters can be processed in a meeting lasting only an hour. The subjects discussed, the decisions made, together with the results of any votes taken (but not the details of the actual discussion themselves) are recorded in the minutes of each meeting, which, in accordance with the principle of public right-of-access, are subsequently made available for anyone wishing to read them.

For the informal evening cabinet sessions Ministers are required to submit the points they wish to see discussed to the Prime Minister's Secretary, at least a day before the meeting (but the Prime Minister does decide on the agenda). Discussion is perceptibly more relaxed than that at official meetings, the aim being to achieve consensus and to reinforce the cabinet's internal solidarity and collective responsibility. Minutes are kept by the Prime Minister's Secretary but, unlike those of the formal sessions, these are not made public.

The Finnish cabinet's activities are conspicuously open. This is due to three factors. First, documents drawn up and produced by the executive, as well as those sent to the government, are *ipso facto* open to public scrutiny. Second, the government has a comprehensive information system at its disposal. Third, the loose nature of coalitions, together with inter-party rivalry, ensures that even confidential discussions and internal government disputes soon leak to the press.

The legally guaranteed public access requirement affects documents arising from official decisions and those received by government officials from private individuals. Matters still under discussion, together with internal reports and memoranda produced by the executive, are not normally made public. Nor are they considered secret, and a Minister can give permission for such information to be released. The President or the cabinet can, in individual cases, declare a document to be secret, but this procedure is usually restricted to foreign policy material.

Official announcements and related public relations questions affecting the government as a whole are handled by a six-person information department based in the Prime Minister's Office. Following every cabinet meeting, the department distributes the relevant documents to radio and television correspondents, the Finnish News Agency (STT) and over 30 newspapers. It also regularly publishes an appendix devoted to State Council affairs in the weekly government gazette, *Virallinen lehti*, which includes a list of the proposals approved by the President and the cabinet over the previous week. Information regarding the cabinet's evening sessions and other informal discussions is given without reference being made to the discussions which took place. This is done by the head of the information department under the instructions of the Prime Minister (*Ministerin käsikirja*, 1987; *Valtioneuvoston esittelijän opas*, 1981).

The same degree of public disclosure does not extend to the cabinet's ministerial committees. The minutes of the Foreign Affairs Committee are secret, although many routine matters handled by the Finance Committee are of little interest to the general public. The activities of the Economic Policy committee raise particular difficulties, as the principle of freedom of access come into direct conflict with the secrecy requirement affecting the drafting process. Many important aspects of government policy and many individual policy decisions are examined in this committee, but very little is reported about its meetings. One ex-Minister has recalled that, at the beginning of the 1980s, the Prime Minister of the day threatened to reduce the number of issues submitted for discussion by the committee unless Ministers – and clearly this was a reference to the Communist Minister concerned – complied with the confidentiality policy he demanded (Kajanoja, 1985). The secrecy surrounding the drafting of the budget has been the subject of some criticism and small leaks to the press occur almost annually.

**Decision-making style**

The State Council is an institution of government, responsible at its official meetings for deciding on a wide variety of individual issues. A sample of cabinet activities over a three-month period in 1958 is shown in Table 13.3 (Nousiainen, 1975).

Table 13.3    Cabinet agenda topics in Finland: October to December 1958

|  | Items | % Total |
|---|---|---|
| Government bills & decrees | 163 | 13 |
| Parliamentary petitions | 18 | 2 |
| Civil service appointments | 210 | 17 |
| Commissions & boards, etc. | 116 | 10 |
| Salaries and pensions | 30 | 3 |
| Financial matters (mostly budget-related) | 405 | 33 |
| Miscellaneous | 273 | 22 |
| Total | 1215 | 100 |

SOURCE:   Jaakko Nousiainen, *Valtioneuvoston historia 1917–1966*, volume III, p. 267 (Helsinki: Government Printing Office, 1975).

According to Cobb and Elder's analysis (1972), the agenda of the cabinet is related to two types of questions – old items (habitual and recurrent) and new items. The latter can include both official reactions to day-to-day events ('fire-fighting activity') and longer-term policy planning.

Normal legislation always includes an element of innovation. Policy decisions breaking new ground have increased in number in the post-war period in comparison to those relating to more routine and formal matters. There has been a two-stage process. The first of these developments took place during World War Two and the early post-war years, when the need to mobilise the country's resources to avert a number of military, foreign policy and economic crises brought about a significant reduction in the level of bureaucratic inflexibility which had previously characterised cabinet activity.

The growth of national income which followed this period led to a new political climate in the 1960s, in which there was a demand for rational management. The role of the cabinet as a planning and policy-making body increased appreciably. This new role has been helped by the emergence of sector-based planning structures oriented towards different areas of social policy (covering such things as education, health care and social security) and by the development of regional planning structures.

The preliminary drafting of planning matters takes places within specialist administrative organs, but decisions can be implemented only when they have been approved by cabinet. Formal procedures had to be adapted to this development, as unofficial and informal discussions and agreements were insufficient. Cabinet decisions in this respect have begun to be referred to as 'statements of principle', which are recorded in cabinet minutes and thereby acquire the status of authoritative and binding declarations of government intent. There is no decision of this type in the material relating to 1958, but subsequently these have become common. A state committee sitting in the late 1970s, which submitted its report in 1978, proposed that cabinet meetings should be less concerned with routine administrative matters and concentrate on forward planning and coordination (*Komiteamietintö*, 1978).

Although one does not know in detail the time-budget of the cabinet, it is clear that the proportion devoted to long-term planning and wider policy problems has markedly increased. The problems which dominate policy discussions within the cabinet essentially revolve around questions of domestic economic, social and cultural policy. Foreign policy, defence, constitutional reform and environmental problems, in contrast, are only raised intermittently.

This general observation is reinforced by an examination of government programmes. Over the course of the last twenty years these have changed from being vague declarations of political intent to detailed and specific documents in which new governments attempt to outline their policy in broad terms for the forthcoming years (Hakovirta and Koskiaho, 1973). Seen from the Prime Minister's position, it was significant that the work of evaluating and monitoring the implementation of programmes was allocated to his department.

Economic and industrial policy, the development of the public sector, inflation, the budget, taxation and social security are among the questions which typically cause disagreement within cabinet. Coalition government abounds with conflicts, most of which are audible and visible to the outside world. Only single-party governments and narrow minority coalitions manage to avoid or to contain conflicts within government ranks. In a situation where the Agrarians represent the interest of agricultural producers and the Social Democrats those of the urban consumer, it has seldom, if ever, been possible for governments, including these parties, to escape from the continuous clashes which take place between them.

Conflicts of this type are solved by votes, mediation, conciliation and compromise. In the heated political atmosphere of the 1950s in particular, government partners were often so sensitive about protecting their own interests that voting was not used as a way of solving problems. The Prime Minister then had to assume the role of conciliator. If he could maintain some measure of government unity, conflicts often shifted to the parliamentary arena. Of the 34 governments listed in Table 13.1, ten collapsed as a result of internal dissension.

When coalitions began to show greater stability, as they did during the second half of the 1970s, more discussion took place about ways of improving the internal solidarity of cabinets and Ministers' perception of the requirements of collective responsibility. Demands voiced by various Prime Ministers for the cabinet to present a united homogeneous face to the outside world reflect not only a move towards the British model, but also the strengthened role of the head of government.

The question of government solidarity has been seen from two perspectives. Those advocating a more liberal approach argue that it is acceptable for open disagreement to exist among members of the cabinet and for recourse to be made to voting to break a deadlock. This comes with the proviso that, after the decision has been taken, those Ministers finding themselves in the minority must accept the majority view, thereby allowing the cabinet to present a united front to Parliament. Those advocating a more rigid arrangement argue that the cabinet should not reveal its internal dissensions on major questions to the outside world, but should always appear unanimous.

In 1983, while presenting his new government which included for the first time Ministers from the Rural Party (a party notorious for its unpredictable parliamentary record) Prime Minister Kalevi Sorsa made it plain that he expected his administration to comply with the stricter of the two interpretations above. 'Prime Minister Sorsa and the leaders of the government parties consistently underlined the fact that the aim of the new government was to remain in office for the entirety of its four year term. Sorsa took it as read that the government would be unanimous in taking decisions on all matters of major importance' (Nousiainen, 1985).

The government succeeded in its aim, although not without difficulties. In a heterogeneous coalition the fulfillment of such a requirement requires extensive confidential negotiations before decisions are taken and a great willingness on the part of coalition members to reconcile their views with those of their partners. It is also likely to cause delays in policy-making and to lead to a narrow governmental agenda which will tend only to deal with questions which are acceptable to all.

In balancing the need for compromise with that of effective decision-making within the context of a multi-party system, the mixture of bureaucracy and informality together with the mixture of presidential leadership and egalitarian cabinet structure have contributed to provide Finland with a working governmental system which, given the divisions of Parliament, might otherwise have been thought impossible.

# Concluding Remarks: A Comparative Approach to the Study of Western European Cabinets

Ferdinand Müller-Rommel

This volume tried to accomplish the necessary first step towards a general understanding of cabinet systems in contemporary Western Europe. The country chapters have given a detailed picture of the way these operate and are affected by such characteristics as the constitutional framework, coalition arrangements or the leadership style of the Prime Minister. This survey did show that our knowledge of cabinet systems across Western Europe is substantial. Although more research has been conducted on cabinets in the Northern area than on the Mediterranean countries, important developments have taken place everywhere.

The bulk of the detailed information is about single systems. This poses a serious problem for comparative analyses, however, as it is difficult at this point to draw general conclusions. What research on cabinet government does therefore need at present is a common approach providing a framework for the analysis on the basis of which it will be possible to summarise, incorporate and interrelate the various characteristics of cabinet structure and cabinet life. The purpose of this chapter is to sketch what this approach might be after reviewing briefly the comparative literature which exists at present.

## COMPARATIVE STUDIES ON CABINET GOVERNMENT

While the literature on single cabinets is extensive, systematic comparative analyses are few. These analyses fall essentially under three headings – namely studies of stability and change, studies on the efficiency of cabinets and studies on ministers.

## 1 Cross-national studies on stability and change

Research on cabinet stability tends to be concerned with the extent of ministerial turnover, the duration of cabinets and the duration of coalitions (Brown *et al.*, 1984; Daalder, 1971; De Swaan, 1973; Dodd, 1984; Lijphart, 1981; Meyer, 1980; Sanders and Herman, 1977; Taylor and Herman, 1971; Taylor and Laver, 1973; Warwick, 1979). It has to be noted that instability results not just from the fact that the turnover of ministers is high, but also from the fact that the maintenance of ministers and of the whole cabinet in office is not predictable.

Some studies have nonetheless argued that most post-war European cabinets have been rather stable on the basis of an empirical measurement of levels of stability and instability. But the country studies in this volume do show that questions of stability and instability go appreciably beyond the examination of ministerial turnover and of cabinet duration. To what might be called a dimension of 'turnover and duration' has therefore to be added a 'conflict' dimension. Such a dimension is concerned with the assessment of the extent to which cabinets can manage conflict situations. An unstable cabinet (unstable, that is, in terms of its duration) might succeed in resolving conflicts which a stable cabinet may not be able to handle.

## 2 Cross-national studies on the effectiveness and efficiency of cabinet government

Some comparative studies have focused on the efficiency of the organisation of cabinets. Research has been conducted, for instance, on the role of Prime Ministers' Offices and of cabinet committees, both being mechanisms designed to solve problems facing the government (Armbruster, 1973; Blondel, 1982; Butler, 1972/3; Campbell, 1983; Mackie and Hogwood, 1985). Yet, despite the fact that these studies are based on substantial evidence, systematic conclusions on cabinet effectiveness and efficiency cannot be drawn at this point – especially with respect to what is the most critical question, namely that of the ability of cabinets to handle political crisis.

Moreover, it is still unclear at this stage how far cabinet effectiveness and efficiency are affected by the political culture, and in particular by the degree of political fragmentation of the society. The single country studies in this volume suggest that such cultural variables may place a considerable part, at least in some cases, in determining cabinet efficiency.

## 3 Cross-national studies of ministers

Only a few studies have thrown light in a comparative manner on the effect which social background may have on the duration in office of ministers. The same remark has to be made about the effect of recruitment (Blondel, 1980; Blondel, 1987; Herman, 1975). The lack of cross-national research becomes even more apparent with respect to the attitudes of ministers. There is, for instance, no empirical study on the role perceptions of cabinet members. We do not know what ministers think about their influence in the cabinet and in the individual departments. These and other questions regarding the possible effect of the background of cabinet members have as yet not been addressed.

Thus, cross-national studies on cabinet government do not provide a comprehensive framework. Indeed, the studies which have just been mentioned examine each problem in isolation, and studies on stability, on effectiveness or on ministerial careers are not related to each other. An effort must therefore be made to combine the structural variables within which cabinets operate with the attitudinal and behavioural characteristics of cabinet members. Only when this is done can the complexity of cabinet decision-making begin to be understood. A new comparative approach has thus to be developed which will take into account the variety of explanatory factors which have so far been used primarily at the single-country level.

## TOWARDS A FRAMEWORK OF ANALYSIS

A framework for the analysis of cabinet government has to be both comprehensive and cross-national. It needs to integrate the major aspects of the cabinet's structure and life in the different countries.

How are cabinets formed? How do cabinets operate? What internal and external factors account for cabinet behaviour? When, how and why do cabinets come and go? These are only some of the questions which need to be investigated both cross-nationally and over time. To answer them, two types of difficulties need to be overcome. First, the unit of analysis has to be clearly defined. Second, the framework for the analysis has to integrate the factors which affect stability, change and the effectiveness of cabinet government.

## 1 The unit of analysis

A comparative study of cabinets cannot be undertaken unless a unit of analysis is selected. There are three main possibilities. The first consists in taking individual ministers as a basis, on the grounds that many aspects of the inquiry refer to ministers (their career is being examined and their views are being sought). Yet such an approach makes it impossible to obtain a picture of cabinets as such and to distinguish between types of cabinets. While it is valuable to use individual ministers as the unit of analysis to the extent that one focuses on the life of government members, we have to look elsewhere if we are to devote our attention to stability, change and the effectiveness of cabinets.

The second possibility consists in considering the nation as the unit and in attempting to contrast country characteristics with respect to cabinet government. Indeed, this is the solution most commonly adopted in ordinary discussions on government. It is implicitly based on the assumption that individual countries have cultural characteristics – a point which has almost certainly considerable validity. There are difficulties with such an approach, however. First, the number of units becomes very small (fifteen in the case of Western Europe) and opportunities for contrasts and for clear-cut conclusions are therefore limited. Second, and even more seriously, characteristics of cabinets vary from one period to another within each country. For instance, there can be coalitions and single-party governments in the same country in succession. Moreover, it becomes difficult to study the impact of leadership, as one would obviously wish to compare and contrast the effect of Prime Ministers on various cabinets.

Thus the only appropriate solution consists in taking *individual cabinets* as the units of analysis. This has the advantage of avoiding the difficulties which country-based studies raise and of increasing the number of observations to a sizeable number. This means not having to dissolve the investigation to the level of individual actors and thus make it impossible to assess the characteristics of the cabinet as a body.

Individual cabinets should therefore be the units of analysis in a comparative study. However, there remain some problems about the precise definition of cabinets. The official list cannot always be used for comparative purposes, as the criteria adopted in different countries vary somewhat (what is merely a reshuffle in one country can lead to the setting up of a new cabinet in another).

There seems gradually to have been agreement on the view that, for purposes of comparative analyses, cabinets should be defined by three criteria, those of the same Prime Minister continuously in office, of the same party or parties in the government and of the same legislative period. On this basis, for the period from 1965 to 1987, for instance, the total number of Western European cabinets is around 160. There are of course substantial variations from one country to another. With Finland having had over twenty and Austria under ten.

## 2   The contextual mapping

Comparative research on cabinets has to list the factors which explain the developments of cabinet systems and their current functioning in each country. The chapters in this volume point out that most European cabinets were formed at the beginning of the nineteenth century. It was also found that the current structure of cabinet governments has been highly influenced by historical events. Indeed, specific historical events were responsible for changes which took place in cabinets from the origin to the present day. In order to understand fully the operation of cabinet governments in the 1970s and 1980s one has therefore, in the first place, to describe the development of cabinets in the context of European history. We shall call this research procedure the *historical dimension* of the comprehensive framework.

Second, the framework which has to be developed has to detail the characteristics which influence the functioning of Western European cabinets today. The chapters in this book have placed a major emphasis on those characteristics. It is not possible here even to summarise the points which are made with respect to all the countries under investigation. There is some evidence that the analysis of contemporary cabinet government in Western Europe has to be conceptualised in terms of a combination of structural variables and of aspects of elite behavior in cabinet. There is, of course, a dynamic relationship between these two types of factors. For instance, the political behaviour and the attitudes of cabinet members are dependent upon institutional matters such as the formal rules of the cabinet.

Structural characteristics of cabinets in turn consist of institutional and political factors. Among institutional factors there are, for example, formal cabinet rules and arrangements. These seem to have been relatively stable over the past 30 years although cabinet systems in different countries have had a stronger or weaker formal organisational structure. Some cabinets have, for instance, a decentralised, others a centralised organisation, with ministers (as cabinet members) wielding more or less power. Comparative research needs to classify the varying formal cabinet rules and structures in Western European systems on what might be termed an *institutional dimension*.

Among the political factors, the question of the type of coalition emerges most prominently. Linked to it is the question whether coalitions have been stable or unstable over time in a given country. Studies in this volume have shown that types of coalition vary both within and among countries. Depending upon the type of coalitions, cabinets are more or less stable and more or less effective and efficient.

Although research on cabinet coalitions has become substantial (Laver, 1986), most analyses remain static. There is work, for instance, on the distribution of cabinet portfolios among coalition partners, or on the number of parties which participate in coalitions, while game-theoretic analyses about behaviour in these parties have been undertaken. However, comparative research on cabinet government has to systematically collect and classify all available data on types of coalition in post-war Europe. We shall refer to this part of analysis as the *political dimension* of the overall framework.

Alongside studies of structural characteristics of cabinet government, which have, as we saw, already been examined intensively and which are not always fully comparative, considerable emphasis should be placed on the analysis of the characteristics of political actors in cabinet. This is to say, on ministers and Prime Ministers. The most important features of these investigations are the background of the ministers, their role perception and the leadership style of the Prime Minister.

There is still no fully comparative study of the social background and the careers of ministers in Western Europe since World War Two. There is still a need to compile a comprehensive data set on Western European ministers. These data will make it possible to determine for each cabinet, for instance, the social background of ministers, their parliamentary experience, their duration in office and the extent to which they moved from post to post.

It is clear that in these matters there are substantial variations across European systems and over time. It is also clear that changes in the background of ministers which might have taken place over the past decades may have had a significant influence on decision-making processes in cabinet. Ministers with greater political experience or greater expert knowledge can be expected to have more influence on policy-making than other cabinet ministers. Therefore, comparative research on cabinet government has to take into account a *ministerial background dimension*, which thus constitutes a further element of the overall framework within which cabinets are to be studied.

Comparative research has not until now been sufficiently devoted to the role perception of ministers. We do not know, for instance, what ministers think about their own work, about the work of their colleagues or about the importance of cabinet meetings. In so far as cabinet decisions matter, cabinet members do too. It is therefore most important to discover the variations in the general political outlook and in the specific concerns of ministers. For example, these may not lend much importance to discussions in cabinet or they may be more or less close to their departments. And/or they may be more or less disposed to be involved in the affairs of other departments.

Comparative research needs to assess the way in which ministers define their own role in cabinet government. Admittedly, to answer these questions one has to interview former ministers in Western Europe – an empirical enterprise which has so far not been undertaken. But the enterprise is a necessity if we are to understand what ministers think. We therefore suggest that a dimension of *ministers' role perception* has to be studied in order to assess the extent to which ministers identify with collective 'cabinet work' or on 'departmental work'.

All the country chapters in this book have given special attention to the role of the Prime Ministers as the head of the cabinet. It is clear that the role and the effect on decision-making of the Prime Minister needs to be examined more closely. Prime Ministers may be 'arbitrators' or 'activists' with respect to policy goals. In the first case, the Prime Minister may not be personally involved in a policy proposal and be content to move the cabinet towards an acceptable solution. In the second case, he or she is deeply interested in particular proposals and attempts to push these through in cabinet.

The way in which a Prime Minister handles policy problems has, of course, an impact on the overall process of decision-making in cabinet. The arbitrating role of Prime Minister may lead to a reduction of collective decision-making if many arrangements are made behind the scenes. An active posture, on the other hand, is often likely to result in tensions. Hence two contradictory tendencies are observable. On the one hand, to the extent that the Prime Minister tries to prevent interdepartmental conflict from occurring, he or she endeavours to reduce tension and limits the collective involvement of ministers. To the extent that the Prime Minister is very active, on the other hand, he or she may increase tension within the cabinet.

Thus it would be wrong to suggest that Prime Ministers currently only attempt to reduce collective decision-making in cabinet. The matter is obviously more complex. What needs to be seen is, for instance, how often different Prime Ministers raise (or support) issues themselves and how far they are primarily concerned with the settlement of matters raised by others. A comparative investigation will have therefore to take into account what might be called the dimension of *prime ministerial leadership*. It will have to examine in detail the ways in which Prime Ministers operate in different countries.

We have argued, first, that research on cabinet government needs to be more precise. In order to be so a unit of analysis, the individual cabinet, has to be adopted. On this basis and in the second place, a 'framework for conceptual mapping' has to be developed within which cabinet government can be analysed according to six dimensions – an historical dimension, an institutional dimension, a political dimension, a social background dimension, a dimension of ministers' role perception and a dimension of prime ministerial leadership.

Such a multi-dimensional analysis constitutes a large undertaking especially since, on a number of aspects, data are not easily available and the principles of classification have also to be refined. Yet, when such an approach is adopted, it will be possible to discover and assess the factors which account for the operation of cabinet governments in different countries and at different points in time and thus even begin to measure levels of efficiency in cabinet government. The importance of these problems is such that it is essential for political science to move in this direction and to embark in a systematic examination of what our governments are, of what they do, of how they do it and of how they can do it better.

# Bibliography

## 1 United Kingdom

BAGEHOT, W. (1963) *The English Constitution* (London: Fontana).

BROWN, A.H. (1968) 'Prime Ministerial Power', *Public Law*, pp. 28–51 and pp. 96–118.

BURCH, M.S. (1983) 'Mrs. Thatcher's Approach to Leadership in Government: 1979–June 1983', *Parliamentary Affairs*, 36, pp. 399–416.

BURCH, M.S. (1987) 'The Demise of Cabinet Government?', in L. Robins (ed.) *Political Institutions in Britain* (London: Longman).

COCKERELL, M., HENNESSEY, P. and WALKER, D. (1985) *Sources Close to the Prime Minister* (London: Macmillan).

CROSSMAN, R.H. (1972) *Inside View* (London: Jonathan Cape).

DE SMITH, S. (1981) *Constitutional and Administrative Law* (Harmondsworth: Penguin) 4th edition.

DONOUGHUE, B. (1987) *Prime Minister* (London: Jonathan Cape).

GORDON WALKER, P. (1973) *The Cabinet* (London: Fontana).

HAILSHAM, Lord (1976) 'Elective Dictatorship', *The Listener*, 21 October, pp. 496–500.

HAINES, J. (1977) *The Politics of Power* (London: Hodder & Stoughton).

HALDANE, Viscount (1918) *Report of the Machinery of Government Committee*, Cd. 9230 (London: HMSO).

HANSON, A.M. and WALLES, M., (1980) *Governing Britain*, 3rd ed. (London: Fontana).

HARTLEY, T.C. and GRIFFITH, J.A.G. (1981) *Government and Law* (London: Weidenfeld & Nicholson) 2nd edition.

HEATH, E. (1976) Radio interview with Edward Heath and Lord Trend, BBC Radio 3, 12 March. See also *The Listener*, 22 April.

HENNESSEY, P. (1985) 'The Quality of Cabinet Government in Britain', *Policy Studies*, 5, pp. 15–45.

HENNESSEY, P. (1986) *Cabinet* (Oxford: Basil Blackwell).

HENNESSEY, P. and ARENDS, A. (1983) 'Mr Attlee's Engine Room: Cabinet Committee Structure and the Labour Government 1945–51', *Strathclyde Papers on Government and Politics* (Glasgow: Strathclyde University) no. 26.

HOME, Lord, (1985) 'The Unknown Premiership', interview with Lord Home, BBC Radio 3, 25 July.

JENKINS, S. (1985) 'The Star Chamber, PESC and the Cabinet', *Political Quarterly*, no. 56.

JONES, G.W. (1985) 'The Prime Minister's Aides', in A. King (ed.) *The British Prime Minister* (London: Macmillan).

KING, A. (1985) 'Margaret Thatcher: the Style of a Prime Minister', in A. King (ed.) *The British Prime Minister* (London: Macmillan).

MACKENZIE, W.J.M. and GROVE, J. (1957) *Central Administration in Britain* (London: Longman).

MACKIE, T.T. and HOGWOOD, B. (1985) *Unlocking the Cabinet* (London: Sage).

MACKINTOSH, J.P. (1977) *The British Cabinet* (London: Stevens) 3rd edition.

MCKENZIE, R.T. (1963) *British Political Parties* (London: Heinemann) 2nd edition.

MARSH, D. (1983) *Pressure Politics* (London: Junction Books).

MARSHALL, G. (1984) *Constitutional Conventions* (Oxford: Clarendon).

MARSHALL, G. and MOODIE, G.C. (1971) *Some Problems of the Constitution*, (London: Hutchinson) 5th edition.

MINKIN, L. (1978) *The Labour Party Conference* (Manchester: Manchester University Press).

MORRISON, Lord (1964) *Government and Parliament* (London: Oxford University Press) 3rd edition.

MOSLEY, R.K. (1969) *The Story of the Cabinet Office* (London: Routledge & Kegan Paul).

NEW STATESMAN (1986) 'The Document Benn Couldn't Disclose', *New Statesman*, 21 and 28 February, no. 14.

NORTON, P. (1980) *Dissension in the House of Commons 1974–1979* (Oxford: Oxford University Press).

NORTON, P. and AUGHEY, A. (1981) *Conservatives and Conservatism* (London: Temple Smith).

POLLITT, C. (1984) *Manipulating the Machine* (London: George Allen & Unwin).

ROSE, R. (1983) 'Still the Era of Party Government', *Parliamentary Affairs*, 36, pp. 282–289.

RUSH, M. (1984) *The Cabinet and Policy Formation* (London: Longman).

SEYMOUR-URE, C. (1968) *Politics, the Press and the Public* (London: Methuen).

TUNSTALL, J. (1970) *The Westminster Lobby Correspondents* (London: Routledge & Kegan Paul).

WRIGHT, M. (1977) 'Ministers and Civil Servants: Relations and Responsibilities', *Parliamentary Affairs*, 30, pp. 293–313.

WILSON, H. (1976) *The Governance of Britain* (London: Weidenfeld & Nicolson).

## 2 Ireland

BARRINGTON, T.J. (1982) 'Whatever happened to Irish Government?', in F. Litton (ed.) *Unequal Achievement: the Irish Experience 1957–82* (Dublin: Institute of Public Administration).

CHUBB, B. (1976) *Cabinet Government in Ireland* (Dublin: Institute of Public Administration).

CHUBB, B. (1983) *Source Book of Irish Government* (Dublin: Institute of Public Administration).

CHUBB, B. (1987) 'Prospects for Democratic Politics in Ireland', in H. Penniman and B. Farrell (eds) *Ireland at the Polls 1981–1987* (Durham, N.C.: Duke University Press).

COAKLEY, J., and FARRELL, B. (forthcoming) 'The Selection of Cabinet Ministers in Ireland, 1922–1982', in M. Dogan and D. Marvick (eds) *Gateways to Power: leadership selection in pluralist democracies* (Berlin, New York: Walter de Gruyter).

COHAN, A.S. (1982) 'Ireland: Coalitions Making a Virtue of Necessity', in E.C. Browne and J. Dreijmanis (eds) *Government Coalitions in Western Democracies* (New York, London: Longman).

FARRELL, B. (1969) 'A Note on the Dail Constitution, 1919', *The Irish Jurist*, 4.1, pp. 127–138.

FARRELL, B. (1970–71) 'The Drafting of the Irish Free State Constitution', *The Irish Jurist*, 5.1, pp. 115–140; 5.2, pp. 343–356; 6.1, pp. 111–135; 6.2, pp. 345–359.

FARRELL, B. (1971a) *The Founding of Dail Eireann: parliament and nation-building* (Dublin: Gill & Macmillan).

FARRELL, B. (1971b) *Chairman or Chief? The role of Taoiseach in Irish Government* (Dublin: Gill & Macmillan).

FARRELL, B. [1983a] *Sean Lemass* (Dublin: Gill & Macmillan).

FARRELL, B. (1983b) 'Coalitions and Political Institutions: the Irish experience', in V. Bogdanor (ed.) *Coalition Government in Western Europe* (London: Heinemann).

FARRELL, B. (1985b) 'Ireland: from Friends and Neighbours to Clients and Partisans. Some Dimensions of Parliamentary Representation under PR-STV', in V. Bogdanor (ed.) *Representatives of the People? Parliamentarians and Constituents in Western Democracies* (Aldershot: Gower).

FARRELL, B. (1985b) 'The Unlikely Marriage: de Valera, Lemass and the shaping of modern Ireland', *Etudes Irlandaises*, 10, pp. 215–222.

FARRELL, B. (1986) 'Politics and Change', in K. Kennedy (ed.) *Ireland in Transition: economic and social change since 1960* (Cork, Dublin: Mercier).

FARRELL, B. (1987a) 'Government Formation and Ministerial Selection', *Ireland at the Polls 1981–1987* (Durham, N.C.: Duke University Press).

FARRELL, B. (1987b) 'Aftermath and Government Formation', in M. Laver, P. Mair and R. Sinnott (eds) *How Ireland Voted February 1987*, (Dublin: Poolbeg).

GALLAGHER, M. (1977) 'The Presidency of the Republic of Ireland: implications of the 'Donegan Affair'', *Parliamentary Affairs*, 30, 4, pp. 375–384.

GIRVIN, B. (1986) 'Social Change and Moral Politics: the Irish Constitutional Referendum 1983', *Political Studies*, 34.1, pp. 61–81.

GIRVIN, B. (1987) 'The Divorce Referendum in the Republic; June 1986', *Irish Political Studies*, 2, pp. 93–99.

KELLY, J. (1984) *The Irish Constitution* (Dublin: Jurist Publishing Company).

LAVER, M. (1986a) 'Politics with some Social Bases: an interpretation based on aggregate data', *Economic and Social Review*, 17.2, pp. 107–131.

LAVER, M. (1986b) 'Politics with some Social Bases: an interpretation based on survey data', *Economic and Social Review*, 17.3, pp. 193–213.

LAVER, M. (1986c) 'Party Choice and Social Structure in Ireland', *Irish Political Studies*, 1, pp. 45–55.

LAVER, M. and HIGGINS, M.D. (1986) 'Coalition or Fianna Fail? the politics of inter-party government in Ireland', in G. Pridham (ed.) *Coalition Behaviour in Theory and Practice: an inductive model for Western Europe* (Cambridge: Cambridge University Press).

LAVER, M., MAIR, P., and SINNOT, R. (1987) *How Ireland Voted: the Irish General Election 1987* (Dublin: Poolbeg for Political Studies Association of Ireland).

MAIR, P. (1987) *The Changing Irish Party System* (London: Francis Pinter).

MOYNIHAN, M. (1969) *The Functions of the Department of the Taoiseach* (Dublin: Institute of Public Administration).

PSORG, (1969) Public Service Organisation Review Group, *Report* (Dublin: Stationery Office).

WHYTE, J.H. (1974) 'Ireland: politics without social bases', in R. Rose (ed.) *Electoral Behaviour: a comparative handbook* (New York: Free Press).

## 3  The Netherlands

ANDEWEG, R.B., VAN DER TAK, Th. and DITTRICH, K. (1980) 'Government Formation in the Netherlands', in R.T. Griffiths (ed.) *The Economy and Politics of the Netherlands since 1945* (The Hague: Nijhoff).

ANDEWEG, R.B. (1985) 'The Netherlands: Cabinet Committees in a Coalition Cabinet', in T.T. Mackie and B.W. Hogwood (eds) *Unlocking the Cabinet: Cabinet Structures in Comparative Perspective* (London: Beverly Hills and New Delhi: Sage).

ANDEWEG, R.B. (1988) 'Centrifugal Forces and Collective Decision-Making: the Case of the Dutch Cabinet', *European Journal of Political Research*, 16, no. 2, pp. 125–151.

BAKEMA, W.E. and SECKER, I.P. (1988) 'Ministerial Expertise and the Dutch Case', *European Journal of Political Research*, 16, no. 2, pp. 153–70.

BARENTS, J. (1952) 'The Dutch Cabinet System', *Public Administration*, 30, pp. 81–87.

DAALDER, H. (1966) Netherlands: Opposition in a Segmented Society', in R.A. Dahl (ed.) *Political Oppositions in Western Democracies* (New Haven: Yale University Press).

DAALDER, H. (1986) 'Changing Procedures and Changing Strategies in Dutch Coalition-Building', *Legislative Studies Quarterly*, 11, pp. 507–31.

DAUDT, H. (1982) 'Political Parties and Government Coalitions in the Netherlands since 1945', *The Netherlands Journal of Sociology*, 18, pp. 1–24.

DE GRAAF, Th.C. and VERSTEEG, A.J.H.W.M. (1985) 'De Staatssecretaris in theorie en praktijk', *Bestuurswetenschappen*, 39, pp. 30–51.

DE JONG, J. and PIJNENBURG, B. (1986) 'The Dutch Christian Democratic Party and Coalitional Behaviour in the Netherlands: a Pivotal Party in the Face of Depillarisation', in G. Pridham (ed.) *Coalitional Behaviour in Theory and Practice: an Inductive Model for Western Europe* (Cambridge: Cambridge University Press).

DE SWAAN, A. (1982) 'The Netherlands: Coalitions in a Segmented Polity', in E.C. Browne and J. Dreijmanis (eds) *Government Coalitions in Western Democracies* (New York and London: Longman).

DOGAN, M. and SCHEFFER-VAN DER VEEN, M. (1957–8) 'Le Personnel Ministériel Hollandais (1848–1958)', *L'Année Sociologique*, 3, pp. 95–125.

DOOYEWEERD, H. (1917) *De Ministerraad in het Nederlandsche Staatsrecht* (Amsterdam: Van Soest).

DREES, W. (1965) *De Vorming van het Regeringsbeleid* (Assen: Van Gorcum).

GEISMANN, G. (1964) *Politische Struktur und Regierungssystem in den Niederlanden* (Frankfurt and Bonn: Athenäum Verlag).

HOEKSTRA, R.J. (1983) *De Ministerraad in Nederland* (Zwolle: Tjeenk Willink).

KOOPMANS, L. (1969) *De Beslissingen over de Rijksbegroting* (Deventer: Kluwer).

LIJPHART, A. (1975e) *The Politics of Accommodation: Pluralism and Democracy in the Netherlands* (Berkeley: University of California Press).

ROSE, R. (1980) 'Government against Sub-Governments: a European Perspective on Washington', in R. Rose and E.N. Suleiman (eds) *Presidents and Prime Ministers* (Washington: AEI).

VAN DEN BERG, Th.J. and VISSCHER, G. (1984) 'Politieke Stabiliteit in de Betrekkingen tussen Kabinet en Tweede Kamer', *Beleid en Maatschappij*, 11, pp. 223–32.

VAN DEN BERG, J.Th.J. (1985e) 'De Regering', in R.B. Andeweg, A. Hoogerwerf and J.J.A. Thomassen (eds) *Politiek in Nederland* (Alphen aan den Rijn and Brussels: Samsom).

VAN DEN BERG, W.A. (1985) 'De Staatssecretaris', *Bestuurswetenschappen*, 39, pp. 192–6.

VAN DEN BOSCH, A. and ELDERSVELD, S.J. (1947) *Government in the Netherlands* (Lexington: Bureau of Government Research, University of Kentucky).

VAN DER VOET, M.J.D. (1974) 'Enige Beschouwingen over de Geschiedenis en de Taak van het Ministerie van Algemene Zaken', *Bestuurswetenschappen*, 28, pp. 142–62.

VAN MAARSEVEEN, H.Th.J.F. (1972) *De Heerschappij van de Ministerraad*, (The Hague: Staatsvitgeverij).

VAN RAALTE, E. (1954) *De Ontwikkeling van het Minister- Presidentschap in Nederland, Belgie, Frankrijk, Engeland en enige andere landen: een studie van vergelijkend staatsrecht* (Leiden: Universitaire Pers Leiden).

## 4 Belgium

BLONDEL, J. (1985) *Government Ministers in the Contemporary World* (London, Beverly Hills, New Delhi: Sage).

BLONDEL, J. (1988) 'Ministerial Careers and the Nature of Parliamentarian Government: the Cases of Austria and Belgium', *European Journal of Political Research*, 16, no. 1, pp. 51–71.

CRISP (Centre de Recherche et d'Information Socio-Politiques) (1972) 'La stabilité gouvernementale en Belgique 1946–1971', *Courrier Hebdomadaire du CRISP*, no. 578.

COVELL, M. (1982) 'Agreeing to Disagree: Elite Bargaining and Revision of the Belgian Constitution', *Canadian Journal of Political Science*, 192, 15, no. 3.

DAS, E. (1987) 'Heij belgisch ministerieele carrierepatroon. Proeve tot internationale vergelyking', *Res Publica*, 24, 2.

DE LICHTERVELDE, L. (1947) 'Le Conseil des Ministres dans le Droit Public Belge', *Bulletin de la Classe des Lettres et des Sciences Morales et Politiques*, p. 21.

DE RIDDER, M., PETERSON, R.L., WIRTH, R. (1978). 'Image of Belgian Politics: the Effects of Cleavages on the Political System', *Legislative Studies*, 3, 1, pp. 83–109.

DE WACHTER, W. (1982) 'Crises macro-sociales et stabilité de l'elite', *Res Publica*, 24, 2.

HOJER, C.K. (1969) *Le regime parlamentaire en Belgique de 1918 a 1940* (Brussels: CRISP).

HUYSE, L. (1981) 'Political Conflict in Bicultural Belgium', in A. Lijphart (ed.) *Conflict and Coexistence in Belgium. The Dynamics of a Culturally Divided Society* (Berkeley: University of California Press).

LIJPHART, A. (1987) 'Introduction: the Belgian Example of Cultural Coexistence in Comparative Perspective', in A. Lijphart (ed.) *Conflict and Coexistence in Belgium. The Dynamics of a Culturally Divided Society* (Berkeley: University of California Press).

MARTENS, W. (1985) *Parole donnée* (Brussels: Hatier).

OBLER, J., STEINER, J. AND DIRICKX, G. (1977). *Decision-Making in Small Democracies: the Consociational Burden* (London: Sage Professional Papers) 01/064.

## 5 France

AVRIL, P. (1987). *La Ve République. Histoire politique et constitutionnelle* (Paris: Presses Universitaires de France).

BODIGUEL, J-L. (1981) 'Conseils resteints, comités interministériels et réunions interministerielles', in F. de. Baecque and J-L. Quermonne (eds) *Administration et politique sous la Cinquième République* (Paris: Presses de la Fondation Nationale des Sciences Politiques).

CHAPSAL, J. (1981) *La vie politique sous la Ve République* (Paris: Presses Universitaires de France).

COIGNARD, S. (1987) MAKARIAN, Ch., 'Le tourniquet des nominations', *Le Point*, 16 March, no. 756.

DUHAMEL, O. (1986) 'Constitution et cohabitation. Cinq innovations de l'alternance', *Le Monde*, 26 March.

DUVERGER, M. (1986) *Les régimes semi-présidentiels* (Paris: Presses Universitaires de France).

DUVERGER, M. (1985) *Le système politique français* (Paris: Presses Universitaires de France).

FOURNIER, J. (1987a) 'Politique gouvernementale: les trois leviers du Président', *Pouvoirs*, no. 41, pp. 63–74.

FOURNIER, J. (1987b) *Le travail gourvernemental* (Paris: Presses de la fondation Nationale dews Sciences Politiques).

HADAS-LEBEL, R. (1986) 'La nouvelle règle du jeu', *l'Express*, 2–8 May.

GICQUEL, J. (1980) *Droit constitutionnel et institutions politiques*, (Paris: Montchrestien).

INSTITUT FRANCAISE DES SCIENCES ADMINISTRATIVES (1986) *Le secretariat général du gouvernement* (Paris: Economical).

PLOUVIN, J-Y. (1980) 'Le Conseil des Ministres, institution seconde', *Revue Administrative*, September–October 33, pp. 485–492.

PORTELLI, H. (1980) 'La présidentialisation des partis', *Pouvoirs*, no. 14, pp. 97–106.

PY, R., *Le secrétariat général du gouvernement* (Paris: La Documentation Française).

QUERMONNE (1987) J-L., *Le gouvernement de la France sous la Ve République* (Paris: Dalloz).

TRICOT, B. (1985) HADAS-LEBEL, R., *Les institutions politiques françaises* (Paris: Presses de la Fondation Natinale des Sciences Politiques and Dalloz).

## 6 Spain

AGUIAR, L. (1980) 'La estructura del proceso de formación del Gobierno. El caso español en el marco del Derecho comparado', *Revista del Departamento de Derecho Politico*; 6, pp. 61–81.

ATTARD, E. (1983) *Vida y muerte de UCD* (Barcelona: Planeta).

BAR, A. (1982) 'El sistema de partidos en España: Ensayo de caracterización', *Sistema*, 47, pp. 3–46.

BAR, A. (1983) *El Presidente del Gobierno en España: Encuadre constitucional y práctica politica* (Madrid: Civitas).

BAR, A. (1984) 'The Emerging Spanish Party System: Is There a Model?', *West European Politics*, 7, pp. 128–155.

BAR, A. (1985a) 'La estructura y funcionamiento del Gobierno en España: una aproximación analítica' in A. Bar *et al.*, *El Gobierno en la Constitución Española y en los Estatutos de Autonomia*, Barcelona, Diputació, pp. 11–61.

BAR, A. (1985b) 'Artìculo 99: Nombramiento del Presidente del Gobierno', in O. Alzaga (ed.) *Comentarios a las leyes politicas: Constitución Española de 1978* (Madrid: EDERSA) VIII, pp. 135–189.

BAR, A. (1985c) 'Articulo 100: Nombramiento y separación de los miembros del Gobierno', in O. Alzaga (ed.) *Comentarios a las leyes politicas: Constitución Española de 1978* (Madrid: EDERSA) VIII, pp. 191–211.

BLONDEL, J. (1982) *The Organization of Governments* (London: Sage).

BLONDEL, J. (1985) *Government Ministers in the Contemporary World* (London: Sage).

CACIAGLI, M. (1986) *Elecciones y partidos en la transición española* (Madrid: CIS).

CHAMORRO, E. (1981) *Viaje al centro de UCD* (Barcelona: Planeta).

CORTES, A. (1965). 'La competencia de los Subsecretarios y Directores Generales en materia de personal', *Documentaciõn Administrativa*, 90, pp. 72–81.

ESTEBAN, J. de, LOPEZ GUERRA, L. (1982) *Los partidos politicos en la España actual* (Barcelona: Planeta).

GUAITA, A. (1978) 'Secretarias de Estado y Subsecretarías', *Revista Española*

*de Derecha Administrativa*, 18, pp. 333–357.
HUNEEUS, C. (1985) *La Unión de Centro Demcratico y la transición a la democracia en España* (Madrid: CIS).
LINZ, J.J and MONTERO, J.R. (1986) *Crisis y cambio: Elecciones y partidos en la España de los años ochenta* (Madrid: CEC).
MARTIN, L. (1980) 'Ante la reforma administrativa: los ministros y otros miembros del Gobierno', *Documentación Administrativa*, 188, pp. 233–346.
MIGUEL, P. de (1972) 'Las comisiones interministeriales', *Revista de Administración Pública*, 67, pp. 457–468.
MOLINA, C.F. (1979) 'Ampliación del nivel político de la Administración española en la actual etapa democrática: los Secretarios de Estado', *Revista de Administración Pública*, 90, pp. 97–166.
MORELL, L. (1980) 'El estatuto de los miembros del Gobierno', *Documentación Administrativa*, 188, pp. 73–104.
MORENA, L. de la (1966) 'Las Subsecretarías en el Derecho orgánico español: apuntes para su configuración institucional', *Documentación Administrativa*, 101–102, pp. 41–67.

# 7 Italy

AQUARONE, A. (1965) *L'organizzazione dello stato totalitario* (Turin: Einaudi).
BARTOLOTTA, F. (1971) *Parlamenti e governi d'Italia dal 1848 al 1970* (Naples: Bianco).
BONANNI, M. (1978). *Governo, Ministri, Presidente* (Milan: Comunità).
BONNANI, M. (1983) 'Il governo nel sistema politico italiano (1948–82)', *Rivista Trimestrale di Scienza dell'Amministrazione*, 33, pp. 1–46.
CALISE, M. and MANNHEIMER, M. (1982) *Governanti in Italia. Un trentennio repubblicano, 1946–1976* (Bologna: Il Mulino).
CALISE, M. and MANNHEIMER, M. (1986) 'Come cambiano i governanti di partito', *Rivista Italiana di Scienza Politica*, 16, pp. 461–483.
CANTELLI, F., MORTARA, V., and MOVIA, G. (1974) *Come lavora il parlamento* (Milan: Giuffrè).
CASSESE, S. (1981) 'Is there a Government in Italy? Politics and Administration at the Top', in R. Rose and E.N. Suleiman (eds) *Presidents and Prime Ministers* (Washington: American Enterprise Institute).
CAZZOLA, F. (1974) *Governo e opposizione nel parlamento italiano* (Milan: Giuffrè).
CIRIELLO, P. (1981) *Ordinamento di governo e comitati interministeriali* (Naples: Iovene).
COTTA, M. (1987) 'Il sotto-sistema governo-parlamento', *Rivista Italiana di Scienza Politica*, 17, pp. 241–283.
DI PALMA, G. (1977) *Surviving without Governing. The Italian Parties in Parliament* (Berkeley: University of California Press).
HERMAN, V. (1975) 'Comparative Perspectives on Ministerial Stability in Britain', in V. Herman and J.E. Alt (eds) *Cabinet Studies* (London: Macmillan), pp. 55–76.
MANZELLA, A. (1977) *Il parlamento* (Bologna: Il Mulino).

MARRADI, A. (1982) 'Italy: from 'Centrism' to Crisis of the Center-Left Coalitions', in E.C. Browne and J. Dreijmanis (ed) *Government Coalitions in Western Democracies* (New York: Longman).

MERLINI, S. (1982) 'Presidente del consiglio e collegialità del governo', *Quaderni Costituzionale*, 2, pp. 7–32.

MERUSI, F. (1977) 'I comitati interministeriali nella struttura di governo', in S. Ristuccià (ed.) *L'istituzione governo* (Milan: Comunità).

MOTTA, R. (1985) 'L'attività legislativa dei governi (1948–83)', *Rivista Italiana di Scienza Politica*, 15, pp. 255–292.

PAPPALARDO, A. (1978) *Partiti e governi di coalizione in Europa* (Milan: Angeli).

PITRUZZELLA, G. (1986). *La presidenza del consiglio dei ministri e l'organizzazione dei governi* (Padua: Cedam).

PRIDHAM, G. (1983) 'Party Politics and Coalition Government in Italy', in V. Bogdanor (ed.) *Coalition Government in Western Europe* (London: Heinemann).

ROTELLI, E. (1972) *La presidenza del consiglio dei ministri* (Milan: Giuffrè).

RUGGERI, A. (1982) special number on 'Struttura costituzionale del governo e 'ragioni' della controfirma del *Premier*', *Quaderni Costituzionali*, 2., no. 1.

RUGGERI, A. (1983) *Il consiglio dei ministri nella constituzione* (Milan: Giuffrè).

SARTORI, G. (1976) *Parties and Party Systems: a Framework for Analysis* (Cambridge: Cambridge University Press).

SPAGNA MUSSO, E. (1979) *Costituzione e struttura del governo. Il problema della presidenza del consiglio* (Padua: Cedam).

ZUCKERMAN, A. (1979) *The Politics of Faction: Christian Democratic Rule in Italy* (New Haven: Yale University Press).

## 8   Austria

ADAMOVICH, L. (1971) *Handbuch des österreichischen Verfassungsrechts* (Vienna: Springer) 6th edition.

BARFUSS, W. (1968) *Ressortzuständigkeit und Vollzugsklausel* (Vienna: Springer).

BERCHTOLD, K. (1974) 'Die Regierung', in H. Fischer (ed.) *Das politische System Österreichs* (Vienna: Europaverlag).

BERNATZIK, E. (1911) *Die österreichischen Verfassungsgesetze* (Vienna: Manz) 2nd edition.

FISCHER, H. (1972) 'Zur Praxis des Begutachtungsverfahrens im Prozeß der Bundesgesetzgebung', *Österreichische Zeitschrift für Politikwissenschaft*, 1, pp. 35–54.

FISCHER, H. (1974) 'Die parlamentarischen Fraktionen', in H. Fischer (ed.) *Das politische System Österreichs* (Vienna: Europaverlag).

GERLICH, P. (1986) 'Die Grenzen der Mehrheitsdemokratie in Österreich', in H. Oberreuter (ed.) *Wahrheit statt Mehrheit?* (Munich: Olzog).

GERLICH, P., GRANDE, E. and MÜLLER, W.C. (1985) *Sozialpartnerschaft in der Krise. Leistungen und Grenzen des Neokorporatismus in Österreich* (Vienna: Böhlau).

GERLICH, P., MÜLLER, W.C. and PHILIPP, W. (1988). 'Potentials and Limitations of Executive Leadership: the Austrian Cabinet since 1945', *European Journal of Political Research*, 16, no. 2, pp. 191–205.

KESSLER, Ch. (ed.) (1983) *The Austrian Federal Constitution* (Vienna: Manz).

LIJPHART, A. (1984) 'Measures of Cabinet Durability' *Comparative Political Studies*, 17, pp. 265–279.

MÜLLER, W.C. (1983) 'Parteien zwischen Öffentlichkeitsarbeit und Medienzwängen', in P. Gerlich and W.C. Müller (eds) *Zwischen Koalition und Konkurrenz. Österreichs Parteien seit 1945* (Vienna: Braumüller).

MÜLLER, W.C. and PHILIPP, W. (1987) 'Parteienregierung und Regierungsparteien in Österreich', *Österreichische Zeitschrift für Politikwissenschaft*, 16, pp. 277–302.

NEISSER, H. (1974) 'Die Rolle der Bürokratie im Regierungsprozess', in H. Fischer (ed.) *Das politische System Österreichs* (Vienna: Europaverlag).

PELINKA, A. and WELAN, M. (1971) *Demokratie und Verfassung in Österreich* (Vienna: Europaverlag).

PFEIFER, H. (1964) 'Über due Beschlußfassung der Regierung und die Verantwortlichkeit ihrer Mitglieder', *Juristische Blätter*, 86, pp. 485–500 and pp. 541–552.

RUDZIO, W. (1971) 'Entscheidungszentrum Koalitionsausschuß – Zur Realverfassung Österreichs unter der großen Koalition', *Politische Vierteljahreschrift*, 12, pp. 87–118.

WALTER, R. (1972) *Österreichisches Bundesverfassungsrecht* (Vienna: Manz).

WELAN, M. (1976) 'Die Kanzlerdemokratie in Österreich', in A. Kohl, R. Pranter and A. Stirnemann (eds) *Um Parlament und Partei* (Graz: Styria).

WELAN, M. and NEISSER, H. (1971) *Der Bundeskanzler im österreichischen Verfassungsgefüge* (Vienna: Hollinek).

## 9 Federal Republic of Germany

ARMINGEON, K. (1986) 'Die Bundesregierungen zwischen 1945 und 1985', *Zeitschrift für Parlamentsfragen*, pp. 25–40.

BLONDEL, J. (1985) *Government Ministers in the Contemporary World* (London: Sage).

BRAUNTHAL, G. (1972) *The West German Legislative Process* (Ithaca: Cornell University Press).

DYSON, K. (1974) 'The German Federal Chancellor's Office', *Political Quarterly*, pp. 364–371.

DYSON, K. (1978) *Party, State and Bureacracy in Western Germany* (Beverley Hills: Sage).

HAUNGS, P. (1986) 'Kanzlerdemokratie in der Bundesrepublik Deutschland von Adenauer bis Kohl', *Zeitschrift für Politik*, pp. 44–66.

JOHNSON, N. (1983) *State and Government in the Federal Republic of Germany* (Oxford: Pergamon Press) 2nd edition.

KÜPPER, J. (1985) *Die Kanzlerdemokratie* (Frankfurt: Peter Lang Verlag).

MACKIE, T. and HOGWOOD, B. (1985) *Unlocking the Cabinet* (London: Sage).

MAYNTZ, R. (1980) 'Executive Leadership in Germany', in R. Rose and E. Suleiman (eds) *Presidents and Prime Ministers* (Washington: American Enterprise Institute).

MAYNTZ, R. and SCHARPF, F. (1975) *Policy-Making in the German Federal Bureaucracy* (Amsterdam: Elsevier).

MÜLLER-ROMMEL, F. (1981) *Innerparteiliche Gruppierungen in der SPD von 1969–1980* (Opladen: Westdeutscher Verlag).

MÜLLER-ROMMEL, F. (1988) 'The Center of Government in West Germany', *European Journal for Political Research*, 16, no. 2, pp. 171–190.

MÜLLER-ROMMEL, F. and SPRENGEL, T. (1986) 'Kabinettsmitglieder in Bonn 1949–1986', *Zeitschrift für Parlamentsfragen*, pp. 41–49.

PATERSON, W. (1981) 'The Chancellor of his Party: Political Leadership in the Federal Republic', in W. Paterson and G. Smith (eds) *The West German Model* (London: Frank Cass).

RIDLEY, F.F. (1966) 'Chancellor Government as a Political System and the German Constitution', *Parliamentary Affairs*, pp. 446–461.

VON BEYME, K. (1983) 'Governments, Parliaments, and the Structure of Power in Political Parties', in H. Daalder and P. Mair (eds) *Western European Party Systems* (London: Sage).

## 10  Denmark

BLONDEL, J. (1986) 'Ministerial Careers and the Nature of Parliamentary Government: the Cases of Austria and Belgium', EUI Working paper, no. 87, 274.

BLONDEL, J. (1986) 'The Analysis of Cabinet Structures and Decision-Making', EUI Working Paper.

BILLE, L. (1980) *Danmark 1945–1980* (Copenhagen: Berg Forlag Aps).

BOGASON, P. (1988) 'Denmark', in D. Rowat (ed.) *Public Administration in the Western World* (New York: Marcel Dekker).

CHRISTENSEN, J.G. (1978) 'Da centraladministrationen blev international. En analyse af den administrative tilpasningsproces ved Denmarks tilslutning til EF', in N. Amstrup and I. Faurby (eds) *Studier i dansk udenrigspolitik* (Århus: Forlaget Politica).

CHRISTENSEN, J.G. (1980) *Centraladministrationen: organisation og politisk placering* (Copenhagen: Samfundsvidenskabeligt Forlag).

FITZMAURICE, J. (1986) 'Coalitional theory and practice in Scandinavia', in G. Pridham (ed.) *Coalition Behaviour in Theory and Practice* (Cambridge: Cambridge University Press).

HOMSTEDT, M. and SCHOU T-L (1987) 'Sweden and Denmark 145–1982: Election Programmes in the Scandinavian Setting', in I. Budge, D. Robertson and D. Hearl (eds) *Ideology, Strategy and Party Change: spatial analyses of post-war election programmes in nineteen democracies* (Cambridge: Cambridge University Press).

JØRGENSEN, T.B. (1981) 'Når staten skal spare' (Copenhagen: Nyt fra Samfundsvidenskaberne).

JØRGENSEN, T.B. (1988) 'Models of Retrenchment Behavior', Working Paper, International Institute of Administrative Sciences.

LASSEN, A. and PEDERSEN, O.K. (1962) *Folkestyrets midler* (Copenhagen: Munksgaards Forlag).

MEYER, P. (1979) *Offentlig forvaltning* (Copenhagen: Gads Forlag) 3rd edition.

OLSEN, S.-O. (1978) 'Regeringsarbejdet og statministeren', *Nordisk Administrativt Tidsskrkift*, no. 2, pp. 55–63.

PETERSEN, N. (1962) 'Oversigt over centraladministrationens udvikling siden 1848', *Betœnkning*, no. 320, 1962, pp. 29–100.

PEDERSEN, M.N. (1983) 'The Defeat of all Parties: the Danish *Folketing* Election of 1973', Odense University Papers, Occasional Paper, no. 10, Department of Public Finance and Policy.

RASMUSSEN, E. (1972) *Komparative Politik* (Copenhagen: Glydendal) no. 2.

SCHOU, T-L, (1972) 'En undersøgelse af ydre faktorers påvirkning af Danmarks markedspolitik', Københavns Universitets Institut for Samfundsfag.

SCHOU, T-L. (1980) 'Norge og EF', Københavns Universitets Institut for Samfundsfag.

SCHOU, T-L. (1981) 'Denmark: the Functionalists', in V. Herman and M. Hagger (eds) *The legislation of Direct Election to the European Parliament* (Aldershot: Gower Publishing Company).

SCHOU, T-L. (1985) 'EF-unionsdebatten i Danmark', in N. Petersen and C. Thune (eds.), *Dansk Udenrigspolitisk Årbog* (Copenhagen: Dansk Udenrigspolitisk Institut).

SCHOU, T-L. and HEARL, D. (forthcoming) 'Denmark', in M. Laver, I. Budge and D. Hearl (eds) *Party Policy and Coalition Government*.

SJÖBLOM, G. (1968) *Party Strategies in a Multi-party System* (Lund: Studentlitteratur).

THOMAS, A.H. (1982) 'Denmark: coalitions and minority governments', in E.C. Browne and J. Dreijmanlis (eds) *Government Coalitions in Western Democracies* (New York).

ØSTERGAARD, H.H.H. (1987) 'Kofoeds kup – eller hvordan finansministeriet blev budgetbissernes hjemsted's *Nordisk Administrativt Tidsskrift*, no. 2, pp. 113–125.

## 11 Norway

ANDERSEN, G. (1984) *Trygve Brateli* (Oslo: Gyldendal and Norsk Forlag).

BLOCH, K.(1963) *Kongens Råd* (Oslo: Universitetsforlaget).

BERGGRAV, D. (1955) 'Regjeringen', in Nordby (ed.) *Storting og Regjering 1945–1986* (Oslow: Kunnskapsforlaget).

BRATBAK, B. *et al.* (n.d.) *Oversikt over et prosjekt finansiert av Radet for forskning for samfunnsplanlegging*, NAVF of Forbruker-og administrasjonsdepartementet.

NORDLI, O. (1978) 'Regjeringens virkemåte', lecture by Prime Minister Nordli given at the University of Bergen.

OLSEN, J. (1980) 'Governing Norway: Segmentation, Anticipation and Consensus Formation', in R. Rose and E.N. Suleiman (eds) *Presidents and Prime Ministers* (Washington: American Enterprise Institute).

OLSEN, J. (1981) 'Regjeringen som samordningsorgan muligheter og begrens-
ninger', *Nordisk Administrativt Tidsskrift*, pp. 363–389.
SOLSTAD, A. (1969) 'The Norwegian Coalition System', *Scandinavian
Political Studies*, pp. 160–167.

## 12 Sweden

AMNÅ, E. (1981) *Planhushållning i den offentliga sektorn? Budgetdialogen
mellan regering och förvaltning under efterkrigstiden* (Stockholm: Horstedt).
BERGSTRÖM, H. (forthcoming) *Rivstarten*.
HAMMERICH, K. (1977) *Kompromissernas koalition, person-och maktspelet
kring regeringen Fälldin* (Stockholm: Rabén & Sjögren).
LARSSON, S-E. (1986) *Regera i koalition* (Stockholm: Bonnier, 1986).
LEIJONHUFVUD, S. (1979) *Ett fall för ministären* (Stockholm: LiberFörlag).
RYDEN, B. (1983) *Makt och Vanmakt* (Stockholm: SNS).
PETERSSON, O. (1979) *Regeringsbildningen 1978* (Stockholm: Rabén &
Sjögren).
SVEGFORS, M. (1982) *Revolution i små steg* (Timbro, Stockholm).
SYDOW VON, B. (1978) *Kan vi lita på politikerna? Offentlig och intern politik i
socialdemokratins ledning 1955–1960* (Stockholm: Tiden).
VEDUNG, E. (1979) *Kärnkraften och regeringen Fälldins fall* Stockholm,
Rabén & Sjögren.
VINDE, P. (1971) *Hur Sverige styres. Central förvaltningen och statens budget*
(Falköping: Prisma).

## 13 Finland

COBB, R.W. and ELDER, C.D. (1972) *Partipation in American Politics: the
Dynamics of Agenda-Building* (Boston: Allyn & Bacon).
FAGERHOLM, K.-A. (1977) *Puhemiehen ääni* (Helsinki: Tammi).
HAKOVIRTA, H., and KOSKIAHO, T. (1973) *Suuomen hallitukset ja
hallitusohjelmat 1945–1973* (Helsinki: Gaudeamus).
KAJANOJA, J. (1985) *Vallankumous ja 10,000 ääntä* (Helsinki: Kirjayhtymä).
LAAKSO, S. (1975) 'Hallituksen muodostaminen Suomessa', *Suomalaisen
lakimiesyhdistyksen julkaisuja A-sarja*, Vammala, no. 110.
LARSSON, T. (1986 *Regeringen och de kansli* (Lund: Studentlitteratur).
LIJPHART, A. (1984) *Democracies: Patterns of Majoritarian and Consensus
Government in Twenty-One Countries* (New Haven, London: Yale University
Press).
LUEBBERT, G.M. (1986) *Comparative Democracy: Policy-Making and Gover-
ning Coalitions in Europe and Israel* (New York: Columbia University Press).
NOUSIAINEN, J. (1971) *The Finnish Political System* (Cambridge: Harvard
University Press).
NOUSIAINEN, J. (1975) 'Valtioneuvoston järjestysmuoto ja sisäinen
toiminta', *Valtioneuvoston historiatoimikunta*, Helsinki.
NOUSIAINEN, J. (1985a) *Suomen presidentit valtiollisina johtajina* (Juva:
WSOY).

NOUSIAINEN, J. (1985b) *Suomen poliittinen järjestelmä* (Juva: WSOY) 6th edition.

NUMMINEN, J. (1985) *Valtioneuvoston ongelmia* (Keuruu: Otava).

NYHOLM, P. (1982) 'Finland: a Probabilistic View of Coalition Formation', in E.C. Browne and J. Dreijmanis (eds) *Government Coalitions in Western Democracies* (New York: Longman).

PAASIKIVEN PÄIVÄKIRJAT (1985–86) 1944–1956 I–II (Juva: WSOY).

PAIGE, G.D. (1977) *The Scientific Study of Political Leadership* (New York and London: Free Press).

PALOHEIMO, H. (1984) *Governments in Democratic Capitalist States: a Data Handbook* (University of Turku, Department of Sociology and Political Science, Studies on Political Science) no. 8.

RUIN, O. (1986) *I välfärdstatens tjänst. Tage Erlander 1946–1969* (Stockholm: Tidens förlag).

TIIHONEN, S. (1985) *Valtioneurosto Koordinoijana Teoria ja käytäntö vuosina 1939–56* (Helsinki: Valtion painatuskeskus).

VALTION KESKUSHALLINTOKOMITEAN II OSAMIETINTÖ, *Komiteanmietintö 1978:22* (Helsinki: Valtion painatuskeskus).

VALTIONEUVOSTON ESITTELIJÄN OPAS (1981) (Helsinki: Valtion painatuskeskus).

VALTIONEUVOSTON HISTORIATOIMIKUNTA (1975) *Valtioneuvoston historia 1917–1966*, I–III (Helsinki: Valtion painatuskeskus).

VALTIONEUVOSTON KANSLIA (1987) Ministerin käsikirja.

VON BEYME, K. (1985) *Political Parties in Western Democracies* (Aldershot: Gower).

VON BONSDORFF, G. (1982) 'Eduskuntaryhmien toiminta ja edustajien muut ryhmittymät', *Eduskunnan historiakomitea*, Suomen kansanedustuslaitoksen historia XII (Helsinki: Valtion painatuskeskus).

# Comparative Bibliography

ARMBRUSTER, F. (1973) 'Ressort-Rotation in Großbritannien und in der Bundesrepublik. Minister: Fachmann oder Politiker', *Zeitschrift für Parlamentsfragen*, pp. 95–110.

BLONDEL, J. (1980) *World Leaders* (London and Beverly Hills: Sage).

BLONDEL, J. (1982) *The Organization of Governments* (London: Sage).

BLONDEL, J. (1985) *Government Ministers in the Contemporary World* (London: Sage).

BLONDEL, J. (1988) 'Ministerial Careers and the Nature of Parliamentary Government: the Cases of Austria and Belgium', *European Journal of Political Research*, 16, no. 1, pp. 51–71.

BROWN, E. *et al.* (1984) 'An "Events" Approach to the Problem of Cabinet Stability', *Comparative Political Studies*, pp. 167–198.

BUTLER, D. (1972/73) 'Ministerial Responsibility in Australia and Britain', *Parliamentary Affairs*, vol. 26, pp. 403.

CAMPBELL, C. (1983) *Governments Under Stress: Political Executives and Key Bureaucrats in Washington* (London, Ottawa and Toronto: Toronto University Press).

COBB, R.W. and ELDER, C.D. (1972) *Participation in American politics: the Dynamics of Agenda-Building* (Boston: Allyn & Bacon).

DAALDER, H. (1971) 'Cabinets and Party Systems in Ten Smaller European Democracies', *Acta Politica*, 6, pp. 282–303.

DE SWAAN, A. (1973) *Coalition Theories and Cabinet Formation* (Amsterdam: Elsevier).

DODD, L. (1984) 'The Study of Cabinet Durability' *Comparative Political Studies*, pp. 155–162.

DUVERGER, M. (1986) *Les régimes semi-présidentiels* (Paris: Presses Universitaires de France).

HERMAN, V. (1975) 'Comparative Perspectives on Ministerial Stability in Britain', in V. Herman and J.E. Alt (eds) *Cabinet Studies* (London: Macmillan).

LAVER, M. (1986) 'Between theoretical elegance and political reality: deductive models and cabinet coalitions in Europe', in G. Pridham (ed.) *Coalition Behaviour in Theory and Practice* (Cambridge: Cambridge University Press).

LIJPHART, A. (1981) 'Power-sharing versus Majority Rule: Patterns of Cabinet Formation in Twenty Democracies', *Government and Opposition*, pp. 395–413.

LIJPHART, A. (1984) *Democracies: Patterns of Majoritarian and Consensus Government in Twenty-One Countries* (New Haven, London: Yale University Press).

LIJPHART, A. (1975e) *The Politics of Accommodation: Pluralism and Democracy in the Netherlands* (Berkeley: University of California Press).

LUEBBERT, G.M. (1986) *Comparative Democracy: Policy-Making and Governing Coalitions in Europe and Israel* (New York: Columbia University Press).

MACKIE, T. and HOGWOOD, B. (1985) *Unlocking the Cabinet* (London: Sage).
MEYER, L.C. (1980) 'Party Systems and Cabinet Stability', in P. Merkl (ed.) *Western European Party Systems* (New York: Free Press).
OBLER, J., STEINER, J. and DIRCKX, G. (1977) *Decision-Making in Small Democracies: the Consociational Burden* (London: Sage) Professional Papers, 01/064.
PAIGE, G.D. (1977) *The Scientific Study of Political Leadership* (New York and London: Free Press).
PALOHEIMO, H. (1984) *Governments in Democratic Capitalist States: a Data Handbook* (University of Turku: Department of Sociology and Political Science, Studies on Political Science) no. 8.
PAPPALARDO, A. (1978) *Partiti e governi di coalizione in Europa* (Milan: Angeli).
SANDERS, D. and HERMAN, V. (1977) 'The Stability and Survival of Governments in Western Democracies', *Acta Politica*, 12, pp. 346–377.
SARTORI, G. (1976) *Parties and Party Systems: a Framework for Analysis* (Cambridge: Cambridge University Press).
ROSE, R. (1980) 'Government against Sub-Governments: a European Perspective on Washington', in R. Rose and E.N. Suleiman (eds) *Presidents and Prime Ministers* (Washington: AEI).
ROSE, R. (1983) 'Still the Era of Party Government', *Parliamentary Affairs*, 36, pp. 282–289.
TAYLOR, M. and HERMAN, V. (1977) 'Party Systems and Government Stability', *American Political Science Review*, pp. 28–37.
TAYLOR, M. and LAVER, M. (1973) 'Government Coalitions in Western Europe', *European Journal of Political Research*, 3, pp. 205 ff.
WARWICK, P. (1979) 'The Durability of Coalition Governments in Parliamentary Democracies', *Comparative Political Studies*, 11, pp. 465–498.

# Index